Software Project Estimation

IEEE PRESS

Software Project Estimation

The Fundamentals for Providing High Quality Information to Decision Makers

Alain Abran

IEEE PRESS

WILEY

Published by John Wiley & Sons, Inc., Hoboken, New Jersey.
Published simultaneously in Canada.

For general information on our other products and services or for technical support, please contact our
Customer Care Department within the United States at (800) 762-2974, outside the United States at
(317) 572-3993 or fax (317) 572-4002.

Wiley also publishes its books in a variety of electronic formats. Some content that appears in print may
not be available in electronic formats. For more information about Wiley products, visit our web site at
www.wiley.com.

Library of Congress Cataloging-in-Publication Data:

Abran, Alain, 1949-
  Software project estimation : the fundamentals for providing high quality information to decision
makers / Alain Abran.
      pages cm
  ISBN 978-1-118-95408-9 (pbk.)
1. Computer software–Development–Estimates. I. Title.
  QA76.76.D47A245 2015
  005.1–dc23
                                        2014033319

Printed in the United States of America.

Contents

2. Engineering and Economics Concepts for Understanding Software Process Performance **32**

3. Project Scenarios, Budgeting, and Contingency Planning **60**

9. Building and Evaluating Single Variable Models   185

10. Building Models with Categorical Variables   205

Foreword

Software project estimation is a challenge in most software organizations – and it is also a challenge to their customers, who endure software projects significantly over budget, with significant delays, less functionality than promised, and with unknown levels of quality.

Is industry better today at estimating software projects than it was 40 years ago, and do today's estimation models perform better?

What has not changed much in software estimation over that period of time?

- Software managers (and their development staff) across the world are still expected to meet budget targets and deadlines typically determined based on imprecise requirements.

- Researchers continue to develop increasingly complex estimation models and techniques in pursuit of 'accurate' estimates.

- Estimation tools are still offered (at a cost by estimation tool vendors or free of charge on the Web and in books), for which there is little or no documented evidence on how these tools have performed on projects completed.

Books and tools on software estimation have been around for four decades now, and a number of solutions (estimation tools, models and techniques) have been proposed to address the challenge of software estimation.

- But how good are these solutions?

- What knowledge is available to assess the estimation tools available?

What do managers typically know about the quality of their estimation process, or about the performance of estimation tools available in the marketplace? Usually not much! Still, management takes a lot of decisions based on the numbers that these estimation tools yield.

In estimation:

- The role of the software estimator is not to promise miracles, but to provide the best and most complete technical *information*, *context*, and *insights*; that is, it is the software estimator's role to provide his manager with *information to support decision making*;

- The role of the manager is to look at all this information, select and allocate a project budget, and then manage the risks associated with it: it is the manager's role to take risks and manage those risks along the way.

When an organization has collected its own data and developed its own set of capabilities for analyzing their data and documenting the quality of their estimation models, then it has developed:

- a key competitive advantage in market-oriented organizations, and
- a key credibility advantage in organizations in non competitive contexts.

When an organization has not measured its own productivity on past projects, it is mostly in the dark about:

- how the organization is performing,
- how much a manager's performance differs from anyone else's, and
- how much the assumptions made in a manager's estimation model differ from those made in someone else's!

In this context, which is typical of many software organizations, using estimation models originating in environments with different productivity performance ratios does not provide real value. This is all the more true when little is known about:

- the quality of the data in these external repositories, or
- the quality of the estimation models in the environments in which they have been built.

Those who might feel good about such models, with all their fancy features and cost drivers, deceive themselves about the numbers coming from these 'black-boxes'.

This book teaches the way to develop _estimation information_ (that is, numbers + context) to be used by managers in making budgeting decisions in contexts of uncertainty.

This book is not about:

- black-box estimation claiming to handle all cost drivers at once;
- a cookbook with estimation recipes;
- a compendium of estimation models, techniques and cost drivers;
- a compendium of hints to handle the detailed planning for each project phase.

This book is about some of the best engineering practices _in software project estimation, including:_

- the right concepts to measure software project productivity – i.e. functional size measurement;
- how to use productivity findings to develop estimation models;
- how to verify the quality of the various components of an estimation process;
- how to provide value (i.e. the right information) to support decision making in software project management (budgeting and control).

... and no, there is no engineering, even in software estimation, without a sound statistical foundation!

SUMMARY

This book is not geared to readers looking for quick one-shot solutions. It is geared to those interested in building a long term and sustainable competitive advantage in software estimation by learning about the best practices and what is needed to implement them (including the necessary effort for data collection and data analysis using simple and sound statistical methods). prior to exploring much more complex statistical approaches, including for instance machine learning techniques or fuzzy logic.

Overview

In this book we share years of experience in the design of credible software estimation processes as decision support tools for managers.

We introduce the basic statistics and economics concepts needed to understand the fundamentals of the design and evaluation of software estimation models, and improvements to them.

Because quantitative data and quantitative models constitute a fundamental concept in engineering, science, and management, this book will be useful to software organizations of all sizes, and managers will find in it effective strategies for improving the quantitative aspects of software project estimation, along with numerous examples.

The book is intended for IT practitioners, managers, and auditors involved in software project estimation, and for students registered in software project management courses.

STRUCTURE AND ORGANIZATION

The book is organized into three parts and thirteen chapters.

Part 1	Part 2	Part 3
Understanding the Estimation Process	Estimation Process: What Must be Verified?	Building Estimation Models: Data Collection & Analysis
Chapters 1 to 3	Chapters 4 to 7	Chapters 8 to 13

Part 1 presents various views of software estimation that both estimators and managers must be aware of when designing and using software estimation models for decision making. It explains the structure of an estimation process, including the productivity models embedded in the estimation process, and clarifies the distinct roles and responsibilities that estimators and managers have. Finally, it introduces a number of economics concepts that must be taken into consideration, such as economies/diseconomies of scale and fixed/variable costs.

Part 2 introduces the concepts and techniques necessary for understanding that the quality of the outcomes of an estimation process depends on the quality of its inputs, of the underlying productivity models it uses, and an understanding of the limitations of the factors added as adjustments for estimation purposes.

Part 3 presents a number of issues related to building estimation models, including data collection and the use of international standards for ease of comparison across groups, organizations, and countries. In addition, it looks at how to build models which have more than one independent variable, using quality data as input and based on a number of economics concepts.

Part 1: Understanding the Estimation Process

Chapter 1: The Estimation Process: Phases & Roles

The estimation process and its various phases is introduced, along with the distinct roles and responsibilities of software estimators and their managers.

Chapter 2: Engineering & Economics Concepts for Understanding Software Process Performance

Some key economics concepts are presented which are useful for understanding, and then modeling, the performance of the development process underlying productivity models. In particular, the concepts of economies/diseconomies of scale and of fixed/variable costs in production models are explained, as well as some characteristics of typical and atypical datasets in software engineering, and the presence of explicit and implicit variables in the productivity model.

Chapter 3: Project Scenarios, Budgeting & Contingency Planning

The impact of the selection of a single budget value among a range of estimates is discussed, including the identification of scenarios and their corresponding probabilities, and the identification and management of contingencies at the project portfolio level.

Part 2: Estimation Process: What Must be Verified?

Chapter 4: What Must be Verified in an Estimation Process: An Overview

The various parts of an estimation process that must be understood and verified when building and using productivity models are identified. We look at models from an engineering perspective, not from a 'craft' perspective.

Chapter 5: Verification of the Dataset Used to Build the Models

The criteria required to analyze the quality of the direct inputs to mathematical models are presented, that is, the independent variables used to predict the dependent variable for estimation purposes.

Chapter 6: Verification of the Models

The criteria required to analyze the quality of mathematical models are presented, along with the outcomes of these models. Then, by way of illustration, these quality criteria are used to evaluate the performance of the models and tools proposed to the industry.

Chapter 7: Verification of the Adjustment Phase

Uncertainties and errors are inherent in measurements and in models of relationships across factors. Some sources of uncertainty and error are presented, and we show how they can accumulate when additional factors are introduced into the estimation process.

Part 3: Building Estimation Models: Data Collection & Analysis

Chapter 8: Data Collection & Industry Standards: The ISBSG Repository

Models for industry usage should be based on well defined and standardized definitions of the parameters included in the estimation process. Some standards for software projects data collection that have been defined by the International Software Benchmarking Standards Group – ISBSG – are introduced. Standardized definitions are, of course, critical for internal and external benchmarking, as well as for building productivity and estimation models.

Chapter 9: Building & Evaluating Single Variable Models

The way to build a model, one independent variable at a time, is illustrated, starting with the variable recognized as the most significant, that is, the size of the software to be delivered. The way to build models using the ISBSG repository of projects is also shown, including data preparation and the identification of relevant samples to handle additional descriptive variables, such as the development environment.

Chapter 10: Building Models with Categorical Variables

A case study on building models with industry data on project size as the key factor is presented, along with a few additional categorical variables, and the way to analyze and understand the quality of such models.

Chapter 11: Contribution of Productivity Extremes in Estimation

An analysis is presented on how projects with the best and worst productivity are identified, and we show how to take advantage of the lessons learned in analyzing their performance and use this information for estimation purposes.

Chapter 12: Multiple Models from a Single Dataset

An analysis is presented on how to identify multiple models from a single dataset by exploring concepts of economies and diseconomies of scale, as well as process performance capabilities and the impact of constraints on productivity.

Chapter 13: Re-Estimation: A Recovery Effort Model

Throughout a software project, a number of factors influence productivity, functions are added and/or modified, risks materialize, and so on. As a result, projects often have to be re-estimated across life cycle phases. An approach to building re-estimation models is presented.

Additional material to complement the information contained in this book can be found at http://profs.etsmtl.ca/aabran/English/Autres/index.html

The table below provides a reading guide for *software managers*.

Chapters to read	Why?	What to do with the information
Part 1 Chapter 1: full reading	Estimation is a multi phases process and estimators and managers have distinct and complementary responsibilities.	Verify that your estimation process covers all the phases described in this chapter & corresponding responsibilities well understood.
Chapter 2: full reading	Economics concepts are useful for estimation purposes: they help explain fundamental issues in the software project cost structure, such as fixed/variable costs and economies/diseconomies of scale in software development.	Ask your software engineers: 1- What are my fixed-variable efforts in software projects? 2- Do we have economies or diseconomies of scale in our software development process?
Chapter 3: full reading	Estimators should provide scenarios and plausible ranges of estimates. From these, business executives should allocate a project budget price, as well as contingency funds at the level of a portfolio of projects.	The manager should be the one to select the project budget (from a range of estimates) and set aside contingency funds to manage the inherent estimation risks.
Part 2 Chapters 4 to 7: quick reading	Estimation models should produce 'credible numbers': the quality of the estimation models must be verified and documented – if not, estimation is reduced to 'garbage in, garbage out'.	Ask your estimators to document the quality controls implemented in your estimation process. Ask for an audit of your estimation process.
Part 3 Chapters: 8 to 13: quick reading	Standardized definitions for the data collected allow performance comparison within your organization and across the industry. Engineering techniques should be used for data analysis and building estimation models.	Verify that your organization is using the best industry standards for data collection. Ask your estimators to implement the best practices recommended in these chapters.

Chapters to read	Why?	What to do with the information
	When project budgets go off-track, regular estimation models no longer work: re-estimation models are needed.	Ask your estimator to develop a re-estimation model.

The table below provides a reading guide for *IT practitioners, IT auditors and undergraduate or graduate students* interested in:

- developing specialized expertise in software estimation,
- verifying the quality of existing software estimation models and processes, or
- designing new software estimation models and processes.

Chapters to read	Why?	What to do with the information
Part 1 Chapters 1 to 3: full reading	Estimation models must be based on a good understanding of the performance of an organization: fixed/variable costs, as well as economies/diseconomies of scale in software development.	When preparing project estimates, use your organization's historical data on fixed/variable costs as the foundation for your estimation process. Clarify the boundaries of the responsibilities between estimator and manager.
Part 2 Chapters 4 to 7: full reading	Estimation models should produce 'information', not only numbers. These 4 chapters illustrate what must be verified and which criteria must be used to document the quality of the outcomes of the productivity models used or to be implemented in your organization. This chapter also illustrates that adding more factors does not automatically increase certainty.	For decision making, you must provide information: i.e. numbers and context. This includes documenting the quality of the inputs to your productivity models, as well as the probable range of estimates.
Part 3 Chapters: 8 to 13: full reading	To design a credible estimation process, you need: – standards for data collection,	At estimation time, use the proposed techniques for building sound estimation models based on relevant data sets.

Chapters to read	Why?	What to do with the information
	– identification of statistical outliers,	
	– select relevant samples for data analysis,	
	– built single and multiple variable models,	
	– take into account non quantitative variables.	
	– And at re-estimation time, a number of additional constraints have to be taken into account.	At re-estimation time, include the relevant additional productivity factors.

Acknowledgments

A number of colleagues in industry and at universities across the world, as well as former graduate students, have helped clarify many of the concepts presented in this book over the years, in particular:

Chapter	Contributors
2 – Engineering and Economics Concepts for understanding Software Process Performance	• Juan Cuadrado-Gallego, University of Alcala (Spain)
3 – Project Scenarios, Budgeting and Contingency Planning	• Eduardo Miranda, Carnegie Mellon University (USA)
7 – Verification of the Adjustment Phase	• Luca Santillo, Agile Metrics (Italy)
8 – Data collection and industry standards: the ISBSG repository	• David Déry (Canada) • Laila Cheikhi, ENSIAS (Morocco)
9 – Building and evaluating single variable models	• Pierre Bourque, ETS – U. Québec (Canada) • Iphigénie Ndiaye (Canada)
10 – Building models with categorical variables	• Ilionar Silva and Laura Primera (Canada)
11 – Contribution of productivity extremes in estimation	• Dominic Paré (Canada)
12 – Multiple models from a single dataset	• Jean-Marc Desharnais, ETS – U. Québec (Canada) • Mohammad Zarour, Prince Sultan University • Onur Demirörs, Middle East Technical University (Turkey)
13 – Re-estimation: a recovery effort model	• Eduardo Miranda, Carnegie Mellon University (USA)

Special thanks to:

- Professor Cuauhtémoc Lopez Martin of the University of Guadalajara and Charles Symons, who have provided very thoughtful comments on draft versions of this book,
- Mr. Maurice Day for improvements to the graphics included in this book.

Above all, this book is dedicated to:

- those who, over the years, have provided me with feedback and insights on software estimation, and who are continuously contributing, each in their own way, to the improvement of software estimation as a foundation for sound, quantitatively based decision-making;
- my PhD students, many with years of industry practice, who have explored various specialized views to develop a more in-depth understanding of software estimation models.

About the Author

$\mathbf{D}$r. Alain Abran is a professor of software engineering at the École de Technologie Supérieure (ETS) – Université du Québec, Montréal, Canada.

Dr. Abran has more than 20 years of industry experience in information systems development and software engineering, and 20 years of university teaching. He holds a PhD in electrical and computer engineering (1994) from École Polytechnique de Montréal (Canada) and Master's degrees in Management Sciences (1974) and Electrical Engineering (1975) from the University of Ottawa (Canada)

He is the chairman of the Common Software Measurement International Consortium (COSMIC) – www.cosmicon.com. He published *Software Metrics and Software Metrology* in 2010, *Management of Software Maintenance*[1] in 2008, both at Wiley & IEEE CS Press, and co-edited the 2004 version of the Guide to the Software Engineering Body of Knowledge (www.swebok.org).

His research interests include software productivity and estimation models, software quality, software measurement, functional size measurement methods, software risk management, and software maintenance management.

Most of his publications can be downloaded from: http://www.researchgate.net

Dr. Abran can be contacted at: alain.abran@etsmtl.ca

---

[1] Co-author: Alain April

Part I

Understanding the Estimation Process

Estimation is not at all about coming up with a magic number to which everyone must commit at the peril of their professional career (which leads to staff members spending lots of overtime attempting to meet unrealistic deadlines.)

Part 1 of this book consists of three chapters, in which some of the key concepts of an estimation process are introduced.

Chapter 1 introduces the estimation process, including:

- the collection of data to be input to the estimation process,
- their usage with a productivity model,
- the adjustment phase to handle project assumptions, uncertainties, and risks,
- the budgeting phase,
- the estimator role: to provide information on a range of estimates,
- the manager role: to select a specific budget from the range of estimates identified by the estimator.

Chapter 2 explains the relationship between the software development life process and the classic model of a process. A number of economics concepts are introduced and illustrated in the context of software projects, such as:

- economies and diseconomies of scale, and
- fixed and variable costs.

Software Project Estimation: The Fundamentals for Providing High Quality Information to Decision Makers, First Edition. Alain Abran.
© 2015 the IEEE Computer Society. Published 2015 by John Wiley & Sons, Inc.

Chapter 3 discusses the impact of the selection of a single budget value from a range of estimates, including the identification of scenarios and their corresponding probabilities, and the identification and management of contingencies at the project portfolio level.

Chapter 1

The Estimation Process: Phases and Roles

OBJECTIVES

This chapter covers

- Two generic approaches to estimation: judgment-based and engineering based
- An overview of the process for estimating software projects
- The foundation: The productivity model
- The phases of the estimation process
- Roles and responsibilities in estimating and budgeting

1.1 INTRODUCTION

When an organization has not measured its own productivity on past projects, it is mostly in the dark about:

- how the organization is performing,
- how much a manager's performance differs from someone else's, and
- how much the assumptions made in a manager's estimation judgment differ from those made in someone else's!

In this context, which is typical in many software organizations, using productivity models originating in environments with different productivity performance ratios does not provide real value. This is all the more true when little is known about

- the quality of the data in these external repositories and
- the quality of the productivity models within the environments in which they have been built.

When an organization has collected its own data and developed its own set of capabilities for analyzing those data and documenting the quality of their productivity models, then it has developed

Software Project Estimation: The Fundamentals for Providing High Quality Information to Decision Makers, First Edition. Alain Abran.
© 2015 the IEEE Computer Society. Published 2015 by John Wiley & Sons, Inc.

- a key competitive advantage in market-oriented organizations and
- a key credibility advantage in organizations in noncompetitive contexts.

Estimation is not at all about coming up with a magic number to which everyone must commit at the peril of their professional career (which leads to staff members spending lots of overtime attempting to meet unrealistic deadlines.)

This chapter presents an overview of the phases of an estimation process and explains the differences between a productivity model and its use in an estimation process. It is organized as follows:

- Section 1.2 introduces two generic approaches to estimation: judgment and engineering.
- Section 1.3 provides an overview of some common practices and expectations involved in estimating software projects.
- Section 1.4 discusses the levels of uncertainty in an estimation process.
- Section 1.5 presents the key concepts of a productivity model.
- Section 1.6 explains the use of a productivity model in an estimation process.
- Section 1.7 discusses the estimation responsibilities in a business context.
- Section 1.8 explains the differences between budgeting and pricing.
- Section 1.9 provides a summary of the chapter.

1.2 GENERIC APPROACHES IN ESTIMATION MODELS: JUDGMENT OR ENGINEERING?

1.2.1 Practitioner's Approach: Judgment and Craftsmanship

In contrast to estimation with mathematical models, where explicit cost drivers are included in the models as either quantitative or categorical parameters, which are manipulated with well-described mathematical equations, the estimation technique often used in practice in industry (also referred to as the *expert judgment estimation approach*) would not typically document which parameters are taken into account, or how they are explicitly combined.

The overall estimation process in the expert judgment approach is similar to the estimation process described later in this chapter, but is much less transparent, of course, and there is no possibility of tracing back to historical data on how the expert judgment models were built. In addition, it is not feasible to gauge the performance of the expert judgment models when there are no objectively quantified and standardized data on key project variables, such as software size:

- A project might appear to be successful if it has respected the "official" budget; however, without the ability to verify that all the promised functions have been delivered, it is a mistake to claim that the estimates were correct: when only a portion of the required functions are delivered, then the expected benefits cannot all be harvested, which destroys the cost-benefit analysis that justified the launching of the project in the first place.

We can conclude from this that analyzing the performance of an expert-based estimate without a corresponding analysis of the functionality delivered is of very limited value.

Of course, the expert judgment approach is highly dependent on the specific expertise of the people participating in the estimation process, and will vary from project to project, making performance assessment challenging.

This dependency of expert judgment on expertise gives the estimation process many of the characteristics of a craft, which is mostly dependent on the abilities of the craftsmen, rather than on a thoroughly tested and well-defined engineering technique.

The decision as to which cost drivers to include, as well as the determination of the values of each interval within a cost driver for particular impact, is most often based entirely on the judgment of a group of estimation tool builders, or even a single tool builder.

Practitioners will also typically attempt to improve conventional software estimation models using a similar approach:

- The addition, modification, and/or deletion of cost drivers is based on a value judgment (also referred to as *expert judgment* or *subject matter expertise*).
- An impact factor is also assigned on this basis.

What this means is that the improvement process is typically subjective and most often undertaken without statistical analysis to support proposed changes.

1.2.2   Engineering Approach: Modest – One Variable at a Time

Building software models from an engineering perspective is based on

- Observation of past projects and quantitative data collection
  - o including identification of the scale types of the variables, and taking them into account to ensure adequate use of those variables in productivity models.
- Analysis of the impact of individual variables, one at a time.
- Selection of relevant samples, and of samples of sufficient size from a statistical viewpoint.
- Documentation and analysis of the demographics of the dataset used.
- Very careful extrapolation to contexts other than those from which the data were collected.

The engineering approach consists of investigating the factors involved and studying them one at a time before combining them.

In this approach, it is not taken for granted that it is feasible for a single model to handle all sets of conditions:

- Instead, a search is conducted for models that are reasonably good within a well-identified and understood set of constraints.

This is the approach taken in this book for building the basis for productivity models:

- Look at the work–effort relationship, one variable at a time, to gain insights for each variable.

Taking this approach means initially obtaining a number of productivity models for each variable, and admitting that

- no one model will be perfect (i.e., it will not take into account the other variables *directly*) and that
- each model will teach us something about the effect of that single variable on the dependent variable, which is effort.

1.3 OVERVIEW OF SOFTWARE PROJECT ESTIMATION AND CURRENT PRACTICES

Here we present an overview of the estimation process, followed by some current practices and expectations.

1.3.1 Overview of an Estimation Process

A high-level view of a software estimation approach is depicted in Figure 1.1:

- **(A)** On the left are the inputs to the software estimation process. These inputs typically consist of
  - Product requirements:
    - ▶ the functional requirements requested by the users and allocated to the software.
    - ▶ the nonfunctional requirements, some of which will be allocated to software, and others to other parts of the system (hardware, procedures manual, etc.).
  - Software development process: typically, a specific life cycle is selected (agile, iterative, etc.), along with its various components, including the development platform, the programming languages, and the project team.
  - Project constraints: these are the constraints externally imposed on the project (predefined deadlines, maximum available budget, etc.).
- **(B)** In the center is a representation of the productivity model used as the foundation of the estimation process, and includes

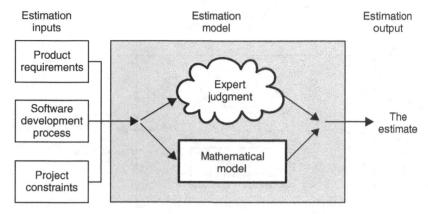

Figure 1.1 One Perception of an Estimation Process

- the "implicit" models of each of the experts participating in the estimation process (typically, the productivity model of the experts is not documented).
- mathematical models: regressions, case-based reasoning, neural networks, and so on.

(C) On the right is the estimation output normally expected, which constitutes

- an estimate of the amount of effort (or cost, or project duration) required to deliver software that will meet the requirements specified in input at the specified level of quality.

1.3.2 Poor Estimation Practices

In the literature, there is a large body of knowledge on project estimation in general, and on software project estimation in particular; however, in practice, the software industry is plagued by a number of poor estimation practices, such as those illustrated in Figure 1.2:

(A) The estimation inputs:

- There is only a very brief description by the customer of the software system expected, usually at a very high level (i.e., poorly defined) and, of course, poorly documented. How many times are software staff asked to provide estimates based on a half-page description of user requirements? This type of estimation input is referred to as a "wish list" in Figure 1.2. Such a list will inevitably change over time, and most probably expand at an unpredictable rate.
- In the hope of offsetting this lack of description of what is expected by users, a software manager will want to take as many cost drivers as possible into account, expecting in this way to lower his estimation risks.

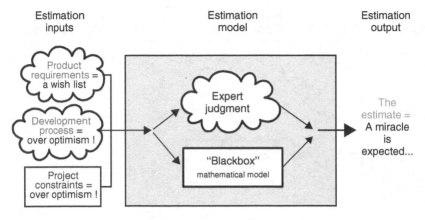

Figure 1.2   Some of the Poor Estimation Practices Observed in Industry

(B) The estimation model:

- A formal or an informal model to mix (in a black-box manner) these ill-defined requirements together through the use of readily available:
  - ▶ local experience: internal or external experience (the expert judgment approach) or
  - ▶ mathematical models described in books or hidden in estimation tools.

(C) The estimation output is made up of

- a single estimate, which is made up of the mandated project budget that must be respected, along with the requirement that the expected functionality be produced within a prescribed period of time;
  - ▶ Note: this figure does not take into account unplanned overtime, for which the development team will not be paid!
- an overly optimistic attitude, which is very common among software professionals, that the development team will outperform any previous historical performance and overcome all constraints in a timely manner; and
- accountability on the part of the software engineer or project manager providing the estimate, in terms of meeting customer expectations and respecting the project budget allocated by senior management.

To summarize, in this worst practice, both customers and senior management expect that their staff (and suppliers) will commit to delivering the expected software functionality on time and on budget, and all this without having themselves worked out the details of what they expect as a well working product and the uncertainties inherent to any new project.

In other words, on the one hand, miracles are expected by customers and senior management, and, on the other, too many software staff, when providing single-point estimates, behave as if they are in the business of continuously delivering miracles!

Some of the Best Estimation Practices in Industry

Mature software organizations consider estimation as a process that gives them a business advantage over their competitors: to acquire this competitive advantage, they have invested in their estimation process to master the key factors, including:

- investment in gathering project requirements and in understanding their qualities;
- use of international standards for software measurement;
- continuous quantitative measurement throughout the project life cycle;
- quantitative analysis of their past performance: that is, how productive were they in terms of delivering past projects and meeting project objectives;
- in-depth analysis of their estimation performance (actual vs estimated).

Some of the Worst Estimation Practices in Industry

- Wishful thinking and single-point estimates.
- Use of estimation black boxes (expert judgment and/or undocumented mathematical models).
- Reliance on others' numbers: no investment in their estimation process to develop a sustainable competitive advantage.

1.3.3 Examples of Poor Estimation Practices

The following are some examples of poor estimation practices – see also Figure 1.3.

(A) Inputs to estimation models:
- Product requirements = Wish list:
  - No measurement of the functional requirements themselves, using international standards.
  - Use of post-project KLOC (thousands of lines of code) without considering the mix of programming languages and their different characteristics.
  - Size units often considered almost irrelevant.
  - Guesstimate of KLOC based on poor requirements and a poor understanding of the relationships between requirements and KLOC in various programming languages.

(B) Development process:
  - Individual descriptive factors transformed into quantitative impact factors without knowledge of their accuracy and variance.
  - No objective quantitative knowledge of the impact of the project variables in their own development environment.
  - Total reliance on outside numbers without strong supporting evidence.

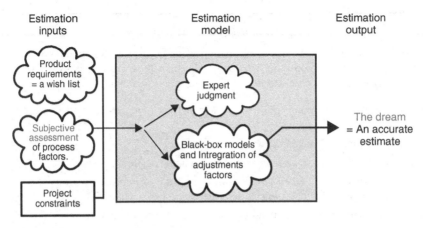

Figure 1.3   The Dream: An "Accurate" Estimate

(C) Productivity model:
- Unknown estimation performance of the so-called experts in the expert-based estimation approach.
- No verification that the assumptions necessary for each statistical technique have been met (e.g., The "normality" distribution of the variables for regression models).
- Too many variables and not enough data points for sound statistical analysis.
- No verification of the size of the software to be delivered in the analysis of the performance of the expert-based approach.
- And so on.

(D) Estimation output:
- The dream: an accurate estimate.
- Limited analysis of the range of candidate values and candidate causes of variations in the estimates.
- Limited documentation of the quality of their estimation outcomes.

1.3.4 The Reality: A Tally of Failures

Software project estimation is a recurrent and important activity in large and small organizations across the world, and a large amount of research has been performed on software project estimation over the past 50 years and a large number of models proposed to industry. The bottom line is, how well is software estimation performing in industry?

The answer is, not very impressively [Jorgensen and Molokken 2006; Jorgensen and Shepperd 2007; Petersen 2011]:

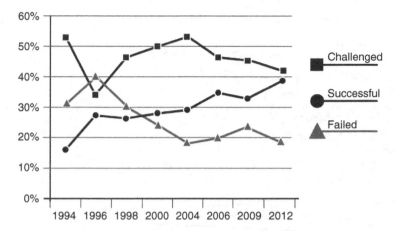

Figure 1.4   Project Success Trends Based on Standish Group Data [Adapted from Miranda 2010].

- Figure 1.4, constructed using data from the Standish Group Chaos Reports cited by [Eveleens and Verhoef 2010], shows that, over the 30-year period, barely 30% of software projects have been delivered on time and on budget:

  o Since the publication of the first Standish Group report in 1995, the software development community has been making some progress in its ability to complete development projects on time and on budget, but almost 70% of software projects still finish late and over budget, or are cancelled.

- The 2008 study by El Eman and Koru [2008] puts the average number of challenged and failed projects at 50%.

1.4 LEVELS OF UNCERTAINTY IN AN ESTIMATION PROCESS

1.4.1 The Cone of Uncertainty

The well-known *cone of uncertainty* attempts to represent the range of expected variations in models across the project life cycle – see Figure 1.5.

At the early, feasibility stage, which is about future projects (i.e., $t = 0$):

- The project estimate can err on the side of underestimation by as much as 400%, or on the side of overestimation by 25% of the estimate.

At the end of a project (i.e., $t =$ the end of the project):

- The information on effort, duration, and costs (i.e., the dependent variables) is now known relatively accurately (with respect to the quality of the data collection process for effort recording).

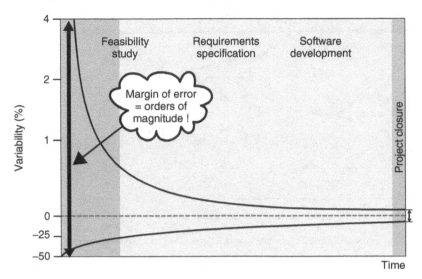

Figure 1.5 Uncertainty Levels in the Project Life Cycle [Adapted from Boehm et al. 2000, Figure 1.2, p. 10]

- The information on the cost drivers (independent variables) are also relatively well known, since they have all been observed in practice – the variables are therefore considered to be "fixed" without uncertainty (many of these are non-quantitative, such as the type of development process, programming language, and development platform.)
- However, the relationships across these dependent variables and the independent variable are far from being common knowledge. *Even in this context of no uncertainty at the level of each variable at the end of a project*, there is no model today that can perfectly replicate the size–effort relationship, and there remains uncertainty in the productivity model itself.

We refer to this stage as the *productivity model stage* (at t = the end of project). The reason why the cone of uncertainty at the extreme right of Figure 1.5 does not infer full accuracy is because all the values in this cone are tentative values provided mostly by expert judgment.

1.4.2 Uncertainty in a Productivity Model

A rough graphical two-dimensional representation of the performance of productivity models (i.e., in a context of completed projects) is depicted in Figure 1.6, where the size of completed projects is plotted along the horizontal axis and the actual effort for the completed projects is plotted along the vertical axis. Each point in this figure corresponds to a completed project (in terms of its size and actual effort) and the slope corresponds to the statistical equation that would best represent this set of completed projects, that is, the corresponding productivity model.

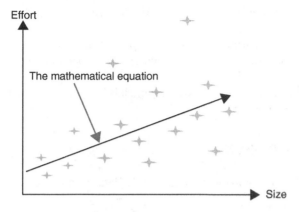

Figure 1.6   A Model with One
Independent Variable

- In other words, the productivity model represents the modeling of the relationships across the two variables in this figure, that is, between the independent variable (the size of the software) and the dependent variable (completed project effort).

It can be observed in Figure 1.6 that most of the actual data do not fall exactly on the mathematical equation (i.e., the slope line), but at some distance from it. This means that the productivity model does not accurately model the size–effort relationship: some actual data are close to the line, with other data quite far apart, even though there was no uncertainty on the inputs to the estimation process.

The current performance targets often mentioned in the literature for such productivity models (with one or multiple independent variables) for modeling the size–effort relationship are something like those in Figure 1.7:

- That is, 80% of the projects fall within 20% of the distance from the equation line, and 20% of the projects outside of this distance (but within an unspecified upper range of variation).

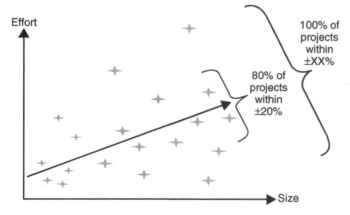

Figure 1.7   Model Accuracy Targets.

The context (and the data collected) used to build a productivity model differs significantly from that in which estimation must be performed: in practice, a project must be estimated fairly early in the project life cycle (i.e., *a priori*), at a time of high uncertainty, in terms of both what software functions must be developed and how they will be developed.

In the next two sections, we discuss both productivity models in more detail, and then their application in an estimation process.

1.5 PRODUCTIVITY MODELS

Researchers typically build their mathematical models using data from completed projects.

- This means that they start with a set of known facts, about which there is no uncertainty – see Figure 1.8.

- Therefore, most of the so-called estimation models in the literature are actually *productivity* models.

The inputs to the models to be built are

- Product requirements: the software that has been built and delivered.
  - The software can be measured very precisely based on the actual software delivered.
  - The software characteristics can also be described, using whatever classification schemes are available.
- The software development process is completed, and can also be described and categorized without uncertainty:

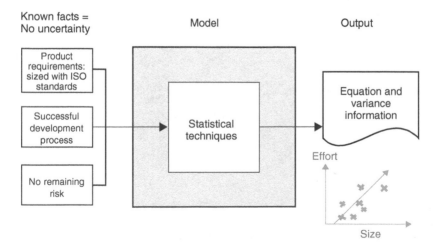

Figure 1.8   The Context of a Productivity Model

- ○ Resources: the relevant staff experience in a business domain, their development expertise, their availability during the project, and so on.
- ○ Process: the development methodology, the development environment, and so on.
- The project constraints are now precisely known, with no remaining uncertainty and no remaining risks: they are constant (i.e., no longer variable).

In summary, these inputs from completed projects can constitute either

- quantitative information (such as software functional size, perhaps measured using an international standard of measurement – such as Function Points or COSMIC Function Points) or
- nominative information (such as the programming language) or nominal categories of information (such as categories of case tools), or ordinal variables (such as levels of complexity, from very simple to very complex).

(A) Mathematical equation models

Estimators have at their disposal a large number of mathematical techniques to help them to determine quantitatively, from a number of completed projects, the relationships between the dependent variable of interest (for instance, project effort or project duration) and the independent variables (the product size and the various cost drivers).

- For instance, the small graph at the bottom right of Figure 1.8 (and Figure 1.6) represents the relationships between the size of the software projects completed and the effort required to deliver these projects:
  - ▶ The horizontal axis represents the size of the software delivered (i.e., the past).
  - ▶ The vertical axis represents the effort expended for each project.
  - ▶ The stars each represent a project tuple (size and effort).
  - ▶ The slope of the graph represents the regression line that corresponds best to the set of points (i.e., the relationships between the independent variable – project size – and the dependent variable – project effort). This regression line, obtained by a statistical model, represents the productivity of projects delivered in the context of the points composing this specific dataset, and so corresponds to the productivity of the past projects for which there is no longer any uncertainty.

Some of the key benefits of these mathematical models of the productivity of past projects are the following:

- The variables in these datasets are described using a documented set of conventions.
- The performance of these mathematical models can be described and analyzed.
  - ▶ For instance, with the regression model in Figure 1.8, the delta of each point to the equation line can be calculated to figure out the "quality" of these models.

- Anybody can use these models for estimating future projects, and, provided the same information is inserted in these models, the same number will come out (in that sense, the models are "objective"). In practice, the estimate will vary when the inputs vary.

Productivity models are therefore *models of past projects built from known information* with

- quantitative variables measured accurately based on what has been implemented in the software (but still with some degree of imprecision in their measurement),
- quantitative variables collected during the project life cycle and archived in the project recording system, or
- other descriptive variables of known information assessed subjectively by project experts, and for which there is no intrinsic uncertainty, the projects being completed.

(B) Expert judgment approach

The expert judgment approach is generally informal, not documented, and is informally derived from past experience based on subjective recollection of past projects, very often without reference to precise quantitative information on the software delivered, nor on precise information on cost drivers.

The only precise information available would typically concern the dependent variables (effort and duration), but not the independent variables (e.g., product size, in particular in terms of the functionality delivered).

In addition, there is usually no precise information on the productivity of past projects and no graphical representation of the performance of a set of projects.

1.6   THE ESTIMATION PROCESS

1.6.1   The Context of the Estimation Process

The typical estimation context is characterized by

- *the imprecise nature of the requirements at estimation time early in the life cycle*:
  - ▶ imprecision of the requirements,
  - ▶ ambiguities and omissions in the requirements,
  - ▶ instability of the requirements across the project life cycle,
  - ▶ and so on.

  Of course, all the above-mentioned statements make it impossible to measure the requirements size accurately at that time, when size can at best be approximated.

- *uncertainty about a number of factors that could impact the project*:
  - ▶ the experience of the project manager,

- ▶ whether or not the new development environment will perform as advertised by its vendor,
- ▶ and so on.

- *a number of risks*:
  - ▶ users changing their minds about the requirements,
  - ▶ an inability to hire competent staff within the planned time frame,
  - ▶ loss of key staff,
  - ▶ and so on.

Estimating future software projects is often, in practice, carried out in such a context, when the information

- is incomplete,
- contains a number of unknowns, and
- is associated with a number of risks.

In this chapter, those needs are addressed through an engineering process to develop an *estimation process* to handle the constraints mentioned above, which are

- incompleteness,
- uncertainty, and
- risks.

1.6.2 The Foundation: The Productivity Model

The productivity model developed from past projects is at the core of an estimation process, whether this model

- is described formally through mathematical equations or
- is hidden beneath the experience-based knowledge of people using the expert judgment approach to software estimation.

Next, the productivity model in Figure 1.8 is used in an estimation context (i.e., the left-hand side of the cone of uncertainty depicted in Figure 1.5) for future projects when

- the inputs (including the size of the product requirements and cost drivers) are unknown precisely and have themselves potentially large ranges of variation and uncertainty.

The expected ranges of variation of the inputs (i.e., future projects) on the horizontal axis will definitively impact the range of variation of the variable estimated in output (for instance, project effort or project duration on the vertical axis) leading to larger candidate variations than the initial productivity models built from past projects.

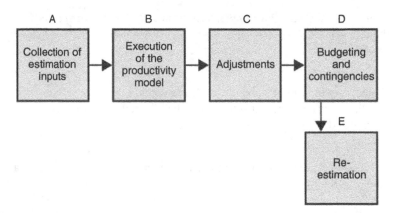

Figure 1.9   The Estimation Process

1.6.3   The Full Estimation Process

The estimation process includes the following five major phases – see Figure 1.9:

(A) Collection of the inputs to the estimation process:

- measurement of the product requirements (or, most often, estimation or approximation of the size of the requirements) and
- assumptions for most of the other cost drivers.

(B) Use of a productivity model (as a kind of simulation model).

(C) An adjustment process to take into account variables and information not included in the productivity model, including:

- identification of uncertainty factors and
- risk assessment.

(D) A budget decision on a single-number budget (at the project and portfolio levels).

(E) Re-estimation when required by project monitoring and control.

Each of these phases is described below in greater detail.

Phase (A) Collection of the estimation inputs – see Figure 1.10
Analysis of the project information and data collection for identifying the cost drivers (Resources, Process, and Products) to be used as inputs to a specific project to be estimated.

Estimation of the values of the cost drivers identified.

▸ At the time an estimate is prepared, the nature of these inputs is uncertain, which is why they have to be estimated.
▸ The uncertainty associated with these inputs should be documented for use in Phase B.

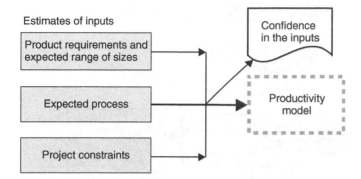

Figure 1.10   Phase A: collection of the Inputs for the Estimation Process

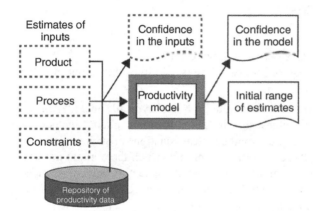

Figure 1.11   Phase B: Execution of the Productivity Model in an Estimation Process

Phase (B) Execution of the productivity model – see Figure 1.11

Execution of the productivity model in an estimation context typically involves two steps:

1. Use of the productivity model (as a kind of simulation model), usually considering only the estimated values of the inputs (and not their ranges of uncertainty).

    a. The productivity model equation will produce a theoretical single estimate on the line represented by the equation.
    b. The information on the performance of the productivity model is used to identify the expected range of variations (based on the historical data used to build the model).

2. Use of the information about the uncertainty and candidate ranges of variation of the estimated inputs to adjust the estimated ranges of the output of Step 1 above. This will generally increase the expected range of variation of the estimates from the productivity model.

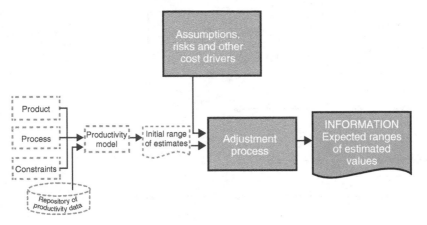

Figure 1.12   Phase C: The Adjustments

Phase (C) The adjustment process – see Figure 1.12

An estimation process is not limited to the blind use of the output of a productivity model:

- On the one hand, the core productivity model typically includes only a limited number of variables, that is, those that are explicitly included as independent variables, in the mathematical equations of such models.
- On the other hand, there are other factors for which there might not have been historical data, as well as a whole set of risk factors that might impact the project over its life cycle (often, many of these factors can be described in a mostly quantitative manner).

  ▶ Software estimators have to identify such factors, as they may impact the project and need to be considered in an adjustment process.

An adjustment process will take into account variables and information not included yet in the estimation process, including:

▶ identification of other cost drivers (i.e., those not included in the productivity model),
▶ identification of uncertainty elements,
▶ identification of risks and probabilities of occurrence, and
▶ identification of key project assumptions.

Note that this process is usually performed on the basis of expert judgment, and would normally affect not only the theoretical estimation of the productivity model, but also its upper and lower limits of estimation, and could provide qualitative information, such as:

- an optimistic estimate (a lowest cost or duration),
- a most likely estimate (with a low probability of occurrence), and
- a pessimist estimate (the highest expected cost or duration).

The output of the estimation process is therefore a set of values, that is, *a set of information* which will be used in the next phase for budgeting and project resource allocation.

Phase (D) The budget decision – see Figure 1.13

The next phase in the estimation process involves selecting a specific value or set of values (on effort and duration) from the ranges proposed and to allocate it to the project, and is the phase in which a decision is made on a project budget.

Of course, the selection of a specific value, often incorrectly referred to as an "estimate," will depend on the strategies of the business manager (i.e., the decision-maker):

- The risk-averter will select a value in the upper range (i.e., a pessimistic scenario).
- The risk-taker will select a value in the lower range (i.e., an optimistic scenario).
- The middle-of-the-road manager will analyze the ranges and their probabilities, and then select a project budget, at the same time setting aside a contingency fund to take into account the probability that he might have selected too low a value.
  - The management of this contingency fund is usually handled at the portfolio level – see also Chapter 3).

Decisions on a specific project budget (incorrectly referred to in practice as a "project estimate") should not be based only on the results of a productivity model.

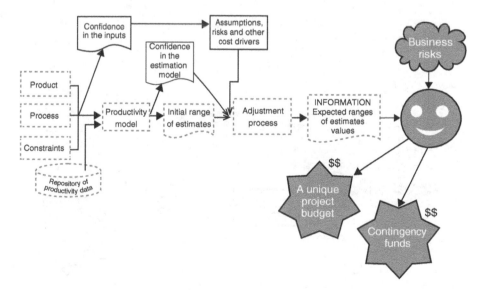

Figure 1.13   Phase D: Budgeting Decision

- The final result of the estimation process cannot be more reliable than the reliability of each subprocess and each component, and is as weak as its weakest component.
- Therefore, the quality of each component must be made known to the decision-makers for prudent use of the outcome of an estimation process.

  Additional concepts related to estimating and budgeting are discussed in Section 1.7.

Phase (E) The re-estimation process – see Figure 1.14
Since uncertainty is inherent to the estimation process, projects must be monitored to verify whether or not they are progressing as planned, with respect to budget, schedule, and expected quality. Whenever major departures from planning materialize, project re-estimation must occur [Fairley 2009; Miranda and Abran 2008]. This is discussed in greater detail in Chapters 3 and 13.

Phase (F) Estimation Process Improvements – see Figures 1.15 and 1.16
At the project level, the direct responsibilities of the project managers cover the five estimation phases described, at which point they move on to the next project.

There is an additional phase typically undertaken at the organizational level, and not at the project level, which involves analyzing the performance of the estimation process itself with respect to the initial estimates once the projects have been completed, and to improve the various phases of the estimation process, from Phase A to Phase E. This we refer to as Phase F: estimation process improvements – see Figure 1.15 for the positioning of this phase and Figure 1.16 for a summary illustration of what this phase includes in terms of inputs and outputs.

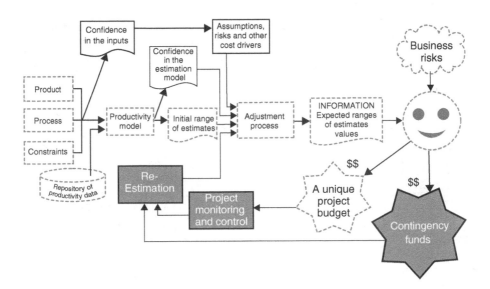

Figure 1.14   Phase E: Re-Estimation

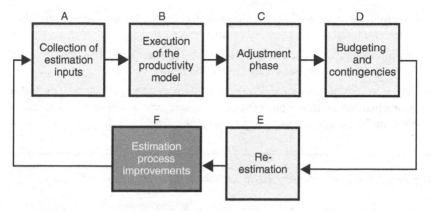

Figure 1.15   Feedback Loop of the Estimation Process

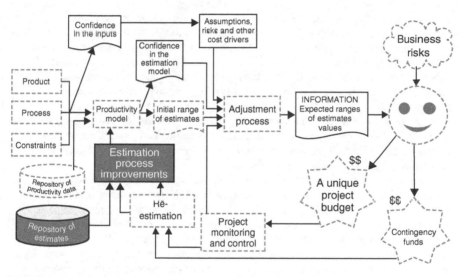

Figure 1.16   Phase F: Estimation Process Improvements

1.7   BUDGETING AND ESTIMATING: ROLES AND RESPONSIBILITIES

1.7.1   Project Budgeting: Levels of Responsibility

The technical part of the estimation process generally leads to a number of scenarios, probabilities, and "estimates."

At this point, a decision must be taken about a specific value, which is commonly referred to as the "project budget" or "project price" in a fixed price management mode.

- The project budget is a single value selected from a large range of candidate values identified by the software estimator!
- This internal project budget, selected by upper management, is then given as the "target" to the project manager (and his team).
- The external project price is determined by upper management, and provided to the customer within a business context, and may be expressed in terms of "time and materials" or as a "fixed price," for instance.

Single-Point Software Project Estimates = A Poor Estimation Culture

Currently, practitioners and managers in the software community provide a "single-point estimate."

However, this practice constitutes a widespread misuse of the concept of estimation, the object of which is to provide a plausible range of values (from a minimum to a maximum, and all the intermediate values – each with a relatively low probability of occurrence), and is the responsibility of the estimator – more on this in Chapters 2 and 3.

Another misuse of the concept of estimation is its improper association with the selection of a specific budget value (which is the role of the manager – see Sections 1.7.2 and 1.7.3), while at the same time risk-taking and the setting aside of contingency funds are addressed at a higher administrative level than that of project manager – more on this in Chapter 3.

Of course, a budget value has a greater probability of being respected than any specific estimate within a range of estimates, mainly because compromises are worked out during the project life cycle, such as reducing the number of functions delivered or lowering quality by skipping some reviews or tests.

Even though a budget value is a single figure, it combines several concepts; for instance, the estimated cost and effort involved in producing a number of deliverables at specified levels of quality at a specified time. The fact that, at the end of the project, the actual cost and effort equal the amounts budgeted does not confirm that the estimates were correct. What is not considered is the possibility that a large number of the required functions might have been delayed to future project phases, and that a great many quality issues might have been shifted to the maintenance category, increasing those costs down the road.

The selection (and allocation) strategy of a project budget will depend on the management culture of the organization and on the industrial context.

(A) *An overly optimistic culture* (or aggressively commercial culture)

In many cases, the basis for the selection of a project budget is the "price to win" (i.e., quotation of the lowest possible price, in order to secure project approval), even though the probability of meeting this budget is almost nonexistent.

- An organization might underbid a project (i.e., put forward a less than reasonable budget) and expect to lose money (i.e., the actual costs will be greater than the accepted budget), but with an expectation of larger profits in subsequent projects.

- An organization might underbid a project initially (i.e., put forward a less than reasonable budget at first), but expect to renegotiate the budget (or prices) upward, based on a number of factors with a high degree of probability of occurrence (such as the addition of functions not initially specified in the bidding process, and at a fairly high cost).

(B) *A very conservative culture*

In a governmental organization with a large number of decision-making levels and long delays for approval, management might present a budget that includes a large number of contingencies in order to avoid going back through the command chain should they have underbudgeted at some point. This would happen, for instance, in organizations operating in a non-competitive environment (such as a commercial monopoly or government agency).

(C) *Any culture between these extremes!*

1.7.2 The Estimator

The role (and responsibility) of the software estimator in the software project estimation process is to

(A) Build the productivity model(s). This includes collecting data from past projects, building explicit models of relationships across dependent and independent variables, and documenting the quality of productivity models.

▶ When the organization does not have data from its past projects, the estimators must find alternative solutions (such as accessing industry data, or gaining access to commercially available estimation tools, and analyzing their performance).

(B) Carry out Phases A–C of the estimation process described in Figures 1.9–1.12, which consists of

▶ collecting data for the project being estimated and documenting them,
▶ feeding these data into the quantitative productivity models as input and documenting the expected ranges of solutions,
▶ carrying out the adjustment process described in Figure 1.12, and
▶ providing this information to decision-makers.

1.7.3 The Manager (Decision-Taker and Overseer)

The manager's responsibility is to take risks and expect to be held accountable for managing them, while minimizing these risks by obtaining as much information as possible with the resources available.

The manager has then to make an informed decision by selecting the "optimal" budget for a specific project in a specific context:

- from the ranges of values provided by the productivity model and the corresponding estimation process

and by committing to a single estimate for a project. This responsibility

- is not in any way an engineering responsibility and
- is clearly a management responsibility.

When a manager forces his technical staff to commit to a single estimate, he is transferring what should be his responsibility to them. This is the inherent risk of decision-making in a context of uncertainty and risk:

- The manager is making the estimator accountable for a decision that he should be taking himself, based on the information that the estimator will have provided.

When a software staffer commits to a single estimate, he is overstepping both his domain of expertise and his domains of responsibility:

- He is acting like a manager, becoming accountable for the risks taken, and he is not being adequately paid for these management duties!

In practice, the business estimation process is much broader than the estimation process, and is not restricted to either a single project or to the software project perspective.

- The outcome of a previous software estimation subprocess cannot not be the only contributor to the decision-making process.

From an organizational perspective, the portfolio of all projects must be taken into account, and, before making a decision on a specific project, managers must also take into account

- the estimated costs,
- the estimated benefits, and
- the estimated risks of all projects.

Decisions on individual projects must be made in the context of a strategy that optimizes the corporate outcome, while minimizing the risks across all projects.

The manager's (i.e., the decision-taker's) additional responsibilities are the following:

- Implementing an estimation process (such as the one described in this chapter), which includes:
  ▶ allocating resources for data collection and data analysis for building the initial productivity model,

▶ allocating resources for integrating this productivity model into the design of the full estimation process,

▶ allocating resources for training on the use of the full estimation process, and

● assigning skilled and trained resources to the estimation process whenever an estimate is required for a specific project.

Example of a High-Risk Project

In a high-risk project situation, with the potential for major benefits, decision-makers will want to provide for contingency funding to ensure project completion, in case the project goes over budget.

Such contingency funding might not be communicated to project management.

This is discussed further in Chapter 2.

1.8 PRICING STRATEGIES

In addition to the estimating and budgeting practices and concepts described in the previous sections, a number of additional practices are referred to (incorrectly) as "estimating" techniques, such as the "win market share" the so-called "estimation technique" – see box below.

Example of a Pricing Strategy: Win Market Share

To win market share, a business decision may be made to underbid for a project by presenting the customer with a "project budget" that may be considerably lower than the expected project cost.

Such a market strategy may hide two other business sub-strategies:

(A) The potential for loss is recognized ahead of time to support the long-term customer relationship, in the form of later and more lucrative projects.

(B) The supplier has realized that, in the course of his project, he has additional ways to increase project costs to recover from the underbid estimates.

This can lead to a situation where perfectly valid ranges of technical estimates are ignored in order to become aligned with business strategies, resulting in project budgets that are unrealistic and unachievable.

1.8.1   Customers-Suppliers: The Risk Transfer Game in Estimation

Almost any customer of a software project is ideally looking for a project at a fixed cost and guaranteed to be *on time* and *on budget*, while implicitly expecting that all the quality targets will be met as well – if not exceeded.

In practice, except in highly competitive markets and in the presence of a great deal of freely available information on the economic factors, this does not happen often because there is an asymmetry of information between customers and producers.

Two generic pricing modes are observed in the software development industry – with a number of variations:

(A) *Time and materials billing mode*

Under this economic pricing model, the customer pays for the effort expended on his project by the software development staff, at an agreed price per staff member throughout the development life cycle. This means that, even though a budget may be allocated ahead of time by the supplier, that supplier is not bound contractually to deliver the described software functions within this budget, by this deadline, and with those quality levels. The supplier is bound to best practices but not to unknown budget figures. In this case, it is the customer who takes on all the budget-related risks. Therefore, providing for overbudgeting is entirely the responsibility of the customer: the customer is basically taking all the business risks.

(B) *Fixed price contract*

Under this economic pricing model, it is the supplier that is legally bound to deliver all of the functionality within the specified budget, deadlines, and quality levels. In such a model, the suppliers is taking all the risks, and correspondingly should have included within the contract, upfront within the agreed price, high contingencies to handle such risks. In such a context, the customer theoretically transfers all the risks to the provider, at a cost of course.

In a context where the economic information between customers and producers is well balanced, the risks across both modes are well managed, but in practice this is not often the case in software development.

1.9   SUMMARY – ESTIMATING PROCESS, ROLES, AND RESPONSIBILITIES

Estimating a fixed effort budget with a fixed duration *accurately* and early on in the budgeting process is not feasible from an engineering perspective:

- The software inputs to the productivity models are far from dependable, and may vary considerably over the project life cycle.
- The available productivity models, built with information from projects completed, are not sophisticated enough to provide a high degree of explanatory power with few independent variables.
- There is, most of the time and in most software organizations, no well-structured feedback loop to improve the foundations of the estimation process.
- Software technology itself is continuously changing, resulting in some of the historical foundations of the productivity models becoming outdated.

Notwithstanding all the above,

- many users still insist that software projects be priced at a fixed cost and be guaranteed to be completed on time and on budget

and

- many project managers commit to completing software projects at a fixed cost and guaranteeing that they will be completed on time and on budget!

This illustrates that beyond the estimation process, there is a business estimation process, distinct from the engineering estimation process.

Business objectives, practices, and policies must also be taken into account when making business decisions.

- Consequently, there are often major differences between the sets of engineering-based estimates and those of the business estimates.

From a corporate perspective, the following two types of estimates should be identified and managed separately:

- engineering estimates and
- business estimates.

This would clarify the decision-making responsibilities and, over time, facilitate improvements to full estimation process.

From an engineering perspective, the software estimation process:

- should not replace the business estimation process

but

- should be a contributor to the full extent of its specialized expertise in terms of providing decision-makers with their professional engineering advice on the estimation of project costs, project uncertainties, and project risks.

This chapter has presented the components that must be implemented to develop a strategy for a *credible and auditable* estimation process.

Key Lessons Learned

In this chapter, we have discussed the fact that the goal of an estimation process should not be to provide a single hard figure, but rather to provide

- information about ranges of plausible values,
- feedback about how good this information is,
- limitations of the information used as input to the estimation process,
- limitations of the information provided as output of the estimation process, and
- analysis and mitigation of risks by documenting the assumptions made about the inputs, and the use of these inputs, in the estimation process.

The realistic expectations of an estimation process must be clarified, as well as what constitutes

- the technical responsibility from an engineering perspective (i.e., the provision of information based on a rigorous process) and
- the managerial responsibility of making a decision on a single-project estimate (from the array of information provided by the productivity model and its context of use for a particular project).

EXERCISES

1. If you do not have quantitative information on your organization's performance in software project delivery, can you expect to have good estimates for the next project? Explain your answer.
2. What are the two broad approaches to software estimation, and what are their differences?
3. Identify some of the *worst* practices with regard to *inputting* to an estimation process.
4. Identify some of the *best* practices with regard to *inputting* to an estimation process.
5. Identify some of the *poor* practices in handling the *outputs* of an estimation process.
6. What do industry surveys tell us about the performance of software projects in meeting their budget and deadlines?
7. What is the difference between a "productivity model" and an "estimation process"?
8. If you know the accuracy of a productivity model, what is the expected accuracy of its use in an *estimation* context?
9. How can you design a productivity model?
10. How do you evaluate the performance of a productivity model?
11. What are the benefits of mathematical productivity models?
12. For estimation, how would you handle *cost drivers* that are not included in the productivity model?
13. For estimation, how would you handle *risk factors* that are not included in the productivity model?

14. How can an organization take into account *potential scope changes* when using its *productivity model* in an *estimation* context?

15. Discuss the key differences between providing an estimate for a project and taking a decision on a project budget. Discuss roles and responsibilities in estimation.

16. What are some of the key characteristics of estimation? Taking into account these key characteristics, what can you deliver when an organization expects accurate estimates from you? Provide your management with a better definition of "accuracy" in this context.

17. When a manager selects a project budget from a range of estimates, what other major decision should he/she take concurrently?

18. How can an organization take into account *actual scope changes* in its *estimation process*?

19. Why should an organization have not only a plain estimation model, but also a re-estimation model?

TERM ASSIGNMENTS

1. Document the estimation process in your organization.

2. Compare the performance of your projects with that documented in industry surveys, such as the Standish Group Chaos Report.

3. Compare the estimation process in your organization with those illustrated in Figures 1.2 and 1.15. Identify improvement priorities for your organization's estimation process.

4. Propose an action plan to address the top three priorities for improving an organization's software estimation process.

5. Compare the estimation process in Figure 1.15 with an estimation model *proposed in a book*. Comment on the similarities and differences. Identify strengths and weaknesses in the productivity model analyzed.

6. Take an estimation model *proposed by a vendor* and compare it to the estimation process in Figure 1.15. Comment on the similarities and differences. Identify strengths and weaknesses in the productivity model analyzed.

7. Take an estimation model that is *available free on the Web* and compare it to the estimation process in Figure 1.15. Comment on the similarities and differences. Identify strengths and weaknesses in the productivity model analyzed.

Chapter 2

Engineering and Economics Concepts for Understanding Software Process Performance

OBJECTIVES

This chapter covers

- The development process modeled as a production process
- Simple quantitative models
- The introduction of economics concepts in software models, such as fixed and variable costs and economies and diseconomies of scale

2.1 INTRODUCTION: THE PRODUCTION (DEVELOPMENT) PROCESS

How can the performance of a development process be estimated in the future if its current and past performances, and variations in those performances, are unknown?

In this chapter, we look into the following questions from an economics perspective:

- How can we figure out the performance of a software development process?

- How can we build quantitative models of development processes?

A development process can be modeled as a production process. This can be illustrated at a very high level with the following main components – see Figure 2.1:

- Process order (in software, the set of requirements)
- Inputs

Software Project Estimation: The Fundamentals for Providing High Quality Information to Decision Makers, First Edition. Alain Abran.
© 2015 the IEEE Computer Society. Published 2015 by John Wiley & Sons, Inc.

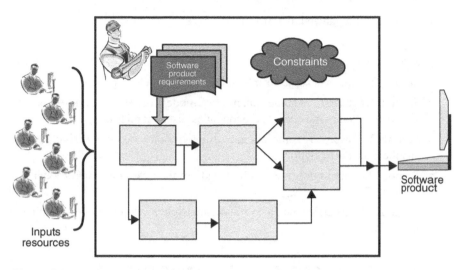

Figure 2.1 A Production Process

- Process activities
- Outputs (the products delivered).

(A) An example of a *process order* in industry would be a car manufacturer producing 100 copies of a car – all the same, or with minor variations. In the case of building a house, the process order would consist of detailed architectural and engineering plans precisely describing the house to be built. In software, the process order corresponds to the set of requirements for the software product to be developed.

(B) The *inputs* to a development process are typically the human resources in software: they are the staff who will be available to work on the development project and perform all the tasks of the subprocesses within the process. These inputs are typically measured in work-hours (or person-days, -weeks, or -months).

(C) In developing software, these *activities* are typically organized according to the development methodology selected by managers, from the waterfall model to the Agile approach. These activities are performed by the developers to transform the requirements into software products. In this context, for each activity in a production process, there are controls that indicate what is expected from the whole production and from each activity. This includes the set of requirements that describes the expected product and its characteristics, as well as any constraints with respect to either the product or the process in terms of the project priorities (costs, quality, and deadlines).

(D) The *output* of a software development process is the operational software that should correspond to the requirements described (i.e., the software product).

This chapter is organized as follows:

- Section 2.2 presents the engineering (and management) perspective of a production process.
- Section 2.3 presents some simple quantitative models of processes.
- Section 2.4 introduces some quantitative models using economics concepts, such as fixed/variable costs and economies/diseconomies of scale.
- Section 2.5 discusses some characteristics of software engineering datasets and their data distribution.
- Section 2.6 highlights the explicit and implicit variables in productivity models.
- Section 2.7 introduces the possibility of multiple economic models within the same dataset.

2.2 THE ENGINEERING (AND MANAGEMENT) PERSPECTIVE ON A PRODUCTION PROCESS

From an engineering perspective, a production process is more complex, and must also include a "monitoring and control" process – see Figure 2.2.

This monitoring and control process must include the following:

- A collection of measurement results about the current and past performance of the production process.

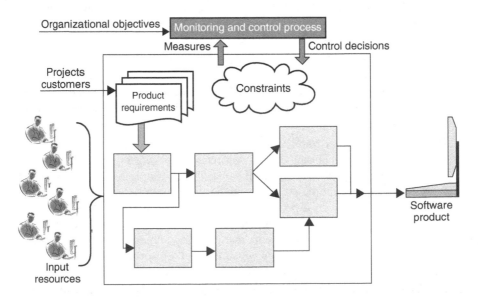

Figure 2.2 A Production Process – the Engineering and Management Perspective

- An analysis of the process performance against the project objectives and the goals of the organization.
- The facility to send back decisions, using various evaluation and decision models, to make adjustments (typically through changes to process activities to alter the performance of the production process).

There are significant differences between *project objectives* and *organizational objectives*.

Project objectives are limited to the specific objectives of the project at hand.

They may involve the delivery of the project according to the priorities identified within the project scope, usually without taking into consideration other organizational constraints beyond the project duration. The project has an estimated end date, and once the project has been completed, the project development team is disbanded: a project has always a closing date.

Project objectives[1] are generally multiple and concurrent, such as to deliver:

- a number of software functions,
- within a specified time frame,
- within a specified (limited) budget, and
- with a level of quality (not always precisely specified).

In an economic context of limited resources, where software project objectives are most often presumed to perform at unrealistically optimized levels (typically using a very optimistic view of the performance capabilities of the process), not all these objectives can be fully met at once.

Priorities must then be assigned to explicitly state:

- which objectives are to be paramount and met as stated and, by contrast,
- which objectives are to be bypassed when a compromise must be made.

Organizational objectives are not limited by the project objectives. They represent a much longer term view with a much broader scope.

- An organizational objective is typically concerned with issues that extend beyond the life of the project itself, such as the impact of the quality delivered by a development project over the many years of maintenance of the software being developed.
- Similarly, the organizational objectives for the project may require that the project follow the standards of the organization, and, even though this might not be optimal for the project at hand, those standards would, when they are closely adhered to, facilitate, for example:
  - ▶ the mobility of staff across projects and
  - ▶ the maintenance of a portfolio of projects developed using the same standards.

---

[1] In the Agile methodology, these correspond to Sprint objectives.

Similarly, it would be important to compare project performance, in terms of evaluating the achievement of organizational objectives, whether the projects use similar or different technologies and development environments:

- Such information could then be used at the organizational level to analyze factors of either low performance or high performance, investigate causes, propose remedial action, and develop improvement programs that may outlive the life span of most projects.

Finally, information collected at the organizational level for each project can be used for external benchmarking purposes and to develop and improve productivity models.

Project Priorities: A Balancing Act

- When the top priority is that all the specified functions be delivered, then, in practice, extension of the project deadline and additional budget expenditures for the project may be required.
- When the top priority is the project deadline (that is, meeting the deadline is paramount), a reduction in the number of functions to be delivered may be required, as well as a compromise on the level of quality to be achieved.

2.3   SIMPLE QUANTITATIVE PROCESS MODELS

2.3.1   Productivity Ratio

In economics, and in engineering as well, *productivity* and *unit cost* are distinct but related concepts.

- *Productivity* is typically defined as the ratio of the number of outputs delivered by a process to the number of its inputs.

$$\text{Productivity ratio} = \frac{\text{Outputs}}{\text{Inputs}}$$

For economic studies, measurement of the outputs must be concerned of what is being produced and be independent of the technology used to deliver a product or a service.

- For a car manufacturing plant:
  - the output for a productivity study might be measured as the number of cars, per category of cars.
    - ▶ The number of tons of steel, fiberglass, and so on., coming out of a car plant would not be used for productivity studies!

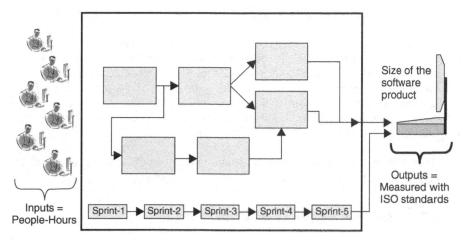

Figure 2.3   The Productivity Ratio

- For software organizations – see Figure 2.3:
  - a measure of what is delivered to users, from the users' perspective, is required for a productivity study.
    - ▶ In software, the productivity ratio is correctly expressed when it uses, as a measurement of the output of the development process, the number of functions delivered (using any such related measures – with preference given to international standards for software measurement) divided by the number of hours worked.
    - ▶ Note that measures of this type are valid for productivity measurement and analysis, since they measure what has been delivered in terms of the needs that are being met by the software, that is, the functions required by the software.

The number of source lines of code (SLOC) is not the best type of measure for a productivity study, as they are highly dependent on programming languages, and on many other factors, such as the programmer's style and standards.

SLOC are useful in organizations with projects developed using a single programming language, but less useful in software projects with a mix of programming languages.

EXAMPLE 2.1

The average productivity of software development organization A is 30 Function Points per person-month when developing a Web-based catalog, and the productivity of software organization B, developing exactly the same type of Web-based catalog, is 33 Function Points per person-month.

The two organizations use the same units of measurement for their inputs and outputs, and their corresponding productivity ratios indicate a 10% difference of productivity within the same application type. This difference indicates that organization B is 10% more productive than organization A; however, it does not explain the reason for this difference, which is typically explained by other factors not included in the productivity ratio per se.

While this productivity ratio quantifies the performance of the process through two explicit variables (input and output), it does not include any direct descriptive or quantitative information about the process itself or about the product developed. The process is therefore only implicit in this ratio.

Productivity ratio comparison is meaningful, since it is independent of the technology and other resources used to develop the product.

2.3.2   Unit Effort (or Unit Cost) Ratio

Unit effort is typically defined as the inverse of the productivity ratio, that is, the ratio of the inputs to the outputs.

$$\text{Unit effort} = \frac{\text{Inputs}}{\text{Outputs}}$$

EXAMPLE 2.2

From Example 2.1, if there are 210 work-hours in a person-month, 30 Function Points per month would correspond to a unit effort of 210 hours/30 Function Points for developing the Web-based software at software organization A, that is, a unit effort of 7 hours/Function Point. For another organization developing software for cash transfer banking operations, the unit effort per Function Point for 210 work-hours could be 210 hours/10 Function Points, that is, a unit effort of 21 hours/Function Point.

This unit effort ratio is often used in the literature and in benchmarking studies. It is also referred to as the "project delivery rate" (PDR) by the International Software Benchmarking Standards Group – ISBSG (wwww.isbsg.org) – see also Chapter 8.

Productivity and Efficiency in Software Development

Henry and Charles each programmed the same set of three functions with a size of 10 Function Points in 60 hours. Henry wrote 600 SLOC (source lines of code) and Charles wrote 900 SLOC in the same programming language.

Productivity: Henry and Charles have the same productivity ratio at 10 Function Points for 60 hours of work (or 1 Function Point per 6 hours of work). Their unit effort per function (the inverse of the productivity ratio) is, therefore, 6 hours per Function Point.

Efficiency: With 600 SLOC for the same set of functions, Henry was more efficient than Charles (with 900 SLOC), using the same programming language for transforming requirements into SLOC: Henry's ratio is 60 SLOC per Function Point, whereas Charles' ratio is 90 SLOC per Function Point.

Therefore, Henry is more efficient than Charles, in terms of transforming requirements into SLOC, although both had the same productivity and the same unit effort.

This example illustrates only short-term efficiency within the project life cycle, but not long-term efficiency across the maintenance life cycle: a function implemented in a highly optimized number of lines of code may be extremely difficult to maintain, lowering long-term efficiency as a result.

Key observations:

(A) SLOC provide a quantitative representation of how something is done in a technology, not what has been produced with that technology. Therefore, SLOC are not an adequate measure for productivity calculation and studies. They are, however, a relevant measure for efficiency studies within the same technology and to compare an aspect of efficiency across technologies.

(B) Measures of functions delivered by software quantify what has been delivered to users, and, from this perspective, they correspond to the output of a software development process, and constitute an adequate concept for productivity measurement and analysis. In addition, international standards for the measurement of software functions facilitate the comparison of productivity ratios and their analysis across contexts and environments.

Efficiency and Performance

Efficiency is not the same as performance, the latter being a much broader term. Efficiency implies fewer resources required to produce something, and, up to a point, lower costs.

For example, a car manufacturing company might be more efficient at building a car than its competitors, but may not perform well in the marketplace: its cars might be less appealing to purchasers, who prefer its competitor's cars, even at a higher price. Similarly, a car manufacturing company might be less efficient, but the best performer in terms of selling cars, and it may be more profitable even though it has the highest unit cost.

In the realm of software, it is important to know something about code readability and maintainability, ease of testing, defect density of delivered products, use of memory, and so on, in order to judge the performances of two programmers or two software organizations.

2.3.3 Averages

In this section, we present an example of a productivity model built using the average productivity of a set of completed projects.

An average is a well-known mathematical function, with corresponding properties (and limitations as well). This average productivity is built by

- calculating the productivity ratios of each individual project in a sample,
- adding them up, and

- dividing the total by the number of projects in the sample.

Note that this average describes the full sample, and not the individual projects in the sample.

In addition, a number of related characteristics are typically provided with the average function as follows:

- Minimum
- Maximum
- First quartile, last quartile
- 1 standard deviation
- 2 standard deviations, and so on
- Skewness
- Kurtosis
- And so on.

A productivity model built using the average productivity is presented in Figure 2.4, where the average, quartiles, minimum, and maximum are represented graphically with a box-plot: the average of a sample is represented by the horizontal line in the brown box that divides the middle quartiles; the maximum and minimum are represented outside these two quartiles.

The *standard deviation* (σ, read as sigma) shows how much variation there is, or dispersion, from the average: a low standard deviation indicates that the data points tend to be very close to the average, and a high standard deviation indicates that the data points are spread out over a large range of values. Figure 2.5 illustrates the standard deviations for a dataset with a Normal (or Gaussian) distribution, where

1. $\sigma = 68.2\%$ means that 68.2% of the data points are within the 1 σ interval across the average
2. $\sigma = 95.2\%$ means that 95.2% of the data points are within the 1 σ interval across the average.

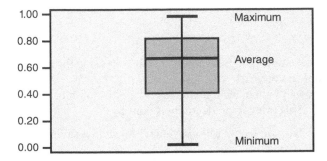

Figure 2.4   Box-Plot: Average and Quartiles

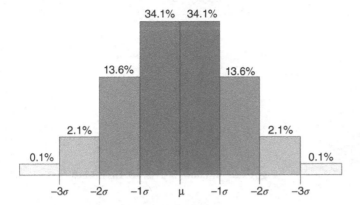

Figure 2.5   A Normal Distribution and the Standard Deviations

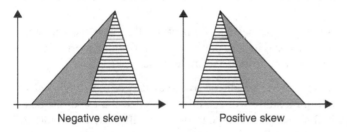

Figure 2.6   Skewness from a Normal Distribution

The distributions of datasets in software engineering are not necessarily Normal, and will often vary. Variations from the normal distribution are commonly characterized by skewness and kurtosis.

Skewness is a measure of the asymmetry of the probability distribution of a random variable with a real value. It can be positive or negative – see Figure 2.6.

- A negative skew indicates that the *tail* on the left-hand side of the probability density function is *longer* than the right-hand side, and the bulk of the values (including the median) lie to the right of the mean.

- A positive skew indicates that the *tail* on the right-hand side of the probability density function is *longer* than the left-hand side, and the bulk of the values lie to the left of the mean.

- A zero value indicates that the values are relatively evenly distributed on both sides of the mean, typically (but not necessarily) implying a symmetric distribution.

Kurtosis is a description of the "peakedness" of a distribution – see Figure 2.7: Similar to the concept of skewness, *kurtosis* is a descriptor of the shape of a probability distribution. In Figure 2.7, both the blue and red distributions would have the same average, but

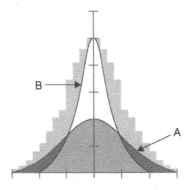

Figure 2.7   Kurtosis in a Normal Distribution

- the distribution of the B curve has a very high peak, which represents high kurtosis, and its data points, which are within the 1 σ interval, would be close to this average,
- the distribution of the A curve has a lower peak for the same average, which represents lower kurtosis, and its data points, which are within the 1 σ interval, would be much further away from the average value.

In summary, productivity models built on averages can be good productivity models, but only under a limited number of conditions: the distribution of the data is normal and there is limited skewness and high kurtosis, as illustrated in Figure 2.7. In all other conditions, when used for estimation purposes, the use of an average is misleading, since the range of estimation errors can be expected to be high.

2.3.4   Linear and Non Linear Models

Figure 2.8 shows a non linear model. How can we obtain a linear model from the dataset containing a number of projects? What statistical techniques can we use?

One technique is statistical linear regression (see any book on statistics that discusses regression techniques). Through a set of iterations, statistical software looks at all the data points in a dataset and calculates the regression equation (which will be a straight line when a linear regression is requested) that models this dataset best:

- It does this by calculating the distance of each data point from the line, taking the sum of these distances over the whole dataset, and, over a number of iterations, finding the line that minimizes the sum of these distances.

The Least-Squares Regression method is typically used to derive the regression equations, because it is relatively simple and produces good results.

- This method involves finding values of a and b that minimize the squares of the differences between the actual and estimated values for each data point.

There are many other types of regression model in the literature, such as the exponential model and the quadratic model.

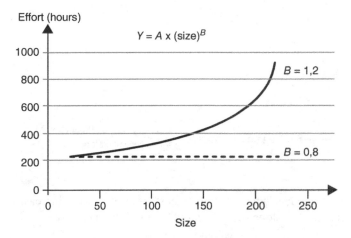

Figure 2.8 Power Models with Exponents Greater than 1 (Solid Line) or Less Than 1 (Dashed Line)

Of course, a production model is not necessarily linear: a production process may behave differently and its model could be represented by any shape. Statistical techniques are available to model production processes of any shape.

A power model, for instance, is represented by the following formula:

$$Y(\text{effort}) = A * (\text{Size})^B$$

Figure 2.8 shows two models with an exponential shape: one where the exponent has a value greater than 1, and another where the exponent has a value less than 1.

- Note that when the value of the exponent is 1, it represents the specific case of a "straight line" model, that is, a linear model.

Of course, there could be other more complex shapes of models, such as quadratic models of the form – see Figure 2.9:

- $Y = A + Bx + Cx^2$

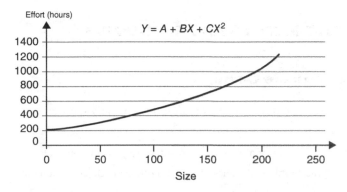

Figure 2.9 A Quadratic Model

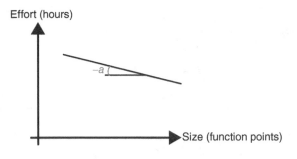

Figure 2.10   A Production Model with a Negative Slope

There could even be models where the total cost decreases with increases in inputs. In these cases, the slope of the model would be negative, as in Figure 2.10.

- This would be surprising in practice, and whenever such models are observed, the practitioners should verify the quality of the data input to their models – see box.

Negative Values in a Model = Warning

Whenever *a negative value* is observed in either the constant or the slope of the model, this should raise a red flag to both practitioners and researchers: the dataset should be closely reviewed to verify the quality of the quantitative data, as well as the presence of significant outliers.

Practitioners should be careful not to use the model for ranges of negative values – for these ranges, the estimated values are meaningless.

Also, they should never use such models outside the ranges for which there exist no data to support them.

2.4   QUANTITATIVE MODELS AND ECONOMICS CONCEPTS

2.4.1   Fixed and Variable Costs

A simple model, such as the one illustrated in Figure 2.11, typically represents the performance of past projects:

- Along the x-axis is the functional size of each software project completed.
- Along the y-axis is the number of hours of effort required to deliver each software project.

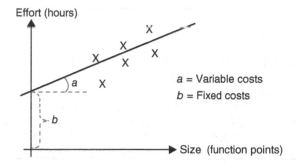

a = Variable costs

b = Fixed costs

Figure 2.11 A Production Model with Fixed and Variable Costs [Abran and Gallego 2009. Reprinted with permission from Knowledge Systems Institute Graduate School.]

Therefore, the points in the graph represent the number of hours[2] it took to deliver the corresponding functional size of the projects completed.

A quantitative model of the performance of a production process is usually built with data from <u>completed</u> projects, that is, when:

- all the information on a project is available,
- there is no remaining uncertainty in either the inputs or the outputs: all the software functions have been delivered, and
- all the work hours for the project have been accurately registered in a time reporting system.

The quantitative model of a production process is represented by the sloping line in Figure 2.11. In a production process, there are typically two major types of cost incurred to produce different sets of the same types of output:

- ▶ *Variable costs*: the portion of the resources expended (i.e. inputs), which depends directly on the number of outputs produced.
  - ▶ In Figure 2.8, this corresponds to the slope of the linear model, that is, slope = a (in terms of hours/Function Point).
- ▶ *Nonvariable costs*: the portion of resources expended (i.e., inputs), *which does not depend on the number of outputs*.
  - ▶ In Figure 2.8, this corresponds to b (i.e. in hours), which represents the point on the vertical axis where the quantitative model crosses this axis when size = 0 on the horizontal axis.

Terminology: Variable and Fixed Costs

In models, this parameter, which represents the portion of the cost *that is not dependent on an increase in the independent variable*, is often referred to as a fixed cost. This common terminology is adopted in this book.

---

[2]Or whatever the unit of work effort: for instance, person-days, person-months, and person-years.

Examples of Fixed Costs in Software Projects

Independently of the size of the projects, the corporate standards of a software organization may require mandatory internal deliverables (project management plans, change control procedures, quality controls, audits, etc.).

In a typical production process, a significant portion of these would be considered the fixed costs of a production run. Similarly for a software project, project management plans do not depend on variations in the functional size of the software delivered to users.

A linear model is one in which the relationship between effort and size is represented by the following formula:

$$Y(\text{effort in hours}) = f(x) = a * \text{Size} + b$$

where

- Size = number of Function Points (FP)
- a = variable cost = number of hours per Function Point (hours/FP)
- b = fixed cost in hours.

In terms of units, this equation gives

$$Y(\text{hours}) = (\text{hours/FP}) \times \text{FP} + \text{hours} = \text{hours}$$

The straight sloping line across the figure represents the performance of the production process, based on the performance of the past projects included in the graph.

- *Fixed cost*: the value of b when $x(\text{size}) = 0$,
  - For example, if $b = 100$ hours on the y-axis, then that 100 hours represents the fixed cost of the production process (i.e., in this organization, a cost of 100 hours of project effort is required to manage a project, according to the corporate standards, independently of its size in terms of functions to be developed).
- *Variable cost*: the slope of the line represents the variable costs, that is, the amount of the dependent variable, y (i.e., the number of work hours) required to produce an additional unit of output, that is, the independent variable, x.

Figures 2.12 and 2.13 represent two other types of production process:

- Figure 2.12 illustrates a production process where there is no fixed cost. In this situation, the production line goes straight through the origin, where effort $y = 0$ when size $x = 0$.
- Figure 2.13 represents a production process where the value on the y-axis at the origin (e.g., $x = 0$) is negative, that is, the number of hours is negative at the origin (i.e., $-b$). Of course, a negative number of hours does not exist in reality.

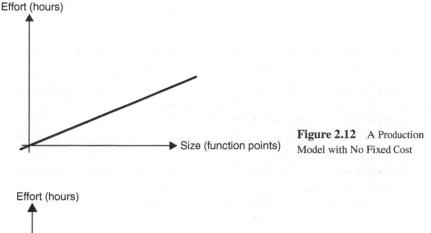

Figure 2.12   A Production
Model with No Fixed Cost

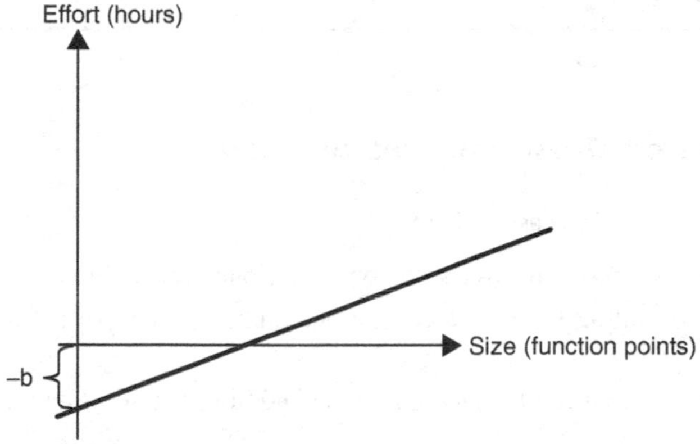

Figure 2.13   A Production Model with a (Theoretically) Negative Fixed Cost

While such a situation can be expressed in a mathematical statistical model, practitioners must be very careful using a model built with data points from industry,
which gives a negative constant at the origin!

- This does not mean that the model is invalid, but rather that it is not valid
  across all size ranges, and cannot be used for small software projects.

Linear Regression Models with a Negative Constant

- For projects smaller than the size at which the linear model crosses under the
  horizontal axis, such models are meaningless.
- For projects larger than the point at which the model crosses the origin, the models
  are meaningful (overall, they provide a positive number of work hours).
- Of course, care should be exercised in the interpretation of models for project sizes
  close to this negative–positive crossing point.

Practical suggestions:

(A) Identify the size at which the model crosses on the horizontal axis on this axis.

(B) Split the dataset into two subsets:

B1: projects sized between 0 and the size threshold at the crossing point on the *x*-axis and

B2: projects larger than the size threshold.

(C) Build two models for each subset (B1: for projects smaller than the threshold and B2: for projects larger than the threshold).

(D) For estimation purposes, select model B1 or B2, depending on the size of the project to be estimated.

2.4.2   Economies and Diseconomies of Scale

In production processes, there can be cases where

- one additional unit of output requires *exactly* one additional unit of input,
- one additional unit of output requires *less than* one additional unit of input, and
- one additional unit of output requires *more than* one additional unit of input.

Economies of Scale

When the increase in output units requires a correspondingly smaller increase in input units, the production process is said to generate economies of scale – see line A in Figure 2.14, as compared to line C:

- For the same increase in outputs, the production process represented by Line A requires much less additional effort (on y-axis) than the production processes represented by either line B or line C.

Diseconomies of Scale

By contrast, when an increase in output units requires a larger increase in input units for each additional output unit, the production process is said to generate diseconomies of scale:

- For each additional unit produced, the production process becomes less productive – see line C in Figure 2.14.

A production process with a similar increase in output units across all size ranges would be represented by line B in Figure 2.14.

For economies and diseconomies of scale, see also Abran and Gallego [2009].

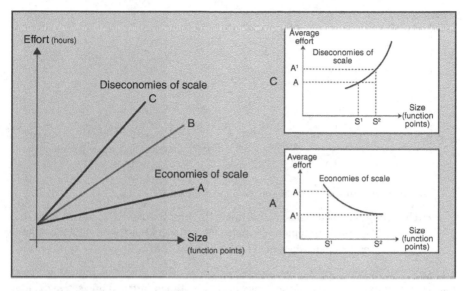

Figure 2.14   Economies (Line A) and Diseconomies of Scale (Line C)

Negative Slopes?

In this type of figure, with size on the *x*-axis and effort (or duration) on the *y*-axis, a negative slope would suggest that, for a large amount of outputs (on the *x*-axis), the process would have required fewer total inputs (here, effort or duration) than smaller projects; of course, this has no practical interpretation in economics, and would suggest instead a problem with the integrity of the data collected.

2.5   SOFTWARE ENGINEERING DATASETS AND THEIR DISTRIBUTION

In this section, we discuss the different types of data distribution observed in the datasets documented in the software engineering literature, as well as in the datasets available in public domain repositories.

2.5.1   Wedge-Shaped Datasets

The type of project distribution illustrated in Figure 2.15 has often been reported in the software engineering literature. We can see here that, as the size increases on the *x*-axis, there is a correspondingly greater dispersion of the data points across the *y*-axis:

- For projects of similar size, there are increasingly wide variations in effort on the y-axis as the projects increase in size.

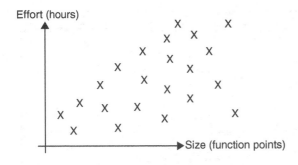

Figure 2.15   A Wedge-Shaped Dataset in Software Engineering

This is often referred to as a wedge-shaped dataset.

- The wedge-shaped dataset was initially observed by Kitchenham and Taylor [1984], and it is typical of many data subsets built with data from large repositories (such as illustrated in Abran et al. 2007).

This type of behavior (increasing dispersion of effort as size increases) indicates that in these datasets, when all the projects are combined into a single set, size alone does not adequately describe the relationship with effort, and that additional independent variables are necessary to do so.

This large dispersion in project productivity would typically be caused by one, or a mix, of the following reasons:

- The project data come from organizations with distinct production processes with correspondingly distinct productivity behavior.
- The project data represent the development of software products with major differences, in terms of software domains, nonfunctional requirements, and other characteristics.
- The development process is out of control, with an almost unpredictable productivity performance (for instance, large productivity variances would be expected from projects developed in an ad hoc manner at Level 1 of the CMMI® model).
- Data collected in an organization based on post-event opinions, outside a sound measurement program, and with ad hoc and local measurement definitions can easily be plagued by data integrity issues, potentially leading to large variations in data behavior.
- And so on.

2.5.2 Homogeneous Datasets

Another type of project distribution is shown in Figure 2.16. Here, the dispersion of the effort as size increases is highly consistent. This would typically indicate more homogeneous datasets, in which the increase in software size explains the increase

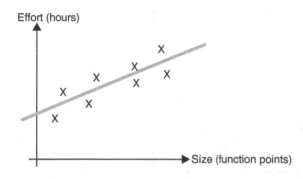

Figure 2.16   A Homogeneous Size–Effort Dataset in Software Engineering

in effort sufficiently well. Such a distribution of software project data also appears in the literature, for example, Abran and Robillard [1996], Abran et al. [2007], Stern [2009], Lind and Heldal [2008, 2010]. In these datasets, the increases in functional size explain 80–90% of the increases in effort, while all the other factors together explain only 10–20% of those increases.

The data points are much closer in these datasets, and the variation in the increase in size leads to consistent variations in the increase in effort, which are, relatively speaking, within the same range and do not exhibit the typical wedge-shaped pattern (as size increases).

- Such datasets would be considered homogeneous with respect to the dependent and independent variables being investigated.

This low dispersion in project productivity is usually caused by one, or a mix, of the following reasons:

- The project data come from a single organization with well-implemented development standards.
- The project data represent the development of software products with very similar characteristics, in terms of software domains, nonfunctional requirements, and other characteristics.
- The development process is under control, with predictable productivity performance (for instance, small process variations from projects developed at Levels 4 or 5 of the CMMi® model).
- The data were collected in an organization based on a sound in-process measurement program, where standardized measurement definitions have been adopted by all project participants, leading to a high level of data integrity.

Note that the datasets in the two examples presented in Figures 2.17 and 2.18 have the following characteristics in common:

- They both represent data for a single organization.
- Both organizations had significant expertise in developing software in a consistent manner, and within basically the same development environment.

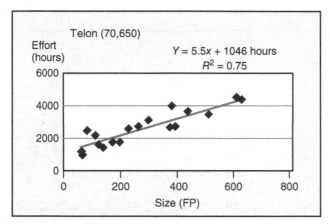

Figure 2.17   The TELON Dataset [Abran et al. 2007. Reprinted with permission from John Wiley & Sons, Inc.]

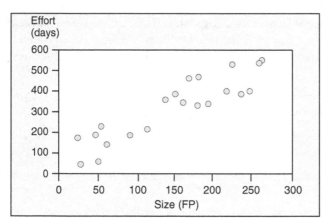

Figure 2.18   A Homogeneous Dataset of 21 projects [Abran and Robillard 1996. Reprinted with permission from an IEEE publication.]

2.6 PRODUCTIVITY MODELS: EXPLICIT AND IMPLICIT VARIABLES

In productivity models represented in two dimensions by a line (a straight line or an exponential line, e.g.), either graphically, as in Figures 2.8–2.16, or by a single independent variable equation, only two explicit variables are modeled:

- The output (size), which is the independent variable
- The input (effort), which is the dependent variable.

What is often forgotten in using and interpreting such models is that there is another underlying, and very important, implicit dimension, which is the process itself.

That process is composed of (or influenced by) a very large number of variables, each of which can have a significant impact on the productivity of the development process.

Examples of Implicit Variables in a Process

- Team experience
- Project manager experience
- Software engineering environment platform
- Design methodology
- Quality controls
- And so on.

- In models with only one independent variable (i.e., the functional size on the x-axis), none of these implicit variables is directly taken into account.
- However, in practice, each of these variables does have an impact on the unit cost of each function developed, and it could be reasonably expected that each variable would have its own range of impact on the dependent variable (i.e., effort).
- The set of these variables, and of their corresponding combined individual impacts, constitutes, then, the variation in the production model that is not entirely explained by the single variable, functional size.

However, if most of these variables in a set of projects are similar for all the projects in the sample, they should have minimal impact on the unit cost:

- In such datasets, it can be reasonably expected that functional size will be the dominant independent variable impacting size.

This set of conditions is illustrated with two examples – see Figures 2.17 and 2.18.

EXAMPLE 2.3

The relatively homogenous dataset in Figure 2.12 is made up of projects from the same organization that developed their software using the same application TELON platform in the late 1990s, with a set of well-documented development and project management procedures, the same teams, and in the same application domain, that is, financial systems. In this dataset, the increase in size alone explains 75% of the increase in effort.

EXAMPLE 2.4

The set of projects in Figure 2.18 comes from a single organization with

- a development process and a project management process documented with a large number of procedural templates, including inspections carried out in multiple project phases (i.e., for requirements documents, design documents, and program coding), as well as extensive testing procedures and
- extensive measurement procedures implemented for both development projects and maintenance activities.

This organization had been assessed at that time with the CMM model as having fully met all the Level 3 Key Process Areas but one, in addition to strong documented evidence of the practices at Level 5.

Therefore, in this organization, the development process was considered under control, with a recognized capacity for estimating adequately and for meeting project commitments in terms of number of functions, delivery date, and levels of quality.

Furthermore, many of these projects had been managed by the same project managers, and with the same staff completing the set of projects, without a noticeable turnover rate, and, of course, using mostly the same software engineering development environment and developing software applications within the same application domain, that is, banking software.

In summary, most of the variables that are significantly different in the datasets of projects from multiple organizations (such as in the ISBSG repository) were, in practice, fixed (e.g., constants) in this development environment. Under these circumstances, it is not surprising that size can explain most of the variations in the dependent variable, that is, project work hours.

When so many cost drivers, or independent variables, do not vary noticeably across projects, they can be considered almost as constants for all projects, with no significant impact across project unit costs.

- This does not mean, however, that size is the only independent variable impacting effort, even in these environments.
- Small variations in the other variables can also have some impact, contributing to the variance not explained by the size variable only.

2.7 A SINGLE AND UNIVERSAL CATCH-ALL MULTIDIMENSIONAL MODEL OR MULTIPLE SIMPLER MODELS?

The Holy Grail of Software Estimation

A single universal model that will predict with (perfect) accuracy any project, any time, and under any circumstances.

The classical approach to building estimation models in software engineering, in industry, and at times in the literature, is to build a single multivariable estimation model and include in it as many cost drivers (i.e., independent variables) as possible (a "catch-all" model).

2.7.1   Models Built from Available Data

The builders of estimation models, who have access to a reasonable set of data points on completed projects, typically attempt to take into account the largest possible number of variables included in the available dataset – or available from the literature – with:

- the authors' own definition of these cost drivers and
- the authors' own measurement rules for these costs drivers, and their own assignment of impact factors for each of them.

This approach, of course, leads to complex models with a large number of variables "n," which cannot be represented in an n-dimensional space. An alternative approach will be discussed later, in Chapter 10, on building estimation models with a larger number of variables.

2.7.2   Models Built on Opinions on Cost Drivers

Another approach often observed in industry is to build models based on practitioners' opinions about various variables and the corresponding estimated impact of each on the development process. This opinion-based approach, which is referred to as the "expert judgment approach," is used when an organization does not collect data.

"Feel Good" Estimation Models

Models that include many opinion-based cost drivers could be characterized as "feel good" models:

- Managers consider that most of the important cost drivers have been taken into account, and hence they believe that the risks associated with their estimates have been reduced.

However, the quality of such models is not supported by empirical evidence, and they typically result in more uncertainty.

The real question is: How good are these models? – see Chapters 4–7 for further details on analyzing the quality of estimation models.

2.7.3 Multiple Models with Coexisting Economies and Diseconomies of Scale

In this book, a modest (and probably more realistic) approach is taken:

- A single model cannot be the best in all circumstances.

Observations in industry and practice *do not currently support* the viability-feasibility of a single and universal model:

- In the field, there is a very large diversity of development processes, different mixes of costs drivers, and most probably different impacts of these cost drivers, depending on the contexts.
    - ▶ The models that both expert practitioners and researchers have come up with have not that much in common, and most cannot be generalized to contexts other than the one on which they were based.
- The datasets in the literature suggest that the classical concepts of economies and diseconomies of scale are applicable to software development processes.

What are the practical implications of these observations?

Let us now revisit the wedge-shaped datasets that are often seen in software projects – see Figure 2.15. When looked at from the perspective of an analytical grid of the concepts of economies and diseconomies of scale, we see that this single wedge-shaped dataset could be split into three subsets for analysis purposes, as follows – see Figure 2.19:

- Zone 1: The lower part of the wedge-shaped dataset, which represents the set of projects demonstrating large economies of scale:

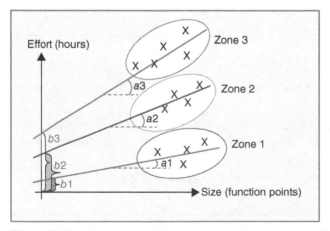

Figure 2.19 A Wedge-Shaped Dataset with Three Data Subsets with Economies/Diseconomies of Scale. [Abran and Cuadrado 2009. Reprinted with permission from Knowledge Systems Institute Graduate School.]

▶ For this subset, even major increases in the number of functions do not lead to noticeably large corresponding increases in effort.

▶ In practice, it is almost as if the effort required in this subset is insensitive to an increase in the number of functions in the software being developed.

● Zone 3: The upper part of the wedge-shaped dataset, which represents the set of projects demonstrating diseconomies of scale with respect to functional size as the independent variable:

▶ For this subset, a small increase in size requires a much larger increase in effort – in either fixed cost or variable cost, or in both.

● Zone 2: Finally, there may be a third subset, which will be found somewhere in the middle of the wedge-shaped dataset.

This could mean that there will be three distinct productivity models within this single dataset:

$f_1(x) = a_1 * x + b_1$, which corresponds to the data sample in zone 1.

$f_2(x) = a_2 * x + b_2$, which corresponds to the data sample in zone 2.

$f_3(x) = a_3 * x + b_3$, which corresponds to the data sample in zone 3.

Each of these three models has its own slope (a_i), as well as its own fixed costs (b_i).

The next question is: What could cause these different behaviors?

Some Candidate Explanations for Economies and Diseconomies of Scale

– Each project within the subset of large diseconomies of scale had very high security constraints, as well as very high safety constraints.

– Each project within the subset of large economies of scale involved the extraction of information from existing databases, that is, there was no need to create and validate new data, and had a very large ratio of reused code and no security constraints.

Of course, the answer cannot be found by graphical analysis alone:

● There is only one independent variable in a two-dimensional graph.

▶ This single variable does not provide, by itself, any information about the other variables, or about similar or distinct characteristics of the completed projects for which data are available.

● However, if the wedge-shaped single data pattern is revisited and is partitioned into data subsets using the concepts of economies and diseconomies of scale (as described in the previous sections of this chapter), then

▶ Through this graphical analysis, the projects in each subset can be identified nominally.

The projects in each subset should be analyzed next to figure out

- Which of their characteristics (or cost drivers) have *similar values* within the same subset?
  - Which characteristics have *very dissimilar values* across the two (or three) subsets?

    Note: Some of these values can be categories (on a "nominal" scale type: e.g. a specific Data Base Management System (DBMS) has been used for one subset of projects, while another subset used another DBMS).

The ability to discover these various values of characteristics can then be used to characterize the datasets, as well as to set the parameters for selecting which of these three productivity models to use later, at estimation time, for estimation purposes – see Chapter 11.

In this chapter, we have looked into some of the key economics concepts at play in production processes, including fixed/variable costs and economies/diseconomies of scale, and we have illustrated these concepts with software engineering datasets that are either wedge-shaped or homogeneous, in terms of the relationship between size and effort.

EXERCISES

1. Provide more detail on the production process presented in Figure 2.1 by suggesting additional inputs, activities, and outputs in the context of a software project.
2. Provide more detail on the evaluation and control process presented in Figure 2.2 by suggesting additional goals, measures, and actions.
3. Provide examples of where organizational goals seem to contradict project objectives. Discuss what actions must be taken by the project manager when this occurs.
4. The average productivity of a software development subsidiary, SoftA, is 30 Function Points per person-month when developing Web-based catalogs, while the productivity of another organizational subsidiary, SoftB, is 10 Function Points per person-month when developing cash transfer banking operations. These two subsidiaries use the same units of measurement for their inputs and outputs. Compare their corresponding productivity ratios when developing Web-based catalogs compared to developing cash transfer banking operations.
5. What is the problem with a productivity ratio based on the number of lines of code? Discuss the pros and cons of such a ratio.
6. In the table below, calculate the productivity ratio and efficiency ratio for Henry and Charles.

Staff	Output (functional size units)	Input (hours)	LOC	Productivity ratio (based on?)	Efficiency ratio (based on?)
Henry	10	60	600		
Charles	10	60	900		

7. What are the other characteristics that should be looked at in addition to a dataset average?

8. What is a Normal (or Gaussian) distribution?

9. Is it prudent to use an average for estimation purposes when it comes from a dataset with major skew?

10. Should you be using an average for estimation purposes when you do not have detailed information about the dataset from which this average has been calculated?

11. If a power model has an exponent of 1.05, does this differ much from that of a linear model?

12. What does it mean when a power model has an exponent of 0.96?

13. If the constant in your linear regression model is negative, is your model wrong?

14. If the slope of your model is negative, what does that mean? What can you do about it?

15. How do you determine whether or not a development process generates economies of scale?

16. Represent graphically the production model of a software development process with diseconomies of scale.

17. At what maturity levels would you expect to see a wedge-shaped dataset and a homogeneously shaped dataset? What would such models say about your organization?

TERM ASSIGNMENTS

1. The evaluation and control process mentioned in Figure 2.2 refers only to a project as a whole. However, such a process can be implemented for each project phase, from the feasibility study to the maintenance phase. Look at your own organization and describe how the evaluation and control process is implemented (or should be implemented) at each project phase.

2. Take the information from the completed software projects in your organization over the past year or two, and put the data on a two-dimensional graph with Functional Size as the independent variable and Effort as the dependent variable. What is the shape of the graphical two-dimensional representation of this dataset? What does that shape say about your development process performance?

3. What is the unit cost of the last three projects you worked on? If you do not have these figures, why is your organization not collecting such basic data?

4. How can you determine the fixed costs of the software projects in your organization?

5. Is the estimation model used in your organization a single catch-all model? If so, how good a model is it?

6. How much data do you have available in your organization to build productivity models for that organization? If there are none available, what is your management's rationale for not having collected such data?

7. If no data are available, where can you look for them? How much is your organization willing to pay for them? If your organization is not ready to pay for them, does this mean that they are of no value to them?

Chapter 3

Project Scenarios, Budgeting, and Contingency Planning*

OBJECTIVES

This chapter covers

- Scenarios for estimation purposes
- Contingency funds and probability of underestimation
- A contingency example at the project level
- Management of contingency funds at the project portfolio level

3.1 INTRODUCTION

In Phase D of the estimation process described in Chapter 1 (see also Figure 1.9 or Figure 1.15), a decision on a specific project has to be made in order to allocate a budget to the software project (or to set a price for it). This decision must be derived from

- an analysis of the uncertainties of the variables in input to the estimation process about the project to be developed,
- an understanding of the strengths and limitations of the productivity model used in the estimation process, and
- the additional contextual information collected by the staff and the estimator, in the form of adjustments and risks, to modify the output of the productivity model.

In line with best practices, two complementary decisions are taken:

A. A budget, at the project level

B. A contingency amount, at the project portfolio level.

---

*See also: Miranda, E., Abran, A., "Protecting Software Development Projects Against Underestimation," Project Management Journal, Project Management Institute, September 2008, pp. 75–85.

Software Project Estimation: The Fundamentals for Providing High Quality Information to Decision Makers, First Edition. Alain Abran.

(A) *Project level*

At the project level, a single project value is typically selected as the project effort budget for which the project manager – and his staff – will be held accountable.

- The selection of a single value from a range of candidate values is no longer an engineering decision:

  ▶ *It is, above all, a management decision* – see also Section 1.7.

(B) *Project portfolio level*

At the project portfolio level, a second type of decision must be made, since, even though senior management may dictate a project effort target, neither senior management nor the project manager

- can resolve all the uncertainties on the inputs at the time a budget is selected,
- can control all the other variables over the course of a project, and
- can foresee all the risks that could materialize over the project life span.

What this means is that, in terms of the current state of the art of software estimation and project management, both at the practice and research levels, there is no possible way of guaranteeing that the project budget selected will be accurate.

There are, however, a number of project management techniques that have been developed to address these issues, since not all the other project constraints, in terms of functionality, deadlines, and quality levels, can be reasonably expected to remain constant over the project life cycle.

In this chapter, we introduce a number of business-related issues in an estimation context as follows:

- Section 3.2: Project scenarios for estimation purposes.
- Section 3.3: The probability of underestimation and the need for contingency funds.
- Section 3.4: An example of contingency funds at the project level.
- Section 3.5: Managing contingency funds at the project portfolio level.
- Section 3.6: Managerial prerogatives: An example in the AGILE context.

Note: A simulation approach to budgeting at the portfolio level is presented in the Advanced Reading section.

3.2   PROJECT SCENARIOS FOR ESTIMATION PURPOSES

In many contexts, project effort and duration estimates must be based on the limited information available in high-level requirements documents, which are notoriously unreliable. The best that estimators can do in these circumstances is to

(A) identify a range of values and

(B) assign a probability to each scenario.

(A) *Identification of a range of values*

The organization identifies a range of values within which they believe they can achieve the objectives of the project – see Figure 3.1. In practice, the range typically consists of at least of three values as follows:

1. The *best-case* scenario, which involves very little effort. This scenario has a low probability of occurrence.
2. The *most likely* scenario, which involves considerable effort. This scenario has the greatest probability of occurrence.

   - Warning: "Most likely" does not mean that the scenario has, for instance, a 50% probability of occurrence. It might have a much lower probability value, 20%, for instance, with all the other values having an even lower probability.

3. The *worst-case* scenario, which involves a very large amount of effort. This scenario also has a low probability of occurrence.

We present an example below illustrating the context in which a productivity model is available (i.e. based on historical data):

- Lower and upper levels of effort can be readily identified for a project with a functional size that is reasonably well known at the time of estimation.

For an expected software size at the time of estimation of, say, 100 FP – see Figure 3.1:

- The least amount of effort for a project of similar size in the data repository would correspond historically to the best-case scenario (i.e., E_{best} on the y-effort axis).
- The largest amount of effort for a project of similar size in the data repository would correspond historically to the worst-case scenario (i.e., E_{worst} on the y-effort axis).

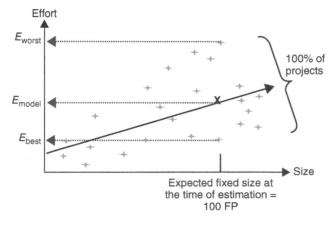

Figure 3.1   Best- and Worst-Case Scenarios

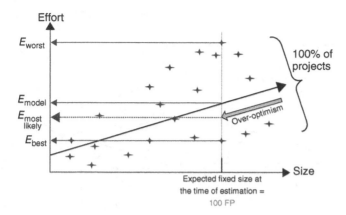

Figure 3.2 Most Likely Scenario and Overoptimism

- The effort produced by the mathematical model (i.e., the equation that best represents the set of points for each value of the independent variable) would give the corresponding effort for the expected size (E_{model} effort on the y-effort axis).

However, this figure will not necessarily correspond to the subjectively determined most likely scenario mentioned in the literature. In fact, in a software industry plagued by overoptimism in its estimation process, there is a fair chance that this value will be lower than the model estimate – see $E_{most\ likely}$ in Figure 3.2.

Figure 3.3 gives an example of where there is additional uncertainty on the expected functional size of the software to be delivered: that is, software size is no longer a constant, but an estimated range of sizes with an expected minimum and an expected maximum.

For instance, the low end of the functional size range in Figure 3.3 could be set at −10%, whereas the high end of the range could be set at, say, +30%, reflecting the fact that there is usually a smaller decrease in candidate size values (with a theoretical minimum lower range extending to zero – negative values having no practical meaning in this context) than a much larger increase in candidate size values (with no theoretical maximum).

- It is obvious from Figure 3.3, then, that this additional uncertainty at the time of estimation on expected software size increases both the lowest and highest limits of effort estimates, leading to a lower E_{best}, and a higher E_{worst}, value.

(B) *Assignment of a probability to each scenario.*Of course, not all the values within the range of estimates have the same probability of occurrence, that is, of being "accurate":

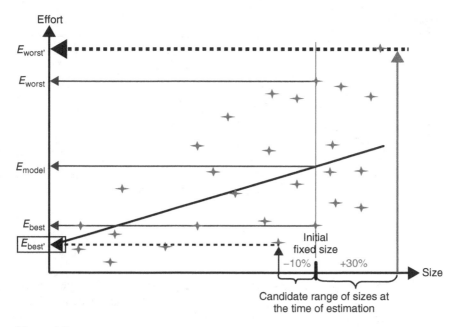

Figure 3.3   Best- and Worst-Case Scenarios and Size Uncertainty

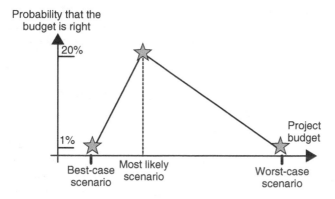

Figure 3.4   Probability Distribution of Scenarios

- Here, "accurate" means that the actual project effort (i.e. the total effort for the project, once completed) corresponds to a single value within the whole range.

By definition:

- Both the worst-case and best-case scenarios should have a very low probability of occurrence (let us say 1% for each in Figure 3.4).

- The most likely scenario should have the highest probability of occurrence (this scenario is arbitrarily assigned a probability of 20% in Figure 3.4.).
- All the other values within the range of estimates should have a decreasing probability from the maximum of the most likely scenario to the lowest probability of either the worst-case or the best-case scenario occurring. This is represented by the triangular probability distribution in Figure 3.4.
    - The selection of a right-skewed triangular distribution is justified for the following three reasons:
        1. While the number of things that can go right in a project is limited, and in most cases have already been factored into the estimate, the number of things that can go wrong is virtually unlimited.
        2. It is simple.
        3. It is as sensible as any other, since the "actual" distribution is unknown.

It is the responsibility of the software engineer in charge of project estimation to identify the estimated values for each of these scenarios and to assign a specific probability (or ranges of probability) to them, as in Figure 3.4.

It is not, however, the responsibility of the estimator to select a single value as the project "estimate," or more appropriately, the project budget.

3.3   PROBABILITY OF UNDERESTIMATION AND CONTINGENCY FUNDS

Whatever the management culture, approach, or strategy (and rationale) for selecting and allocating budgets, similar behaviors generally result:

- Choosing the best-case scenario will almost certainly lead to cost overruns and to shortcuts being taken, as this scenario always has an extremely low probability of occurrence [Austin, 2001].
- Choosing the worst-case scenario might result in failure to get the job (i.e. too much money for extras and gold-plating, and not enough focus on high priority and high value added functions, lack of focus generally, too long a schedule, and loss of business opportunities) and, almost certainly, overspending [Miranda, 2003].
- In practice, the most likely scenario is often selected, since it is also perceived to have the greatest chance of being "accurate"; however, in a software estimation context, it is typically biased toward the most optimistic scenario (rather than being biased toward the worst-case scenario):
    - Software staff are usually optimists – even though most of their project estimates are wrong!

  o A number of software staff may be influenced either by customers or man-
    agers, or both, looking for the best deals (i.e. project effort as low as possi-
    ble).

* When looked at objectively, the most likely scenario has a single value and
  probability value. Even though it may have a higher probability than any other
  scenario, the combination of the probabilities of all those scenarios combined
  would typically be much larger. Therefore:

  o the odds that a specific most likely scenario will not happen are very large
    and
  o the odds of it happening are only a fraction of that!

The problem of underestimation is illustrated in Figure 3.5, where the project
estimate is represented by the dashed line on the left, while the unknown final project
cost is represented by the dashed line on the right. Of course, at budget time, this
actual value is unknown, and this is why it is referred to in Figure 3.5 as the "actual
unknown cost."

In Figure 3.5, the project budget selected is a little higher than the most likely scenario, and the actual reported project effort is significantly to the right of the budget.
The difference between the budget and the actual cost, when it is known, is referred
to as the Underestimate (u).

The probability distribution (i.e. $p(u)$) of the underestimation, u is similar to the
effort distribution in Figure 3.4, but shifted by the project budget.

In summary, whatever estimated value is selected as the "budget" there is a high
probability in software projects that it will be proven to be inaccurate. In practice,
as mentioned in Section 1.3.4 and illustrated in Figure 1.4, in the software industry,
most projects are underfunded when project budgets are set up.

If underestimation is expected to happen in most projects, how can this be
managed?

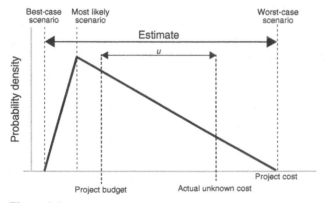

Figure 3.5   The Budget as a Target from a Large Number of Estimated Values [Miranda and Abran
2008. Reprinted with permission from John Wiley & Sons, Inc.]

Underestimation is not a new issue in project management, and, in the past, a number of approaches have been developed by the engineering and management communities. These have been included in the Project Management Body of Knowledge (PMBOK), published by the Project Management Institute [PMI 2013].

According to the Project Management Institute (PMI), a *contingency reserve* is "the amount of funds, budget, or time needed above the estimate to reduce the risk of overruns of project objectives to a level acceptable to the organization" [PMI 2004, p. 355].

- Contingency funds are meant to cover a variety of possible events and problems that are not specifically identified, or to account for a lack of project definition during the preparation of planning estimates.
    - ▶ When the authority for the use of the funds is above the project management level, it may be called a *management reserve*.

In practice, contingencies are added to projects using heuristics, such as 10% or 20% of the project budget, or by accruing percentage points on the basis of responses given to a risk questionnaire.

- More mature organizations might even run Monte Carlo simulations to calculate expected values.

Whatever the approach chosen, the human and organizational considerations that dictate decision-making in real-world projects in terms of the size of contingency funds and how to administer them cannot be ignored, specifically,

- management's preference for schedule over cost,
- their tendency toward inaction, and
- the money allocated is money spent (MAIMS) behavior [Kujawski et al. 2004].
    - o With this behavior, once a budget has been allocated, it will, for a variety of reasons, tend to be spent in its entirety, which means that funds not spent as a result of cost underruns are seldom available to offset overruns.
        - ▪ This negates the basic premise that contingency usage is probabilistic, and hence managing funds over and above the project level becomes the obvious and mathematically valid solution for its effective and efficient administration.

3.4   A CONTINGENCY EXAMPLE FOR A SINGLE PROJECT

In this section, we present an example of the level of contingency funds management could set aside when selecting a single budget value from a large number of estimated values, each with a small probability of occurrence. Consider, for illustrative purposes:

- an optimistic estimate of 200 person-months,
- a most likely estimate of 240 person-months, and
- a pessimistic estimate of 480 person-months.

Figure 3.6 shows an illustration for the ranges of estimates in the 20 person-month interval in linear form. Figure 3.6 also presents an example of a nonlinear set of contingency amounts that could be required by each level of funding. As expected,

- when the project is budgeted at its most optimistic estimate (i.e. 200 months), the contingency is at its maximum = 240 person-months and
- when the project is budgeted at its most pessimistic level (i.e. 480 months), the contingency is zero.

While the project manager is responsible for the project budget allocated to him, it is the senior management's responsibility not to be blindsided by the low probability budget value, and to set aside the necessary, but reasonable, contingency funds for adequately handling the project funding in a context of uncertainty.

In the example, the minimum total cost is achieved for a budget allocation of 320 person-months – the upper line in Figure 3.6.

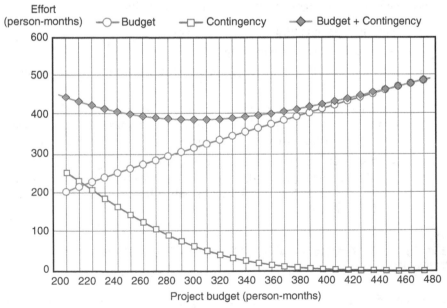

Figure 3.6   Breakdown of Total Project Costs (Budget + Contingency) as a Function of the Budget Allocated to the Project [Miranda and Abran 2008. Reprinted with permission from John Wiley & Sons, Inc.]

Note: In contrast to most figures in this book, the numbers provided in this example and in Figure 3.6 are illustrative and do not come from actual project data.

3.5 MANAGING CONTINGENCY FUNDS AT THE PORTFOLIO LEVEL

The MAIMS behavior could be explained by Parkinson's Law and budget games such as expending the entire budget to avoid setting precedents [Flyvbjerg, 2005].

- If the MAIMS behavior is prevalent in an organization, all the funds allocated to a project will be spent, irrespective of whether or not they were needed, and so there are never cost underruns, only cost overruns.

This negates the basic premise that contingency use is probabilistic.

The obvious and mathematically valid solution for the effective and efficient management of the funds is to maintain them at portfolio level, distributing them to individual projects on an as-needed basis.

This is illustrated in the Further Reading section with an example comprising a simulation of a portfolio consisting of three projects identical to the one in the example in Figure 3.6 under four different budget allocation policies (i.e. scenarios) as follows:

1. Scenario 1 shows the results of the simulation when projects are allocated a budget equal to that of the best-case scenario.
2. Scenario 2 corresponds to a budget allocation equal to that of the most likely scenario.
3. Scenario 3 corresponds to a budget allocation that minimizes the expected contingency.
4. The budget allocation for Scenario 4 is set at the worst-case scenario.

3.6 MANAGERIAL PREROGATIVES: AN EXAMPLE IN THE AGILE CONTEXT

It is widely held that software size is a significant driver of project effort, and this view is strongly supported by a number of research reports based on statistical studies.

This is illustrated in Figure 3.7, which shows product requirements driving product size, which in turn drives project effort. To be precise, product size is the independent variable and project effort is the dependent variable.

However, it is also considered that size is far from being the only driver (independent variable) at all times, and that a number of other factors (development tools, programming languages, reuse, etc.) can be taken into account to improve the modeling of the relationship with effort.

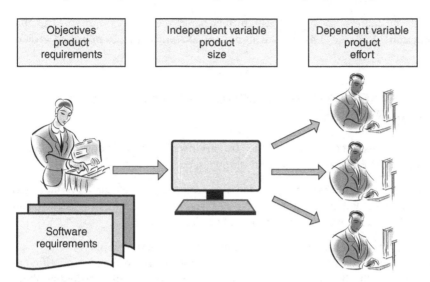

Figure 3.7   Product Size as the Key Driver of Project Effort and Duration

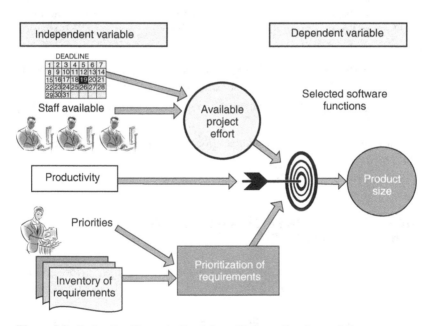

Figure 3.8   Project Deadline as the Key Driver of Software Functions and Size

In addition, software size may at times become a dependent variable, such as when a project deadline is the key driver (i.e., project priority number 1). In this specific context – see Figure 3.8:

(A) The project deadline is a driver (i.e. an independent variable) and the maximum number of people who can reasonably be assigned to the project within that time frame (another independent variable) will together determine the maximum possible project effort within that time frame.

(B) The list of requirements and their corresponding effort estimates, along with their respective priorities, could constitute another set of independent variables.

(C) The independent variables from both A and B are then taken into account to select which product features will be implemented with the people available within the time frame, and this will drive the product size delivered (the dependent variable) – see Figure 3.8.

The Agile approach is aligned with this managerial prerogative.

3.7 SUMMARY

In this chapter, we have shown that the estimation of a project comprises a range of values and probabilities within which an organization believes it is possible to achieve the project's objectives with a defined probability.

The selection of a single number (from a large range of estimated values) as the project budget (i.e. the target) is the result of a business and management decision and consists of the allocation to the project of an amount of money or effort within the estimated range:

- A low budget will have a high probability of underestimating the actual effort required.

- A large budget will almost certainly result in gold-plating and over-engineering.

FURTHER READING: A SIMULATION FOR BUDGETING AT THE PORTFOLIO LEVEL

The obvious avenue to the effective and efficient management of contingency funds is to maintain them at portfolio level, distributing them to individual projects on an as-needed basis.

This is explored in the following example,[1] comprising a simulation of a portfolio of three projects (identical to the ones in the example in Figure 3.6) under four different budget allocation policies (i.e. scenarios).

Figure 3.9 shows the probability of delivering the product on time and the expected portfolio cost for each scenario. This figure shows the following probabilities:

---

[1] For more details, see Miranda, E., Abran, A., "Insuring Software Development Projects Against Underestimation," Project Management Journal, Project Management Institute, September 2008, pp. 75–85.

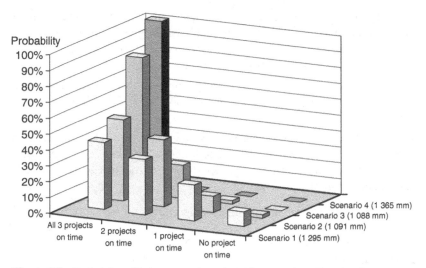

Figure 3.9   *Probability of Delivering on Time for Different Budget Allocation Scenarios*. Note – The Numbers in Parentheses Represent the Expected Portfolio Cost [Miranda and Abran 2008. Reprinted with permission from John Wiley & Sons, Inc.]

(A) None of the projects will be delivered on time.

(B) One project will be delivered on time.

(C) Two projects will be delivered on time.

(D) All three projects will be delivered on time.

The portfolio cost includes the allocated budget for the three projects plus their recovery costs, or, whenever it is not possible to recover from the underestimation, the penalties.

Scenario 1 shows the results of the simulation when projects are allocated a budget equal to that of the most optimistic estimate (i.e. 200 person-months).

- This is probably the worst policy of all. Not only does it yield the second highest portfolio cost, but also projects completed the latest.

  ▶ Despite the projects being allocated the minimum budget, recovery costs and penalties drive the cost up.

Scenario 2 corresponds to a budget allocation equal to that of the most likely estimate (i.e., 240 person-months).

- In this case, the portfolio cost is lower than it was in the previous scenario, and the probability of delivering on time is higher.

Scenario 3 corresponds to a budget allocation that minimizes the expected recovery cost (contingency), as shown in 3.9.

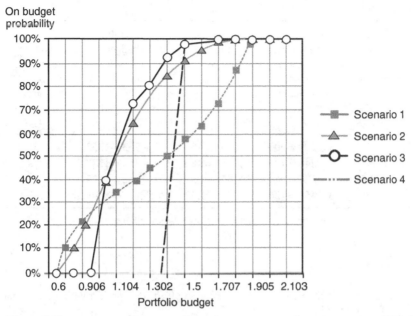

Figure 3.10 Distribution of Portfolio Costs for Each Scenario [Miranda and Abran 2008. Reprinted with permission from John Wiley & Sons, Inc.]

- With a total cost of 1088 person-months, this scenario offers the lowest expected total cost with a high probability of delivering the three projects on time.

The budget allocation for Scenario 4 is set at 455 person-months, the 99% quartile of the estimate distribution.

- In this scenario, all the projects are completed on time, but at the highest cost.

Figure 3.10 shows the distribution of portfolio costs for each of the scenarios.

- What is important to look at here is the steepness of the curve. Steeper curves are the result of a smaller variation in portfolio costs for a given scenario.
  - ▶ Scenario 4 has the lowest variation, since the large budgets allocated to the projects preclude underestimation.
  - ▶ The opposite is the case for Scenario 1, which has the largest variation as a result of each project having been underestimated at one simulation iteration or another.

The importance of curve steepness is that the steeper the curve, the higher the level of safety per dollar or person-month added to the project budget. The results are summarized in Table 3.1.

In fact, Scenario 3 offers the most efficient policy, with a 71% probability of the project being on-budget for an expected portfolio budget of 1125 person-months.

Table 3.1   Summary of Budgeting Policies

Scenario	Expected portfolio cost (from simulation) (person-months)	Budget for the three projects (person-months)	Contingency funds (person-months)	Portfolio budget (person-months)	Probability of not exceeding the portfolio budget (%) (Fig. 3.6) ($\cong$)
1	1,295	$3 \times 200 = 600$	$3 \times 251 = 753$	$600 + 753 = 1353$	55
2	1,091	$3 \times 240 = 720$	$3 \times 150 = 450$	$720 + 450 = 1170$	68
3	1,088	$3 \times 320 = 960$	$3 \times 55 = 165$	$960 + 165 = 1125$	71
4	1,365	$3 \times 455 = 1365$	$3 \times 0.5 = 1.5$	$1365 + 1.5 = 1366.5$	99

Miranda and Abran 2008. Reprinted with permission from John Wiley & Sons, Inc.

EXERCISES

1. In Figure 3.1, what is the best-case and worst-case effort for a project with a functional size of 50 Function Points?

2. What is usually the probability that the most likely scenario will be successful in project management? Why?

3. If the size of the software to be developed is not precisely known at estimation time, but an expected size range can be identified, what is the impact of this on the estimation outcome?

4. What are the risks of selecting an optimistic scenario in software estimation? Who is responsible for mitigating risk when an optimistic scenario has been selected?

5. Is the probability of underestimation the same across all scenarios (best case – most likely case – worst case)? What is the impact of underestimation on the contingency reserve?

6. What is the MAIMS behavior in project management?

7. Identify some of the biases in the business decision step when allocating a budget to a project. For each of these biases, what is the impact on the project manager and on the project team members?

8. In the example presented in Figure 3.6, what are the conditions for the minimum total project effort?

9. In a well-run software organization, at what management level is the contingency fund handled?

10. The development of scenarios and the assignment of probabilities to budget values should involve the analysis of past data. Identify from Figures 1.12 to 1.16 the necessary data repositories and feedback loops that should be taken into account.

TERM ASSIGNMENTS

1. If in your organization you develop project budget scenarios (best-case, most likely case, and worst-case), what is the process for doing so? Is it mostly based on opinion or on analysis of past projects?

2. Knowing your organization's experience in meeting effort and schedule estimates, what is the (true) probability that the most likely scenario will be achieved?

3. For the current project you are working on, what are the best-case, most likely, and worst-case scenarios? What probability of achieving each one would you currently assign to these scenarios?

4. For the above-mentioned project, for which you have identified various scenarios and corresponding probabilities, calculate what contingency amount should be held to fund a backup solution?

5. In your organization, who determines the amount of the contingency funds, and who manages them?

6. You, in the project management (PM) office, are responsible for monitoring a number of projects. Identify for each project its probability of underestimation, and calculate the contingency funds that should be available to provide additional funding in a timely manner.

Part II

Estimation Process: What Must be Verified?

Productivity models are at the core of an estimation process, and their users must understand their strengths and weaknesses, while the builders of such models should analyze and document their strengths and limitations.

In Part 2 of this book, we look into some of the quality issues arising in an estimation process. Specifically, we view the estimation process from an engineering perspective, and not from a "craft" perspective. All the verification criteria presented should be investigated and documented when any estimation process is designed or selected, and the verification results should be made available to those using the process for any new project to be developed.

Chapter 4 presents an overview of the various parts of the estimation process that must be understood and verified, first when building productivity models, and then when using them in an estimation process.

Chapter 5 discusses the necessary verification of the direct inputs used to design productivity models, that is, the independent variables that are explicitly taken into account in parametric statistical models.

Chapter 6 presents some of the criteria used to verify that the conditions for using the statistical techniques have been met, as well as the criteria for identifying the ranges of estimates and the estimated errors on the model parameters.

Software Project Estimation: The Fundamentals for Providing High Quality Information to Decision Makers,
First Edition. Alain Abran.
© 2015 the IEEE Computer Society. Published 2015 by John Wiley & Sons, Inc.

Chapter 7 discusses some of the elements of the Adjustment phase of the estimation process. This includes the identification and necessary understanding of the sub models behind what is typically referred to as "cost drivers" in the traditional approach to estimation. This chapter also includes an introduction to the impact of the uncertainty of measurements when a multitude of factors are introduced into productivity models. Does this action add more precision, or does it compound the uncertainty and error ranges?

Chapter 4

What Must be Verified in an Estimation Process: An Overview

OBJECTIVES

This chapter provides an overview of what must be verified at each phase of an estimation process, including

- the direct inputs used to build an estimation process
- the use of the productivity model itself
- the adjustment phase
- the budgeting phase

4.1 INTRODUCTION

Should you care about how good an estimation process and its underlying productivity model are?

Software engineers and managers use an estimation process to make commitments that are

- financially significant for their organization and

- professionally important for their own career.

Are these highly skilled professionals behaving like wise and well-informed consumers?

In daily life, at home and at work, consumers know that they must be aware of the quality of the products and services they purchase and use.

Software Project Estimation: The Fundamentals for Providing High Quality Information to Decision Makers,
First Edition. Alain Abran.
© 2015 the IEEE Computer Society. Published 2015 by John Wiley & Sons, Inc.

Buying a Car is Not to Be Taken Lightly!

When thinking about buying a car, most consumers read about cars extensively, find out about their technical performance (i.e., quality characteristics), and compare prices before making a purchasing decision.

This includes, for instance, getting hold of consumer reports on cars, as well as specialized magazines on comparative car performance, both within car categories and with respect to a number of variables considered important for both driver and passengers.

How Good are Software Project Estimates?

Most of the time, software projects require a great deal more funding than a car purchase.

Does your organization really know about the quality and performance of the estimation tools and techniques it is currently using or is planning to use?

Estimation models can be obtained from a variety of sources, such as

1. The Web, sometimes in the form of no-fee estimation software.
2. Vendors of estimation software tools, typically in the form of black-box estimation software tools, for which neither the internal mathematical equations nor the dataset on which they are based is available for independent analysis.
3. Books, magazines, and refereed publications.

Whatever their source, these estimation tools are used to make financially important decisions on the resources to be allocated to a project:

- How often are such estimation tools (including mathematical models) used without first verifying their quality and understanding their limitations?

Users of software estimation tools should be very concerned about the quality of the tools: a great deal of organizational time and money is at stake.

Estimation processes (and their related software tools) are much like any other technology:

- Not all of them are good and able to perform adequately in a particular context.
- Like any other process or model, the estimation process is highly dependent on the quality of its inputs (i.e., "garbage in, garbage out").

In this chapter, we identify the elements that should be verified to make an estimation process credible and auditable. This includes overviews on

- the quality of the input measures (products, process, and resources),

- the criteria that the productivity models at the core of an estimation process must meet,
- the quality of the derived inputs for an estimation model, and
- the other inputs to the estimation process (key assumptions, constraints, and expert judgments).

Details of the above-mentioned points will be presented in Chapters 5–7. This chapter is organized as follows:

- Section 4.2 verifies the direct inputs to the estimation process; for example, product size.
- Section 4.3 verifies the model itself.
- Section 4.4 discusses the verifications in the adjustment phase.
- Section 4.5 discusses the budgeting and re-estimation process.
- Section 4.6 introduces the continuous improvement of the full estimation process.

4.2   VERIFICATION OF THE DIRECT INPUTS TO AN ESTIMATION PROCESS

The first verification step consists of identifying the inputs to the estimation process (i.e., the information available at the time the estimate is being prepared) and documenting the quality of those inputs when estimating a specific project for a specific context.

4.2.1   Identification of the Estimation Inputs

The estimation inputs are typically of two types as follows:

- quantitative product information for the independent variable and
- descriptive process information for the selection of a specific model, when a number of models are available.

Product Information

Information about the software *product* to be developed is gathered, including

- the functional requirements (which can be measured with any of the international standards for functional size measurement),
- the nonfunctional requirements (typically in a textual description, since few corresponding international standards exist), and
- the relationships between the system view and the software view (i.e., software is to be developed for an environment which will consist of a set of procedures to allow the software to interact with manual or automated procedures, with or without interactions with hardware).

As much as possible, such product information should be quantitative and well documented for each development life cycle phase.

Process Information

This is information related to the expected characteristics of the development *process* and implementation platform.

- Process information includes known constraints with respect to a single technical environment, such as DBMS, programming languages, and programming standards.

Resource Information

At the early stages of the estimation in the analysis phase, estimation should be performed independently of the specific human resources to be allocated to a project.

4.2.2   Documenting the Quality of These Inputs

It is not sufficient to merely identify the inputs. The key independent variables are not necessarily known with certainty at this point, and there might be significant plausible variations in the input variables, including functional size, which will introduce a large range of plausible variations in the estimation outcomes. The estimator is expected to provide an assessment of the quality of the information available to quantify such inputs when the project is estimated: any such assessment of the quality of the estimation inputs should always be documented for traceability purposes and for understanding the candidate ranges of uncertainty before the models are used – see Figure 4.1.

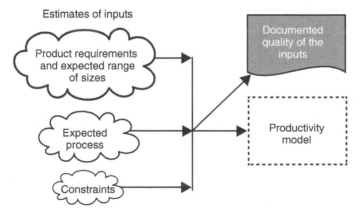

Figure 4.1   Verification of the Inputs to Productivity Models

For example:

(A) The measurement of the functional size of the requirements should indicate the quality and completeness of the Functional User Requirements[1]:

- For example, if a size of 377 Function Points (FP) has been assigned to the inputs to the model, there should be an indication that this figure is based on functional specifications which

  ▶ have been inspected to ensure completeness, consistency, and unambiguousness, and so providing the necessary conditions for accurate and adequate measurement of functional size, or

  ▶ have been described in conformity with international standards, such as IEEE 830 on Software Requirements Specifications [IEEE 1998], or

  ▶ are described to such a high level that precise measurement is not feasible, but rather only an approximation of size is feasible, with an unknown range of accuracy.

(B) When the requirements are not detailed enough to allow the measurement of the Functional User Requirements using the rules prescribed by international standards, the estimator may use any of the approximation approaches available in the literature or from ISO standards support groups.

The outcome of this first step should be a report documenting

(A) the measurement results of the inputs to the estimation process and

(B) an appreciation of the quality of these measurement results, including the assumptions made throughout this step, in particular when the specifications were at too high a level or too ambiguous for accurate sizing.

Are Function Points Accurate as Estimation Input?

For projects to be estimated:

(A) When *all the requirements are detailed and available*, Function Points can be measured quite accurately and used with confidence as inputs to an estimation process.

(B) When *not all the requirements are detailed,* there *are techniques for approximating can*didate size ranges – see, for example, the document "Guideline for Approximate COSMIC Functional Size Measurement" [COSMIC 2014a].

---

[1] The functional requirements as defined in IEEE 830 are also referred to as "Functional User Requirements – FUR" in the ISO standards for the measurement of the functional size of software, such as the ISO 14143 series [ISO 2007a] and in ISO 19761 and ISO 20926. We have adopted FUR terminology in this book, which uses ISO standards extensively, since it considers software size as the key independent variable in productivity models.

4.3   VERIFICATION OF THE PRODUCTIVITY MODEL

The productivity model is not verified each time an estimate is made for a project. Typically, it is verified only once, when the productivity model is first built, or when an estimation tool is selected from external sources. This more complex verification consists of two steps as follows:

- Analysis of the data used as input to the design of the productivity model – see Chapter 5.
- Verification of the productivity model itself – see Chapter 6.

4.3.1   In-House Productivity Models

An in-house productivity model will ideally have been built using

(A) the organization's own historical data and

(B) its quality as a model documented on the basis of such historical data.

In practice, there are additional constraints in estimation; the two major ones being the following:

1. The project being estimated may face conditions or constraints not included in the model, that is, the model may not be completely representative of the project to be estimated:
   - If the model has been built using all the data points from 0 to 100 CFP (COSMIC Function Points[2]), it cannot represent points outside that range (i.e., it could not be relied on to estimate a project of, say, 1200 CFP) – see Figure 4.2.
     (Note that this step corresponds to the use of the productivity model as a simulation model.)
2. It cannot be expected that the outcome of a model will be a unique and guaranteed (i.e., accurate) number:
   - Typically, a model provides a range of plausible values (along with a range of probabilities in some models).

A model used in an estimation process should therefore include – see Figure 4.3:

- Documentation of the ranges of expected values – for further details, refer to Chapter 6.
- Warnings about its use in the context of the project being estimated if the conditions of that project differ significantly from those in which the model was derived.

Further details are provided on the analysis of quality of models built using statistical analysis of historical data in Chapter 6.

---

[2]CFP = COSMIC Function Points measured on the basis of ISO standard ISO 19761 [COSMIC 2014b]; [ISO 2011].

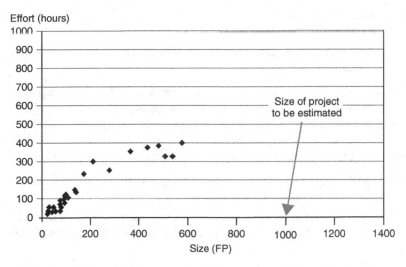

Figure 4.2   The Representativeness of a Model Depends on Its Population Sample

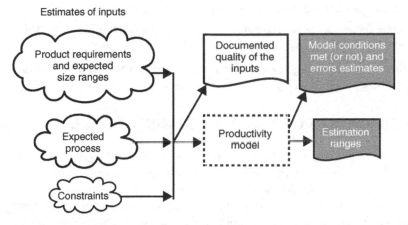

Figure 4.3   Verification of the Execution of the Productivity Models

4.3.2   Externally Provided Models

Organizations *without their own repository of completed projects* will typically use

- models stored in other repositories, such as the repository of the International Software Benchmarking Standards Group – ISBSG,
- models embedded within software estimation tools[3]:

---

[3]What we call "productivity models" in this book are often referred to more generically as "estimation tools" or "productivity models" in the literature and by vendors.

> ▶ from vendors – at a cost or
> ▶ from the Web – free of charge,

- models and mathematical formulas from the literature (e.g., the COCOMO81 and COCOMOII models).

It is not reasonable to expect that these external models, built in other organizational contexts and different types of projects, can be mapped perfectly to the projects to be developed in a specific organization with its own culture and technological environment.

Therefore, the use of an external model in an estimation context should be

- analyzed to determine its power of predictability for the organization using it and

- calibrated to the business environment in which a business decision has to be made, and resources should be committed on the basis of the outcomes of such a model.

To analyze the power of predictability of an external model, an organization can

- take information from one or more of its recently completed projects,

- use this information as inputs to the external model, and

- compare the results of the estimate against the actual effort of the projects fed as inputs to the external model.

With this information, organizations can get a good feel for the power of predictability of the external models for their organization.

4.4 VERIFICATION OF THE ADJUSTMENT PHASE

In the previous verification step, both the in-house and external models take into account *only the variables that are explicit within their mathematical equation.*

However, productivity models are limited by the number of independent factors taken into account in the mathematical formula. Of course, it is a recognized fact that a large number of other independent factors may impact the relationships with the dependent variable, and these may be added in the adjustment phase of the estimation process – see Figure 4.4.

For instance, a specific project may have a number of product, process, and resource characteristics that are not taken into account by these productivity models.

A verification step is required (see also Section 1.6.3 and Figure 1.12)

- to identify, document, and "qualify" the additional variables, information, and constraints,

- to prepare an assessment of the individual impact of the additional variables, and

Estimates of inputs

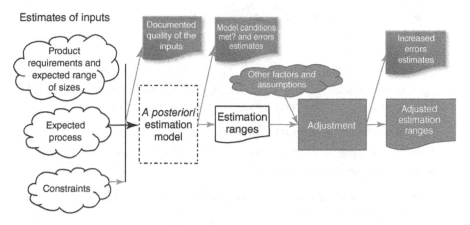

Figure 4.4   Verification of the Adjustments Phase

- to introduce these adjustments to the models used, whether in-house or external.

This means that the output from the previous step of the model is only one of the inputs for the verification of the adjustment phase. The basis for these adjustments, as well as for the quality of the predictive impact of such adjustments, should be documented.

- The many books that discuss adjustments and their impact are typically based only on expert opinion, and not on reasonably controlled experiments or industry data with a sufficiently large sample to be meaningful from a statistical viewpoint.
  - ▶ The error range of adjustments is usually not discussed, nor is the impact of adjustments on estimates.

This topic will be discussed specifically in Chapter 7.

4.5   VERIFICATION OF THE BUDGETING PHASE

The verification process should take into consideration additional elements that might pose a risk in a project, namely:

- Technological:
  - ▶ a selected technology might not deliver as promised,
- Organizational:
  - ▶ an experienced employee will not be available at critical steps in the software development life cycle,

▶ illness and the departure of key employees,

▶ hiring difficulties,

▶ and so on.

The optimistic, the most likely, and the pessimistic estimated values are often expressed as three distinct figures. However, they should ideally lie in ranges of values on a continuum, each corresponding to a probability of occurrence.

- A range of optimistic estimated values
- A range of most likely estimated values
- A range of pessimistic estimated values.

This type of verification is more related to the management domain, and is not addressed further in this book.

4.6 RE-ESTIMATION AND CONTINUOUS IMPROVEMENT TO THE FULL ESTIMATION PROCESS

Improving an estimation process and its underlying productivity models depends on the following – see Figure 4.5:

- The data collected at the completion of a project when there is no longer uncertainty about the project deliverables (number of functions delivered, duration, and quality levels achieved).
- The skills of the people integrating this information into the productivity models to improve them.

Improving models is hard to achieve in industry, and is much less frequently attempted in the software industry. It has a number of particular challenges as follows:

- There is rarely a single estimated budget.
    ▶ In practice, since the estimation process is so poor in the software industry, the project budget in often re-estimated a number of times over the course of the project's life cycle.
- The information used as input to the estimation process is often not documented.
    ▶ Its quality and completeness are neither recorded nor analyzed.
- Assumptions made during the estimation process are not all documented.
- "Scope creep" during the life cycle is rarely measured or controlled – See the SouthernSCOPE approach for the management of scope throughout a project life cycle [Victoria 2009].

Ideally, all the information mentioned above should be recorded in a repository of information on the estimation process, and then used to evaluate the performance of that process.

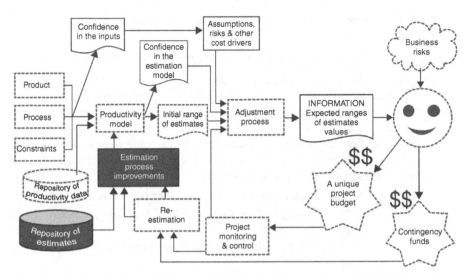

Figure 4.5   The Full Estimation Process with the Feedback Loop (and the Historical Database of Estimates on Past Projects)

At project completion, actual budgets and estimates (not only of effort, but of all the other product measures) should be compared to provide feedback on the quality of the estimation process.

This could provide valuable information for

- documenting the current quality and predictability of the estimation process,
- improving the estimation process itself, and
- training, using the steps of the estimation process as an example.

Actual data should be fed back to the model for improvements.

This final step is included in Figure 4.5, and completes the view of the verification of the full estimation process.

FURTHER READING: THE ESTIMATION VERIFICATION REPORT

The full estimation process, with all its components, should be verifiable, auditable, and audited. In this section, we present a structure of what should be included in a quality assessment report of the *full estimation process* described in Figure 4.5. It should include *verification sections* on

A. The inputs to the estimation process

B. The outputs of the mathematical models used in the estimation process

C. The inputs and outputs of the adjustment phase

D. The decisions taken at the project and portfolio levels, along with the basis justifying those decisions

E. Re-estimation and verification of the business decision-making process.

(A) *Verification of the direct inputs (i.e., the independent variables)*
The quality of the direct inputs to the productivity model used in the estimation context is recorded in the verification section – see Chapter 4.2 for more details.
In this section, comments on the status (accuracy and completeness) of the documentation relied on to determine the functional size of the software to be developed should be provided as follows:

o the status of the documents used as a basis for measurement:

– a finalized Software Requirements Specifications document (e.g., inspected and approved),
– a draft of high-level requirements (those not yet reviewed and approved),
– and so on.

o the range of expected variation when functional size is approximated, rather than measured.
o life cycle activity: feasibility, planning, analysis, and so on.
o experience of the functional size measurers, and so on.

(B) *Verification of the use of the productivity model*
In this section of the verification report, the documentation on the quality of the productivity model – described in Chapter 6 – should be available.
It should compare the project being estimated and the projects used for designing the productivity models:

• When the project to be estimated *is not* in the same context and the same size range, additional uncertainties are introduced, which should be noted.
• When the project to be estimated *is* in the same context and the same size range, the information about the quality of the model can be used to describe the expected range of variance of the estimates produced by the model.
• When the inputs have to be approximated (instead of being measured precisely), there is uncertainty and a lack of completeness of the data used as inputs to the productivity model, and the additional range of variation that results must be assessed.

(C) *Verification of the Adjustment Phase*
This section of the verification report should document

• all the inputs to the process of adjusting the outputs of the productivity model,
• the rationale for the adjustments made on the basis of the judgments of the practitioners and managers who have to deliver the project results and make commitments, and
• the expected impact of these adjustments, as well as the expected ranges of additional variations in the estimates provided.

Comparison with a historical estimation database
Ideally, there should be a historical database of past project estimates, including

- iterative estimates and
- detailed information on incremental changes of

  o project outputs and
  o productivity factors.

Analysis of the project characteristics relative to those of previous projects could provide additional insights for the preparation of the estimation confidence report.

Sanity check
A sanity check on the ranges of estimates and adjustments should be carried out by comparing them with the practitioners' estimates – see Chapter 7 for more details.

(D) *Verification of the budgeting phase*
The inputs to the budgeting phase should be highly visible. They should include documentation of

- key assumptions,
- uncertainty factors,
- risk factors, and
- recommended use of the outcome of the estimation process.

Uncertainty factors
The sooner in a project life cycle an estimate is prepared, the higher the degree of uncertainty will be on all the inputs to the estimation process. This should be fully highlighted.

Recommended use of the budgeting outcome
The report on the outcome of a budgeting process should clearly spell out, in an objective manner

1. the details of an unbiased assessment of the current life cycle phase of the project being estimated and
2. the recommended use of the estimation ranges and budgeting scenario results in the decision-making process.

For example, in their budgeting report, business managers should provide an indication of the types of decisions that should be taken based on the quality of the information available, such as

- high-level budget provisions (e.g., to ensure adequate funding of priorities),
- funding of the next project phase only (e.g., when product description is incomplete or unstable), and
- final phase funding (when a detailed product description is available and stable, and to which there is full commitment).

The estimators should stress the iterative nature of the estimation process throughout the project life cycle.

This verification report should document

- additional factors taken into account in decision-making,
- decisions made at the project level, and
- any contingency identified at the portfolio level and the strategy used to determine that contingency.

(E) *Re-estimation and verification of the business decision-making process*
The business estimation process can only be assessed over a fairly long period of time and over a large set of projects. It could be divided into two major components:
For *each project*: cleanliness checks (i.e., practitioners' judgments) on

- the assessment of risks and then the management of those risks,
- the assessment of benefits and then the management of those benefits.

For the *portfolio of projects*: cleanliness checks (i.e., practitioners' judgments) on

- the assessment of risks and then the management of those risks across the portfolio,
- the assessment of benefits and then the management of those benefits across the portfolio.

This assessment is very important from a corporate strategy viewpoint, but is outside the scope of this book.

EXERCISES

1. Can all the aspects of verification be performed at the same time in an estimation process? What should the sequence of those aspects be?
2. What should be included in the verification of the variables in the inputs to an estimation process?
3. What should be included in the verification of the use of an in-house productivity model?
4. What should be included in the verification of the use of a vendor estimation model?
5. How can you verify an estimation model picked up free of charge from a book or from the Web?
6. What should be verified in the adjustment phase of the estimation process?
7. What should be documented when a specific decision is made on a project budget?
8. What type of information must be kept to analyze the performance of project estimates and to make improvements to the full estimation process?

TERM ASSIGNMENTS

1. Document the quality controls in the estimation process in your organization.
2. Identify the strengths and weaknesses of your organization's estimation process.
3. Identify the improvement priorities for your organization's estimation process.
4. Propose an action plan to address the top three priorities.
5. Design a template for the quality assurance of a productivity model.
6. Design a template for the quality assurance of a full estimation process.
7. Select three estimation models proposed in the literature. Even though the authors may claim that their models are to be used for estimation, are those models based on productivity studies or on opinion? If the latter, what would be your confidence level using them for estimation purposes?
8. Compare the verification steps in Figure 4.5 with the verification recommended in the literature on software estimation. Comment on the similarities and differences. Identify strengths and weaknesses of the model analyzed.
9. What has been done in your organization over the past 12 months to analyze the quality of its productivity model and estimation process? Why? Is it because estimates are (or are not) important to your organization?
10. For estimation purposes, how would you handle *cost drivers* not included in the productivity model?
11. For estimation purposes, how would you handle *risk factors* not included in the productivity model?
12. Identify some of the biases inherent in the business decision allocating a budget to a project. For each of these biases, what is the impact on the project manager and on the project team members?
13. How can an organization take into account potential scope changes in its productivity model and estimation process? How should an organization manage and control the scope of change during project execution?

Chapter 5

Verification of the Dataset Used to Build the Models

OBJECTIVES

This chapter covers

- Verification of the quality of the dataset used to build the productivity models.
- Verification of the distribution of the input variables, including graphical and statistical analyses and identification of outliers.
- Verification of the inputs derived from conversion formula.

5.1   INTRODUCTION

Understanding the quality and level of performance of any technology is important to its users. This is also true of productivity models, whether they include statistical techniques or are judgment-based.

The specific focus on this chapter is on the verification of the inputs to productivity models based on statistical techniques.

- While this book does not focus on estimation based on expert opinion, most of the concepts presented here, and in this chapter, also apply.

Many of the below-mentioned verification steps should be carried out only when the productivity models are being built, and the verification findings should be made available to those who will be using them for estimating a specific project with its unique set of constraints.

A productivity model based on statistical techniques consists of the following – see Figure 5.1:

1. Inputs, that is, the dataset of:
   ▶ independent variables and

Software Project Estimation: The Fundamentals for Providing High Quality Information to Decision Makers, First Edition. Alain Abran.
© 2015 the IEEE Computer Society. Published 2015 by John Wiley & Sons, Inc.

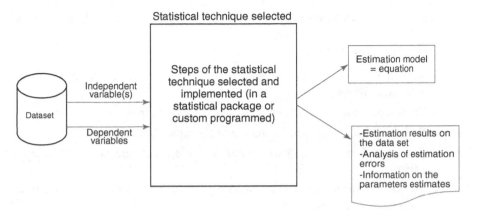

Figure 5.1 An Estimation Model as a Process

    ▶ dependent variables.
2. Steps specific to the statistical technique used.
3. Outcomes that include:
    ▶ the mathematical equation of the productivity model built,
    ▶ the estimation results on the dataset used, and
    ▶ the information on the estimation errors of the model on the original dataset.

The proper use of a statistical technique therefore requires three distinct types of verification as follows:

1. Verification of the characteristics of the input variables in the dataset:
    ▶ to gain an understanding of the dataset itself and
    ▶ to ensure that the conditions for appropriate use of the statistical techniques are met:
       ■ It is often forgotten in the analysis of the statistical test results that these are valid provided that the conditions on the inputs to the statistical techniques used are met.
2. Verification of the proper execution of the steps of the statistical techniques:
    ▶ When well-known statistical software packages are used, this verification step can be skipped with confidence.
    ▶ When the steps are executed by custom-built programs, extensive testing should be conducted using well-executed testing procedures.
3. Verification of the characteristics of the output variables:
    ▶ This provides an understanding of the true statistical significance of the outputs of the productivity model.

This chapter focuses on verification of the inputs that were used, or are to be used, to build a productivity model.

It is organized as follows:

- Section 5.2 verifies the relevance and quality of the direct inputs to an estimation process.
- Section 5.3 discusses the graphical analysis of the inputs.
- Section 5.4 analyzes the distribution of the input variables.
- Section 5.5 introduces two-dimensional graphical analysis of the input variables.
- Section 5.6 discusses issues related to the use of size inputs derived from conversion formulas.

5.2 VERIFICATION OF *DIRECT* INPUTS

5.2.1 Verification of the Data Definitions and Data Quality

In this section, we present a number of aspects that must be analyzed to determine the relevance and quality of the inputs to productivity models, that is, on both the independent and dependent variables used to build the productivity models.

- It is important for users of productivity models to understand the quality of these inputs, since they strongly influence the quality of the outputs of the models.

All mathematically based estimation techniques (statistical techniques, regressions, neural networks, case-based reasoning techniques, etc.) do the following:

- Use the data that are fed to them.
- Make an implicit assumption that these inputs are correct and reliable.

Since models and techniques cannot recognize bad data coming in, the following question arises:

- Is it up to the builders of the models or the users of the models, or both, to ensure the quality of the inputs to their estimation techniques and corresponding models?

The colloquial expression, "garbage in, garbage out," is relevant in building, as well as in using, estimation models – see the box below. How can "accurate" estimates be expected from an estimation process if what is put in is itself highly inaccurate (i.e., of poor quality)?

"Garbage In, Garbage Out"

If the data used to build a productivity model are of poor quality (both on their own and relative to the statistical techniques used to build the model), good results cannot be expected:

- Numbers will come out of a model, but, if garbage is fed in, there is no reason to expect anything but garbage coming out!
- Numbers derived from statistical techniques are valid only provided that a number of fairly strict conditions of use are met, and that the data used are valid and truly representative of the phenomenon being modeled (i.e., the specific types of projects for which the estimate is sought).

Examples of poor-quality data:

- Data from which part of the content is missing; for example, unrecorded overtime effort.
- Data with major time lags in collection; for example, effort data recorded based on staff recollections months after the completion of a project will be of much lower quality than effort data recorded on a daily basis.

It is important to fully understand the specific definition of each input parameter, and of the characteristics that could lead to meaningful and significant variations in the data collected.

Examples of Data Definitions From the ISBSG

See Chapter 8 on the ISBSG repository for examples of well-defined data definitions and related data collection procedures, in particular for effort data and size data.

5.2.2   Importance of the Verification of the Measurement Scale Type

Models are built with numbers:

- Of course, not all numbers (e.g., measures) are created equal, particularly in software engineering, where the measurement of software is still in its infancy:
  - ▶ Numbers must have strong properties if they are to be used properly as foundations for models.

In software practice, as soon as "something" is expressed by a number, it is referred to as a "metric," and there is a strong (implicit) assumption by most people in the software field that if it is expressed by a number, then that number will automatically be of the highest quality, that is:

- the number is necessarily accurate,
- the number is necessarily relevant, and
- the number necessarily means the same thing to everybody who collected it and are using it.

However, not all numbers can be used for mathematical operations (i.e. addition, subtraction, multiplication, and division):

- In the Capability Maturity Model, the numbers 1–5 are only correctly used as ordered labels to "qualify" the maturity levels.
- However, when the similarly ordered number labels 0–5 assigned to the 14 general systems characteristics in Function Point Analysis are multiplied by impact factors, this is without doubt an inappropriate mathematical operation – see (Abran 2010, Chapter 8).

Maturity Models – Capability Levels

With regard to the numbers 1–5 assigned to the well-known levels of the software Capability Maturity Model:

- They do not have the properties of the ratio scale type, which allows numerical operations. Therefore, no mathematical operations are admissible.
- Even though expressed with a number, these levels only represent information on an ordinal scale type, where level 2 strictly means that it is considered more mature than level 1 and less mature than level 3.

The numbers 1, 2, and 3 in this case merely represent an ordering: they do not even represent determined quantified intervals across such an ordering.

For each data field collected and used in a productivity model, the scale type should be clearly identifiable and understood:

- Nominal
- Ordinal
- Interval
- Ratio.

Numbers on the ratio scale can be added and multiplied, but not on all the other scales. Therefore, care must be exercised to take into account the scale type of each variable used as input to a statistical technique [Abran 2010; Ebert et al. 2005]:

- A variable such as functional size, quantified with an international standard, such as the COSMIC-ISO 19761 measurement method, is of the ratio scale type, and can be handled by statistical regression techniques.

- A variable such as a programming language is of the nominal scale type, and cannot be handled directly in statistical regression techniques. In this case, dummy variables must be introduced to adequately handle information about the categorical value of the programming language – see Chapter 10.

Measurement of a Single Attribute: A Base Quantity

A single attribute, or property, of an entity (including that of a physical object or a concept) is typically measured through a base quantity. In the sciences and in engineering, the domain of metrology has been developed over centuries to ensure the quality of the measurement results of single attributes.

The quality criteria of base quantities have been described in the ISO International Vocabulary of Metrology (VIM) [ISO 2007b], and include

- accuracy,
- precision,
- repeatability,
- reproducibility,
- and so on.

ISO Metrology Definitions in the VIM 2007 [ISO 2007b]

Accuracy: closeness of agreement between a *measured quantity value* and a *true quantity value*.

Precision: closeness of agreement between *indications or measured quantity values* obtained by replicate *measurements* on the same or similar objects under specified conditions.

Repeatability: *measurement precision* under a set of *repeatability conditions of measurement* (i.e., out of a set of conditions that includes the same *measurement procedure*, operators, *measuring system*, operating conditions, and location, and replicate measurements on the same or similar objects over a short period of time).

Reproducibility: *measurement precision* under *reproducibility conditions of measurement* (i.e., out of a set of conditions that includes different locations, operators, *measuring systems*, and replicate measurements on the same or similar objects).

The metrology domain has also recognized that there is always a certain level of uncertainty in measurement results, as well as various types of errors:

- systematic errors,
- random errors,
- and so on.

Furthermore, international measurement standards-etalons have been developed in metrology to ensure consistency of measurement across countries and contexts: kilogram, meter, second, and so on.

Well-designed measurement methods for base quantities have two very important properties:

- They are all expressed with *a single measurement unit.*

- The numbers obtained from the measurement methods are not to be interpreted in the specific context of measurement, but rather with *traceability to the international standards-etalons.*

The benefits are obvious:

- Instead of measurement results, which are meaningful only among a small group of people who defined them at some point, measurements based on international standards:
    - allow meaningful comparisons to be made across groups, organizations, and time;
    - provide the foundation for objective comparison, including against targets, while measurements based on individual definitions erect barriers to objective comparisons across groups and organizations, and so erect barriers to both oversight and objective accountability.

5.3   GRAPHICAL ANALYSIS – ONE-DIMENSIONAL

The values of the inputs can be presented in tables, along with some statistical information, such as *average*, *median*, and *standard deviation.*

However, it is often easier to grasp the information about the values when they are presented graphically, either one at a time or in a two-dimensional representation with two axes.

One-dimensional graphical analysis will typically provide the user with an intuitive feel about the data collected, one data field at a time.

From the visual analysis of the dataset, the general distribution of the data points can usually be determined, in forms as follows:

- Ranges of values: min, max;
- Dispersion of the values and the density of the ranges of data values: a large population of data points, sparse ranges of values, ranges without values;
- Gaussian distribution: skewness, kurtosis, normality tests, etc.;
- Candidate outliers on a single dimension;
- And so on.

Table 5.1 presents an example of a dataset of 21 data points, with information on both functional size (in COSMIC Function Points) and effort (in hours). In this

Table 5.1   Dataset: Effort and Functional Size ($N = 21$)

ID of the data item	Functional Size for the independent variable (CFP units)	Effort for the dependent variable (hours)
1	216	88
2	618	956
3	89	148
4	3	66
5	3	83
6	7	34
7	21	96
8	25	84
9	42	31
10	46	409
11	2	30
12	2	140
13	67	308
14	173	244
15	25	188
16	1	34
17	1	73
18	1	27
19	8	91
20	19	13
21	157	724
Total ($N=21$)	1526	3867
Average ($N=21$)	**73**	**184**

table, the data are presented together, in the typical sequential order of the project identification numbers, at the bottom of the table with simple summary statistics:

- Average functional size: 73 COSMIC Function Points (CFP)
- Average project effort: 184 hours.

Figure 5.2 presents a graphical representation of this dataset of 21 projects, with functional size on the horizontal axis (in CFP) and effort (in hours) on the vertical axis. We can see that

- on the x-axis, the size of most projects varies from +0 to around 200 CFP, although there is a much larger project, the size of which is over 600 CFP and
- on the y-axis, the effort for most projects varies from 30 to 400 hours, although for two projects, the effort is over 700 hours.

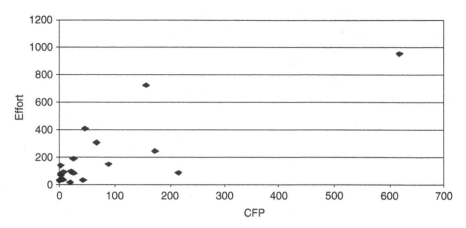

Figure 5.2   Two-Dimensional Graph of the Dataset in Table 5.1

Key Learning: Always plot data to understand it

5.4   ANALYSIS OF THE DISTRIBUTION OF THE INPUT VARIABLES

5.4.1   Identification of a Normal (Gaussian) Distribution

Some statistical techniques require that the input data be normally distributed (i.e., a Gaussian distribution – see Figure 5.3). This requires that the distribution of the input variables in the dataset be investigated to verify whether or not they have a normal distribution.

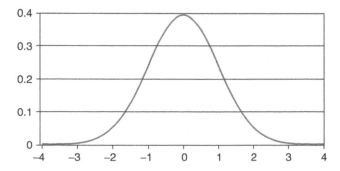

Figure 5.3   Example of a Gaussian (Normal) Distribution

- Software engineering data repositories often contain a large number of small projects and few large and very large projects. Such a dataset would not typically have a Gaussian distribution.

Some of the tests used to verify the normality of a data variable are

- standard deviations
- skewness and kurtosis (see Section 2.3)
- normal distribution and statistical outliers.

For instance, the distributions can be tested for normality using a skewness statistic ($\sqrt{b_1}$) and a kurtosis statistic ($b2$). A further omnibus test ($K2$), capable of detecting deviations from normality due to either skewness or kurtosis, can be calculated. Other tests mentioned in the literature are

- Grubbs test
- Kolmogorov–Smirnov test
- Shapiro–Wilk normality test (e.g., when W is significantly smaller than 1, the assumption of normality is not met).

Subsection 5.4.2 illustrates the use of these normality tests with the two variables in Table 5.1.

What Does a Non-Normal Distribution Represent for Practitioners?

A non-normal distribution does not mean that the resulting regression model is of no use to practitioners.

It does, however, let practitioners know that the regression model is not equally representative across all ranges of the variables modeled.

Of course, the model will be more representative for the range of values with more data points, and less representative for the sparsely populated ranges.

With a non-normal distribution of data points, under no circumstances should the representativeness of the productivity model be extrapolated to ranges without data points.

5.4.2 Identification of Outliers: One-Dimensional Representation

The relevance of the values of the data in input that are significantly far from the average of the population of the dataset, that is, the candidate outliers, must also be verified.

- A candidate outlier would be typically at least one or two orders of magnitude larger than a data point closer to it.

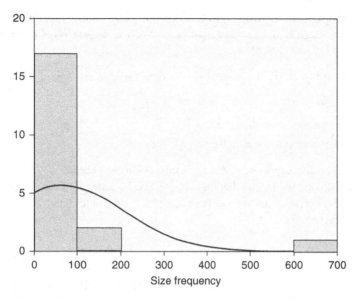

Figure 5.4   Frequency Distribution of the *Size* (Independent Variable) in Table 5.1 with $N = 21$

- For someone with limited knowledge of statistics, it is often easier to identify candidate outliers from a graphical representation than a tabular format, such as in Table 5.1.

Figures 5.4 and 5.5 present the one-dimensional representation of the independent size variable and the dependent effort variable, respectively from Table 5.1. It can be observed graphically

- from Figure 5.4 that a project of over 600 CFP is quite far away from the other projects (as it is around three times larger than the next largest project) and
- from Figure 5.5 that the project with an effort of almost 1000 hours is also far from the other projects in terms of hours: this project is then a good statistical outlier candidate, to be confirmed by appropriate statistical tests.

In software datasets, the distribution is often skewed to the left:

- ▶ There are often many smaller projects (in terms of either effort or functional size) than much larger projects.
- ▶ Negative values for either effort or size have no practical meaning (and if such negative values were found, it would be a clear indication of a bad data field).

With a feel for candidate outliers, it becomes a straightforward matter to run the relevant statistical tests to verify whether or not these data points are true statistical outliers.

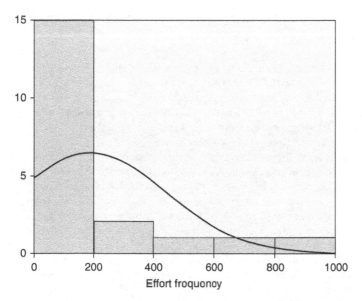

Figure 5.5   Frequency Distribution of the *Effort* (Dependent Variable) in Table 5.1 with $N = 21$.

- The presence of outliers can be analyzed with the Grubbs test also referred to as the ESD method (Extreme Studentized Deviate).
- The studentized values measure how many standard deviations each value is from the sample mean.
  - ▶ When the P-value for the Grubbs test is less than 0.05, that value is a significant outlier at the 5.0% significance level.
  - ▶ Values with a modified Z-score greater than 3.5 in absolute value may well be outliers.

There are a number of statistical tools on the Web for performing such tests. Some examples are as follows:

- For the Grubbs test:
  http://www.graphpad.com/quickcalcs/Grubbs1.cfm
- For linear least squares regression:
  http://www.shodor.org/unchem/math/lls/leastsq.html

Of course, professional statistical software packages offer more extensive and comprehensive options and facilities.

On the dataset in Table 5.1, the Kolmogorov–Smirnov test indicates that

- the size variable is not normally distributed – see Figure 5.4 and
- the effort variable is not normally distributed – see Figure 5.5.

Identification of Outliers in Table 5.1

The Grubbs test on the dataset in Table 5.1 and Figure 5.4 indicates that the first variable, *functional size*, of project no. 2 at 618 CFP is significantly larger than all the others: it is more than three standard deviations from the average of 73 CFP.

When there are good reasons to believe that such outliers are not representative of the dataset under study, they should be taken out of the sample being analyzed.

When project no. 2 is taken out of the sample, it can be verified again that the *size* variable in the sample of 20 projects has a normal distribution, based on its Kolmogorov–Smirnov test, which gives a significant P-value (high).

The Grubbs test on the second variable, *effort*, indicates that both project no. 2 (with 956 hours) and project no. 21 (with 724 hours) are far from the set of observations: from Table 5.1 and Figure 5.5, the distance of these two projects from the average of the population at 184 hours can be measured in terms of multiples of sigma (the standard deviation of the variable), two standard deviations in this case, which means that these two projects can be considered as outliers in the population under study for this input parameter.

As indicated in Table 5.2, the averages for both functional size and effort are significantly reduced when these two outliers are excluded: from 184 to 115 hours on average for the effort variable and from 73 down to 40 CFP for the functional size variable.

Without these two outliers, the distributions of the sample ($N = 19$) for each variable separately become closer to a normal distribution – see Table 5.3, based on the Kolmogorov–Smirnov test: a nonsignificant (high) P-value (here $P = 0.16$, which is higher than the threshold of $P < 0.05$), which allows us to assume that the variable is distributed normally.

Table 5.2   Analysis of the Impact of Outliers in the Dataset

Identification	Effort (hours)	Functional size (CFP units)
Total ($N = 21$)	3867	1526
Average ($N = 21$)	184	73
Total ($N = 19$) excluding outlier nos. 2 and 21	2187	751
Average ($N = 19$)	115	40

Table 5.3   Kolmogorov–Smirnov Test of the Normal Distribution – Reduced Set: $N = 19$

Variable	N	D	P
Effort	19	0.27	0.16
Size in CFP	19	0.28	0.10

5.4.3   Log Transformation

Since variables that are not normally distributed offer weak support for linear regression, mathematical transformations may be performed on these datasets.

- The log transform is often used to obtain normal distributions for either the size or the effort variable, or both.

Figure 5.6 presents the initial wedge-shaped dataset of project effort with respect to project duration, while Figure 5.7 presents the log transformation of both axes [Bourque et al. 2007].

- On the one hand, the log transformation will often lead to normal distributions of the variables and to the satisfaction of the normality assumption for the use

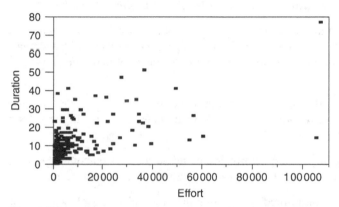

Figure 5.6   Scatter Plot of Project Effort Versus Duration ($N = 312$) [Bourque et al. 2007, Fig. 2. Reprinted with permission from Springer Science+Business Media B.V.]

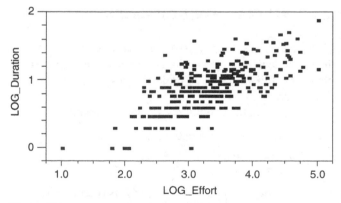

Figure 5.7   Log Transform of Figure 5.6 on LOG (Effort) and LOG (Duration) [Bourque et al. 2007, Fig. 7. Reprinted with permission from Springer Science+Business Media B.V.]

of regression models. Log transformation will also often lead to regression models with a higher coefficient of determination than models built with the nontransformed data.

- On the other hand, the weaknesses in the distribution of the underlying data still exist and must be taken into account in the practical analysis of the quality of these models, and in their practical use.

For software engineering practitioners, these log transformations are not very useful:

- The large gaps in data points in the original size format still exist, and *log-log models (such as non-log-transform models) are not representative of data points in such gaps*:
- *Productivity models like these should not be used to extrapolate the behavior of the dependent variable in these gaps in the independent variables.*

Any practical use of the outcomes of such estimation log models requires that the data be transformed back into their initial form: in practice, software engineers and their managers work in terms of hours, days, or months (and not log-hours, log-days, or log-months).

- ▶ It is also much easier to grasp the true magnitude of errors in the raw data when the data have not been transformed, than with the log-transform values.

For all intents and purposes, practitioners should be concerned about the quality of a model proposed to them where the units used are in log-transform form.

- ▶ This should serve an immediate warning that the practical quality of the log model could be much lower in the regular scale than that reported in the log scale.

5.5 GRAPHICAL ANALYSIS – TWO-DIMENSIONAL

Multidimensional graphical analysis will typically provide an intuitive feel for the relationships between the dependent variable and independent variable. Figure 5.2 presented this relationship for the full dataset of 21 projects, while the set without the two outliers is presented in Figure 5.8.

Note that the scales on the axes in the two figures are not the same:

- For the full dataset of $N = 21$ projects (Figure 5.2):
  - ▶ size varies from +0 to 700 CFP and
  - ▶ effort varies from +0 to 1200 hours.
- For the dataset without the two outliers of $N = 19$ projects (Figure 5.8):
  - ▶ size varies from +0 to 250 CFP and
  - ▶ effort varies from +0 to 450 hours.

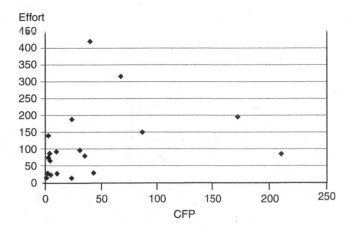

Figure 5.8   Dataset Excluding Two Outliers ($N = 19$)

Identification and impact of outliers:

- A true statistical outlier would noticeably change the slope of the regression model.
- If it does not change the regression model slope, then it is not necessarily an outlier.

Additional graphical analyses could help identify the presence of candidate multiple submodels based on various concepts typically found in production processes, as explained in Chapters 2, 10, and 12:

- Candidate subsets of data points (i.e., distinct samples) on the dependent variable, in particular on economies and diseconomies of scale
- Whether or not it is better to segregate the sample into two subsets using the density of data points within some ranges:
  - a densely populated sample within a range (typically small- to medium-sized projects) or
  - a sparsely populated sample of larger projects within a larger range.

Such a graphical analysis will provide insights into whether or not it is wise to generalize the model in the nonpopulated interval.

For instance, in Figure 5.9

- *most of the data points* are within the +0 to 100 CFP size range,
- there is *a sparsely populated interval* between 100 and 400 CFP,
- there are *no data between* 400 CFP and 600 CFP, and
- there is a *sparsely populated interval* between 600 and 800 CFP.

While a single productivity model could be constructed including all the data points at once, using the economics concepts described in Chapter 2, there could well be three more specific models – see Figure 5.10

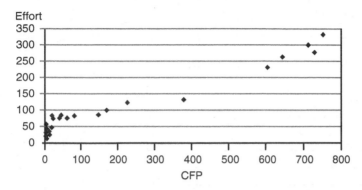

Figure 5.9   Dataset with a Sparsely Populated Size Interval (Between 250 and 600 CFP)

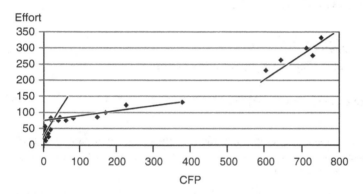

Figure 5.10   Candidate Productivity Models by Size Range

- for small projects (1–30 CFP): diseconomies of scale, and variable effort
- for medium-sized projects (30–400 CFP): large economies of scale (same fixed effort and a small effort increase due to increases in size)
- for large projects (600–800 CFP): some economies of scale (fixed effort, larger than for medium-sized projects)

Key Learning

In this particular example, there are not enough projects in each size range to confirm that the candidate models are statistically significant, but the visual analysis provides insights that will make it possible to develop more refined productivity models over time based on the specific characteristics of a software organization and its context.

5.6   SIZE INPUTS DERIVED FROM A CONVERSION FORMULA

Many of the software estimation models and software tools proposed in the literature and by tool vendors have been built based on inputs measured in lines of code (LOC), and are used in an estimation context with estimates of LOC.

With the growing popularity of Function Points in the 1990s and 2000s, a number of conversion ratios have been published to convert FP into LOC for various programming languages in order to take this type of input into older estimation models. These conversion numbers are readily available on the Web, and are, of course, easy to use.

- However, does quick-and-easy really improve the quality of the estimation process?

In practice, both practitioners and researchers must be extremely careful when using such conversion factors for estimation purposes and they should be particularly careful when using estimation models requiring LOC-FP conversion ratios.

The published conversion ratios are taken as "averages" of Function Points to a number of Lines of Code in a specific programming language. However, it is fairly risky to use any average for decision-making without considerable knowledge about it, including all of the examples mentioned earlier (size of samples, statistical deviations, outliers, context, etc.)

This is illustrated in Figure 5.11 with two normal distributions which have exactly the same average value, but major differences in their standard deviations:

- Distribution A has a fairly large dispersion of its data points across its average in this distribution.

- Distribution no. 2, represented by the blue line, has the same average, but a much higher distribution peak, indicating that most of the data points are close to this average:

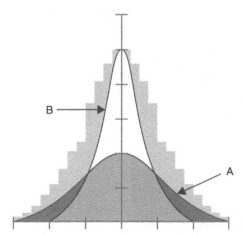

Figure 5.11   The Same Average, But Very Different Variations from the Average

- ○ When the conversion factor comes from a distribution such as Distribution B then the average value represented by the conversion factor introduces only a minor candidate variation in the conversion from Lines of Code to Function Points.

  - ■ In contrast, the use of the average from a distribution such as Distribution A in Figure 5.11 introduces a much larger range of variation into the conversion results, to the point of being dangerous to use for estimation purposes since it increases uncertainty, rather than contributing to its reduction.

Without information on both the sample size and the deviation from the averages, the published conversion factors are *numbers without any intrinsic qualities*, and cannot be considered as valuable information for decision-making purposes.

Backfiring: Converting Lines of Code into Function Points

The use of conversion factors to express LOC in Function Points is often referred to as *backfiring*.

According to measurement experts in the field, *backfiring will backfire!*

5.7 SUMMARY

As of now, there is still no reliable, documented statistical study available on the convertibility of Function Points to LOC across programming languages.

- Without documented evidence, there is no support for a professionally sound use of such conversion factors.

These are examples of the missing information that makes the use of these conversion factors less reliable:

- Unknown size of the samples used to derive them
- Unknown statistical deviations from the published averages
- Unknown presence (or absence) of outliers in the datasets
- No indication of the potential causes of significant variations from the published averages.

SUMMARY

For all these reasons, it is imprudent, even highly risky, to use any of these ratios, unless an organization has a sophisticated statistical analyst at its disposal who can provide the specialized knowledge required to adequately take into account such uncertain information in a decision-making context.

FURTHER READING: MEASUREMENT AND QUANTIFICATION

(A) **Introduction**

The development of productivity models in the sciences and in engineering has benefited from two major advantages:

- A considerable amount of time, money, and expertise has typically been invested to ensure, through experimentation, the quality of productivity models and to document limitations.
- A very sound foundation for the measurement concepts, measuring units, and measuring tools used in the design of their productivity models.

By contrast, software engineering suffers from the following major weaknesses when it comes to building productivity models:

- A very weak foundation of software measures for ensuring accuracy, repeatability, and reproducibility of the data collected for experimentation and usage.
- A lack of attention to the properties of the numbers in these productivity models.
- A lack of experimentally verified productivity models:
  - ▶ The models proposed to practitioners are typically not based on sound and well-documented experimental data:
    - Too many are typically based on personal opinion and theories that have not been quantitatively and independently verified.

This Advanced Reading section presents some of the key concepts required to understand some of the strengths and weaknesses of the measures used in input to productivity models – for further details, see the book, *Software Metrics and Software Metrology* [Abran, 2010].

(B) **Base and derived quantities**

There are seven *base quantities* in the International System of Quantities as follows:

- Second for time
- Meter for length
- Kilogram for mass
- Ampere for electric current
- Kelvin for the thermodynamic temperature
- Candela for luminosity intensity
- Mole for the amount of substance.

A base quantity cannot be expressed in terms of the others.

Combinations of base quantities are considered *derived quantities* and are defined, by convention, to represent a combination of multiple concepts of interest.

Examples of Base Quantities

Time and distance are base quantities: a measurement of each represents a quantification of the respective agreed-on concept measured using their respective measurement standards-etalons of second and meter.

Examples of Derived Quantities

– Speed is defined as the distance traveled over a period of time. It is therefore defined as a combination of the concepts of distance and time, and is quantified as the ratio of these two base quantities. Speed is therefore a derived quantity.

– The Earth's gravity is defined as $G = 9.81$ m/s^2.

The metrological properties of this quantification in a derived quantity are directly dependent on the quality of the base quantities that compose it. Therefore, the accuracy of the measurement of speed depends on the accuracy of the measurement of both time and distance, and the accuracy of gravity depends on the accuracy of both length and time.

It can be observed that measurements with derived quantities have two very important properties as follows:

- They are all expressed with *a combination of measurement units.*
- The numbers obtained from the measurement procedures are not to be interpreted within the specific context of measurement, but must be interpreted with traceability to the international standards-etalons *of the base units used.*

Software engineers should beware when

- measurement units are not well defined, such as in the Cyclomatic Complexity Number, and for which there is ambiguity in the admissible mathematical operations (see Chapter 6 in *Software Metrics and Software Metrology* – [Abran, 2010]);
- mathematical operations do not take into account the measurement units, such as in the "effort" metrics of Halstead (see Chapter 7 in *Software Metrics and Software Metrology* – [Abran, 2010]);
- the design of a software measure includes a number of inadmissible mathematical operations of measures that are not of the ratio scale type, such as in Use Case Points (see Chapters 8 and 9 in *Software Metrics and Software Metrology* – [Abran, 2010]).

(C) **"Feel good" Adjustments and Weights**

In both software measurement methods and software productivity models, there is often an *adjustment factor* for combining and integrating a number of concepts. However, a look at many of these adjustment factors reveals that they disregard both the measurement units and the scale type to obtain what is often referred as *points*: for instance, object points, use case points, etc.

An adjustment in a "software metrics" or in estimation models is typically composed of multiple factors, multiple ways of quantifying these factors, and multiple ways of combining these factors into a single end number to represent the adjustment to the estimation equation. These adjustments are either designed by an individual or by a group of practitioners.

An example of a group view of an adjustment is the size Adjustment in the first generation of the functional size methods, which transforms the Unadjusted Function Points into Adjusted Function Points, using 14 factors and a linear transformation. This example is selected here because its structure has influenced a large number of variants, not only in size measurement methods, but in estimation models as well.

In the design of this type of Adjustment, there are serious methodological weaknesses in the use of quantities with distinct scale types:

(**A**) Each of the 14 factors is classified into one of the five classifications:

- When a factor is absent, it is assigned a classification of 0.
- When the factor is present at its maximum, it is assigned a classification of 5.
- Various other criteria are provided to assign the intermediate classifications 1, 2, 3, and 4.

This classification from 0 to 5 constitutes an *ordered set*, where each value from 0 to 5 is considered greater than the previous value; however, the intervals for the classification are typically

- irregular within each factor and
- different across all 14 factors.

Therefore, these 0, 1, 2, 3, 4, and 5 do not represent numbers on a ratio scale, but rather *ordered labels* (i.e., labels with an ordering scale type).

(**B**) In the next step for calculating the Adjustment, the classification in the previous step is multiplied by a "degree of influence" of 0.1. The design of this measurement step contains a number of incorrect and inadmissible operations:

   a. All 14 factors have different definitions and distinct interval ranges: there are no *a priori* reasons to assign the same 0.1 to the 14 distinct factors, each with their own distinct irregular intervals of classification.

   b. A multiplication usually requires that the numbers being multiplied are at least on a ratio scale. This is obviously not the case here: the values of 0–5 of the previous steps are not on a ratio scale, but are merely ordered labels, which have no precise quantitative meaning; their addition or multiplication is mathematically invalid.

(**C**) In the final step, all the numbers obtained in the previous step for each of the 14 factors are added together and included in a linear transformation to allow an impact of ±35% to the unadjusted functional size.

Even though practitioners might "feel good" that their sizing or estimation models take into account a considerable number of factors or
characteristics, these adjustment are of little value.

There are similar mathematical issues in the use of the so-called "weights" in
measurement methods – for a more detailed discussion on these issues, see
Chapter 7 in *Software Metrics and Software Metrology* – [Abran, 2010]).

(D) Verification of the data collection procedures

It is not enough to have good data definitions and adequate measurement
scale types. Every organization must also implement good data collection
procedures to ensure the high quality of the data collected. To achieve this,
information such as the following should be documented for the data collected
and the inputs to the estimation process:

- The raw information on each data point
- The measurement method used as well as the detailed measurement proce-
  dure
- The specific context as well as the conditions of measurement and data
  collection
- The potential biases in the data collection process for each input variable
- An indication of the error range for each input variable.

Examples of Data Quality Controls from the ISBSG

See Chapter 8 of the ISBSG repository for examples of administrative procedures, and
related data fields, to ensure the quality of the data collected and the documented analysis
of those data.

EXERCISES

1. When you are building a productivity model, why do you need to verify each input to your
   model?
2. Can models and techniques recognize bad input data?
3. Give five examples of bad or poor data input to productivity models.
4. Give two examples of independent and dependent variables used as inputs to productivity
   models.
5. Why is the scale type of an input variable important in a model?
6. Give an example of the misuse of a scale type in an input variable.
7. What mathematical operations can you perform with the CMMi® maturity level numbers?
8. Productivity models are built with numbers and they produce numbers. Under what conditions can you add and multiply numbers in a software productivity model?

9. Why is it important to use international standards for the measurement of input variables for estimation purposes?

10. List some of the verification procedures that can be implemented to improve the quality of the inputs to a productivity model?

11. How do you verify that the data points for a variable have a normal distribution?

12. Why is a normal distribution important for models?

13. What is a statistical outlier in a dataset?

14. How do you identify a statistical outlier in a dataset?

15. Discuss the perils for practitioners of using models built on the basis of log transforms.

16. Are there outliers in the dataset in Table 5.1? Use both a graphical analysis and some statistical tests to support your answer.

17. What are the necessary conditions for the use of the LOC-Function Point conversion ratios by programming languages?

TERM ASSIGNMENTS

1. Measure the functional size of the software project you are currently working on. What is the most probable error range in your measurement result? Comment.

2. Look at the documentation associated with the estimate preparation of three recent projects in your organization. Comment on the quality of the inputs to the estimation model used (including the inputs for estimating based on expert judgment). What lessons can be learned from this?

3. Carry out a literature review of software estimation models. Of those that you have come across, which use measurement units recognized as international standards? When the estimation models do not use standards for their measurement units, what is the impact in practice?

4. Access three estimation models available on the Web. Document the basis for experimentation provided by the designers of each of these publicly available estimation models. To what point can you trust them? Explain your point of view to your management and customers. Look back at the reasons supporting that point of view and classify them as engineering-based or opinion-based.

5. Access some of the Web information on conversion factors from Lines of Code to Function Points (or vice versa). What is their documented quality? How much more uncertainty is introduced into your estimation model if you use any of these conversion factors?

EXERCISES – FURTHER READING SECTION

1. Select one software estimation model. Do the units of the independent variables (e.g., the cost factors) added and multiplied in that model lead to the units of the dependent variable that it attempts to estimate (e.g., effort in hours or duration in months)?

2. What is the unit of a Use Case Point? What is its scale type? What is the impact of the scale type when use case points are used as inputs in estimation models?

3. Provide examples of the software size units used in three estimation models.

TERM ASSIGNMENTS – FURTHER READING SECTION

1. Select two estimation models. Identify the base measures (or base quantities) and the derived measures (or derived quantities) in each model. In these models, what is the impact if the derived measures are not based on international standards of measurement? What is the impact if different measurement units are used?

2. All software estimation models use a measure of size. Select five estimation models and list the software size measurement method they use. What is the impact on the estimate produced if you use a different software size unit?

3. Take the mathematical formula for gravity. In your own words, describe how much time and experimentation was required to quantitatively figure out the relationship among the elements in this formula. Describe how much care is taken by industry to measure the various elements to determine gravity in a specific context (e.g., in rocket launches). Next, take the software estimation model used in your organization, and do the same as you did earlier for the mathematical formula for gravity.

Chapter 6

Verification of Productivity Models

OBJECTIVES

This chapter covers

- The criteria for evaluating productivity models.
- Verification of the assumptions of the productivity models.
- Evaluation of models by their own builders.
- Independent evaluations: small- and large-scale replication studies.

6.1 INTRODUCTION

In this chapter, we present a number of criteria that should be documented to provide information on the performance of a productivity model, in terms of the ranges of estimates and uncertainties inherent in such models. Various examples are provided.

For the sake of simplicity, all the examples presented in this chapter are simple linear regression models with a single independent variable; however, the verification criteria discussed are also relevant for nonlinear and multiregression models with many independent variables – see Chapter 10.

This chapter is organized as follows:

- Section 6.2 presents a number of criteria that describe the relationships across the variables in productivity models.

- Section 6.3 provides examples of the verification of the assumptions in productivity models.

- Section 6.4 gives some examples of the verification of productivity models by their model builders.

Software Project Estimation: The Fundamentals for Providing High Quality Information to Decision Makers, First Edition. Alain Abran.

- Section 6.5 provides examples of independent evaluation of productivity models already built: small- and large-scale replication studies.
- Section 6.6 presents some lessons learned, and in particular the existence of distinct models by size range.

6.2 CRITERIA DESCRIBING THE RELATIONSHIPS ACROSS VARIABLES

Productivity models are built to represent the relationships of a dependent variable (for instance, project effort) with respect to a single independent variable, or a number of them (software size, team size, development environment, etc.).

In this section, we present some of the criteria recommended by Conte *et al.* [1986] to analyze the relationships across the variables in productivity models built from a dataset.

6.2.1 Simple Criteria

Coefficient of determination (R^2)

The coefficient of Determination (R^2) describes the percentage of variability explained by the independent variable(s).

- This coefficient has a value between 0 and 1:
  - ▶ An R^2 close to 1 indicates that the variability in the response to the independent variable can be explained by the model.
    - That is, there is a strong relationship between the independent and dependent variables.
  - ▶ An R^2 close to 0 indicates that the variability in the response to the independent variable *cannot* be explained by the model.
    - That is, there is a no relationship between the independent and dependent variables.

Error of an Estimate (E)

The actual value minus the estimated value of the dependent variable equals the error of the productivity model on a single project:

- For example, when project effort is the dependent variable, E (i.e., error) is the difference between the known project effort of a completed project (i.e., actual value) and the value calculated by the model (i.e., estimated value).

$$Error = E = \text{Actual} - \text{Estimated}$$

Relative Error (RE)

The relative error (RE) gives an indication of the divergence between the values estimated by the model and the actual values, expressed as a percentage. This relative error can be either positive or negative, representing either an overestimation or an underestimation by the model.

$$\textit{Relative error:} \ \mathrm{RE} = \frac{\mathrm{Actual} - \mathrm{Estimate}}{\mathrm{Actual}}$$

Magnitude of the Relative Error (MRE)

The magnitude of the RE (MRE) gives an indication of the divergence between the values estimated by the model and the actual values, expressed as a percentage.

- Perfect estimates would give an MRE of 0%.

$$\textit{Magnitude of the relative error:} \ \mathrm{MRE} = |\mathrm{RE}| = \left| \frac{\mathrm{Actual} - \mathrm{Estimate}}{\mathrm{Actual}} \right|$$

$$\textit{Mean magnitude of the relative error:} \ \mathrm{MMRE} = \overline{\mathrm{MRE}} = \frac{1}{n} \sum_{i=1}^{n} \mathrm{MRE}_i$$

Some of the key concepts underlying REs and MMREs are illustrated in Figure 6.1:

- Each star represents an actual tuple (size, effort) of a completed project.
- The blue linear regression line represents the productivity model derived from the actual (i.e., each point on the linear model represents the model estimate of the effort for each size on the x-axis).

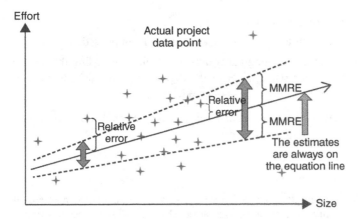

Figure 6.1   Mean Magnitude of Relative Error – MMRE

- The relative error (i.e., actual value − estimated value) is the distance of each actual point to the estimation line.
- The MMRE is the mean magnitude of relative error across all the data points, and is represented by the dashed lines.
  - The MMRE does not represent the extreme of the estimate errors, only the mean; therefore:
    - there are estimates that are further away from the actual than the MMRE and
    - others that are closer to the estimate of the regression line.

Prediction Level of the Model

The prediction level of a model is given by $PRED(l) = \frac{k}{n}$, where k is the number of projects in a specific sample of size n for which MRE $\leq l$.

It is not sufficient for a productivity model to perform well with the dataset used to build it, but it also has to perform well with other data (e.g., predictability), and this is very dependent on the number and quality of the data sample in input to these models. To analyze the predictability of a productivity model, the model has to be tested with projects other than the ones that contributed to its design.

For such a predictability analysis, model builders would typically build the models using a large subset of the projects (say 60%), and then test the performance of the model with the subset of hold-out projects (i.e., the 40% not used for building the model). Another method is the so-called leave-one-out strategy, where the models are built with $n−1$ data points, and tested with one left out. This is done iteratively with a different data point left out at each iteration.

6.2.2   Practical Interpretation of Criteria Values

In practice, a model is considered as good when:

(A) it is based on high-quality data,

(B) the data assumptions of the statistical models have been proved, and

(C) the outcomes of the model adequately describe reality, including the related uncertainties in the relationships across the dependent and independent variables within the context of the data collected.

The next three examples illustrate criteria values expected in distinct contexts.

EXAMPLE 6.1

An organization has its software development process assessed as being at the high end of the CMMi® process capability maturity model (i.e., at Level 4 or 5). With project data from a homogeneous environment and considerable development process expertise, a model built with one or two independent variables (including software size) would be expected to have an $R^2 \geq$ 0.8 and a PRED(0.20) = 0.80. that is, in such an environment, software size is often observed as expressing most of the variability of the process effort in one type of development project, while all of the other factors combined have much less impact on the dependent variable than software size alone.

EXAMPLE 6.2

In the same organization as in Example 6.1, and for another dataset of projects with brand new technologies and a variety of development environments, an estimation model would be expected to have much lower criteria values, such as an $R^2 \geq 0.5$ and a PRED(0.20) = 0.50. These ranges of values could be considered to adequately represent the uncertainty of such innovative projects, which allows management to identify an adequate level of contingency planning across such a portfolio of innovative projects – see Chapter 3 for further insights into contingency planning, including the Further Reading section.

EXAMPLE 6.3

An organization's software development process is rated at Level 1 on the CMMi® rating scale, which means that it is developed in an ad hoc manner, without the support of well-established organizational processes, including well-proven project management practices. Such a development environment is typically risky and unpredictable. An estimation model with one or two independent variables built from data from such an environment would usually have a fairly low R^2 (i.e., $R^2 < 0.5$).

- Should models from such an organization have a very large R^2 (≥ 0.8), this would be highly suspicious and the quality of the input data should be cross-checked for inconsistencies or errors:
  - ▶ The dataset includes one or more outliers, which should have been excluded for statistical analysis,
  - ▶ Some data points might come from nontrustworthy sources,
  - ▶ Data collection procedures might not have been properly followed,
  - ▶ And so on.

Is There Such a Thing as a "Good" Model?

In the software literature, a model is often qualified as good when the MRE (Mean Relative Error) is within ±25% for 75% of the observations, or PRED(25%) = 75% [Conte *et al.*, 1986].

Sometimes the following criteria are also used:

- PRED(20%) = 80%
- PRED(30%) = 70%.

There is, however, no theoretical foundation for such threshold values: productivity models with lower values still provide an organization with a great deal of information on the expected variability, and ranges of variations, of their development processes.

A productivity model based on the statistical analysis of a data sample is considered good when its input data are of high quality, *when the model's assumptions are met, and the model provides the right information on the relationships across the variables investigated, including on the related uncertainties.*

In summary, a productivity model is good when it provides the right information, not when it provides a specific number or meets specific threshold values.

6.2.3 More Advanced Criteria

Some more advanced criteria are presented in Conte *et al.* [1986]:

The root of the mean square error: $\text{RMS} = (\overline{\text{SE}})^{1/2} = \sqrt{\dfrac{1}{n}\sum_{i=1}^{n}(\text{Actual}_i - \text{Estimate}_i)^2}$

The relative root of the mean square error: $\text{RRMS} = \overline{\text{RMS}} = \dfrac{\text{RMS}}{\dfrac{1}{n}\sum_{i=1}^{n}\text{Actual}_i}$

P-Value of the Statistical Parameters

The coefficients of the independent variables in models can be assessed using the P-value statistical parameter, which expresses the statistical significance of the coefficients of the models.

- Commonly, values of P lower than 0.05 are considered statistically significant.

Testing the Significance of the Model

These tests relate to the significance of the variables.

- The t-test: explains whether or not a coefficient of *a given independent variable* differs from zero.
  - ▶ Rule of thumb: if the t-value calculated exceeds two, then the coefficient is significant.
- The F-test: tests for the significance of *the model as a whole.*

Analysis of the Residuals

Three additional tests can be conducted to assess the quality of a model:

- The residuals are normally distributed
- The residuals are independent of the independent variable
- The variance of the residuals is constant over the range of the dependent variable.

However, these tests are not sufficient by themselves to verify models. The inputs should be of high quality, and the model's assumptions must be satisfied – see next section.

While these criteria are at times used in the literature, they are rarely used in current industry practices.

6.3   VERIFICATION OF THE ASSUMPTIONS OF THE MODELS

In a number of studies on estimation models, some authors report that their models perform well on many of the criteria mentioned in Section 6.2. However, this is not enough. To be valid, statistically based models must meet the fundamental statistical assumptions for such models – see the following for further discussion.

6.3.1   Three Key Conditions Often Required

Productivity models built using simple parametric regression techniques require:

- a normal distribution of the input parameters – see Section 5.4.1:
  - ▶ for both the dependent and independent variables;
- no outlier that influences the model unduly – see Section 5.4.2;
- a large enough dataset to build them:
  - ▶ typically, 30 data points for each independent parameter included in the model.

All the above-mentioned conditions must be met concurrently to give users confidence in the results of the tests documented by the statistical tools and to make generalizations on the goodness and usefulness of regression-based productivity models.

Builders of a model, as well as users, should verify that those conditions are verified and documented, and that the model building process meets the minimal requirements before claiming that their models have "good predictability":

- If these conditions are not met, generalizations made by the builders regarding such models are unsound, and users should not rely on them.

6.3.2 Sample Size

The size of sample required for meaningful statistical regression results means, for example, that:

- Building each independent parameter with a sound basis for statistical test validity typically requires 30 projects when random data are involved.
- It is still feasible to build regression models with fewer data points, but authors should not venture into broad generalizations if the model is built based on a sample with fewer than 15–20 projects – see the recommendations of the International Benchmarking Standards Group – ISBSG – on sample size for external data in the box below.
- Of course, models built with only 4–10 data points should be considered without underlying statistical strength (even when the criteria have high value, high values do not correspond to statistical validity).
  - This does not mean, however, that these models are meaningless and not useful to the organization that provided the data. On the contrary, even such small samples can provide an organization with an objective, quantitative view of the performance of their development processes from which they can derive insights on what can be reasonably expected of subsequent projects, in terms of productivity performance.
    - Within their own organization, these data points are not random, but rather they are representative of the projects completed within their context and data collection time frame.
  - Of course, for organizations that did not provide such data, the models based on a small sample do not hold generalization value (i.e., the odds are small that these results are relevant, even to their own context).

ISBSG Recommendations on Sample Size for Statistical Analysis

"For regression to make sense, you need quite a lot of data. A sample size of 30 or more is desirable, although a sample size of 20 or more should provide reasonable results."

"Not much can be concluded from a sample size of less than 10 projects."

"There are several other restrictions on when regression can be used. For example, the data should be 'normally distributed' (this is not the case in the common situation where there are many small values and only few large ones); and should not show a fan-shaped pattern (small spread for small values, and a large spread for large values). These restrictions are often violated in software engineering datasets."

> *"Before performing a regression analysis, you need to study your data carefully to make sure they are appropriate. For more information, consult any standard textbook on statistics."*
>
> Source: Guidelines for use of the ISBSG data [ISBSG 2009].

Examples of regression models that meet, or do not meet, the above-mentioned criteria are presented in the next sections.

6.4   EVALUATION OF MODELS BY THEIR OWN BUILDERS

The information on the variation ranges and levels of uncertainty of models should normally be documented by those who design and publish them (i.e., the model builders). When the details of such models are documented, we can refer to them as "white-box" models, in contrast to "black-box" models, in which their data, the models themselves, and their performance on specific datasets are hidden.

EXAMPLE 6.4   *Function Point-Based Models and Multi-Organizational Datasets*

The [Desharnais 1988] study was conducted with a multi-organizational dataset of 82 MIS projects.

For the productivity model built on the full multi-organizational dataset (i.e., 82 projects), the variation in functional size explains 50% of the variation in project effort, that is, $R^2 = 0.50$.

When subdivided into more homogeneous samples by development environment platform, the reported performances of the corresponding productivity models are as follows:

- With 47 projects on the mainframe platform: $R^2 = 0.57$
- With 25 projects on the mid-range platform: $R^2 = 0.39$
- With 10 projects on the PC platform: $R^2 = 0.13$.

The productivity models built on this dataset can be considered as white-box models, since all the detailed data used to build them are documented and available for independent replication studies.

EXAMPLE 6.5

The study reported in Abran and Robillard [1996] was conducted with a dataset of 21 MIS projects from a *single* organization. This dataset represents a fairly homogeneous environment from an organization, which at the time was well on its way to being rated (by an externally certified assessor) at Level 3 on the SEI's Capability Maturity Model scale.

In this context, the productivity model built using functional size as the single independent variable explains 81% of the variation with project effort ($R^2 = 0.81$).

The productivity models built on this dataset can be considered as white-box models, since all the detailed data used to build them are documented and available for independent replication studies.

EXAMPLE 6.6

The study in Stern [2009] reports on five datasets varying from 8 to 30 real-time embedded software projects measured in COSMIC Function Points. Each dataset originates from a *single (but distinct)* organization, each representing a fairly homogeneous development environment. The productivity models built using functional size as the single independent variable are presented graphically and explain from 68% to 93% of the variation with project effort (i.e., the R^2 range from 0.68 to 0.93).

6.5 MODELS ALREADY BUILT–SHOULD YOU TRUST THEM?

6.5.1 Independent Evaluations: Small-Scale Replication Studies

In this book, the term "white-box models" refers to models for which the detailed internal structure that converts the estimation inputs into an estimate is known and documented; that is, the detailed equations of the white-box model, and the corresponding parameters, are described, and the information about the dataset from which these equations were derived is provided.

In contrast, the term "black-box models" refers to models whose internal structure is hidden from both users and researchers, and for which nothing specific has been made available about the datasets from which they were derived.

Whether the models proposed are white-box or black-box models, they should be evaluated using different datasets from the ones that were used to build them:

- This type of verification addresses a key concern of users of these models: how do they perform for projects developed in other environments, and their own in particular?

Such verification is typically performed independently of the model builders:

- by independent researchers using the empirical datasets at their disposal or
- by practitioners who have access to historical data within their own organizations and who want to test the performance of such models when data from their own completed projects are fed into these productivity models.

Tests with Other Datasets

This is, of course, the fundamental test of how "good" the proposed models are: no one should use them without first verifying their performance against their own datasets.

The classic example of the small-scale independent evaluation of software models is Kemerer's study, in which data from 15 projects originating from many organizations were used to analyze the performance of a number of models reported in the literature, including COCOMO 81, ESTIMAC, and SLIM [Kemerer 1987].

- For example, the performance reported for the Intermediate COCOMO 81 model is $R^2 = 0.60$ and an MRE of 584%.

- In contrast, the performance of the function points-based regression model built by Kemerer directly from this multi-organizational dataset of 15 projects was $R^2 = 0.55$ with an MRE of 103%. In summary, the model built directly from Kemerer's dataset had a much smaller range of estimation errors than the models tested.

Key Lessons Learned

When you have enough data points, it is much better to build your own productivity models based on your own data than using someone else's models.

Expect wider ranges of variation in models built based on multi-organizational datasets. The performance spread will be wider for a variety of reasons: real differences in performance between organizations, different constraints, different nonfunctional requirements, etc.

6.5.2   Large-Scale Replication Studies

The generalization power of small-scale studies is limited, owing to the small samples usually used for these studies.

A larger-scale replication study is reported in Abran Ndiaye and Bourque [2007] using a much larger dataset of 497 projects, further subdivided by programming language. This large-scale study took into account verification of the regression model assumptions by identifying the ranges of values of the independent variable, the number of data points within each range, and the presence of outliers (i.e., the conditions of validity of the statistical regression models used).

However, this larger scale study investigated only a single black-box estimation tool from vendors included in Kemerer [1987].

This study reported on the performance of both

- a black-box model from a software vendor for each of the samples identified in the large-scale replication study and
- the productivity models derived directly, in a white-box manner, for each of the samples.

Results from both the black-box and white-box approaches were compared using the RRMS (or $\overline{RMS}$: the lower, the better) and a prediction level to within 25% [i.e., PRED (25%): the higher, the better].

The results are presented in Table 6.1 for the set of samples that excluded outliers (refer to Section 5.4). Note that the row headings in Table 6.1 indicate, for each sample:

- the size ranges of the data from which the regression models are built, and for which the productivity models are valid.

For example:

- For the Access language, the data points available were within the 200–800 Function Point interval.
- For Oracle, the data points available were within the 100–2000 Function Point interval.
- For the C++ language, there were two distinct intervals of data points within the 70–500 Function Point interval and data points within the 750–1250 Function Point interval with a distinct productivity model and a distinct estimation performance within that range.

(A) *Estimation performance of the black-box estimation tool*

For most of the programming languages for which there were enough data points for a statistical analysis – see columns (1) and (3) in Table 6.1, the black-box estimation tool produced:

- estimation (RRMS) errors in column (1) varying from a minimum of 89% for Cobol II (within the 80–180 FP interval) up to a maximum of 1653% for C (within the 200–800 FP interval), with both very large underestimation and overestimation when the actual values are taken into account, rather than only the magnitude of the errors;
- not a single PRED(25%) estimate for the majority of the samples (i.e., 0% in column 3), and the best PRED (25%) performance for only 20% of the estimates within the PL1 [550, 2550] sample.

This large-scale replication study confirmed the findings of the small-scale study of Kemerer [1987] for this vendor estimation tool; that is, in both studies (small scale and large scale), the estimation errors were considerable, with both very large underestimates and overestimates, in a somewhat random manner.

Table 6.1   Comparison of Results – RRMS and PRED(0.25) (Samples Excluding Outliers)

Sample characteristics: Programming language, size range [in Function Points]	RRMS		PRED(0.25)	
	(1) Vendor's black-box estimation tool (%)	(2) White-box models built directly from the data (%)	(3) Vendor's estimation tool (%)	(4) White-box models built directly from the data (%)
Access [200,800]	341	**15**	**0**	**91**
C [200, 800]	**1653**	50	11	22
C++ [70, 500]	97	86	8	25
C++ [750, 1250]	95	24	0	60
Cobol [60, 400]	400	42	7	43
Cobol [401, 3500]	348	51	16	35
Cobol II [80, 180]	**89**	29	0	78
Cobol II [180, 500]	109	46	17	33
Natural [20, 620]	243	50	10	27
Natural [621, 3500]	347	35	11	33
Oracle [100, 2000]	319	**120**	0	**21**
PL1 [80, 450]	274	45	5	42
PL1 [550, 2550]	895	21	**20**	60
Powerbuilder [60, 400]	95	29	0	58
SQL [280, 800]	136	81	0	27
SQL [801, 4500]	127	45	0	25
Telon [70, 650]	100	22	0	56
Visual Basic [30, 600]	122	54	0	42
Min	**89**	**15**	**0**	**21**
Max	**1653**	**120**	**20**	**91**

Abran et al. 2007. Reprinted with permission from John Wiley & Sons, Inc.

Documentation of the Performance of Estimation Tools

Do you purchase a car only because it looks good? Don't you first check the consumer reports on their technical performance and safety track records?

Most of the estimation tools that are freely available on the Web, as well as black-box estimation tools from some vendors, typically do not provide supporting evidence documenting:

- how such models have performed using historical datasets using the widely accepted criteria listed in this chapter,
- how well practitioners should expect them to perform on other datasets.

Should you trust them?

Not at all. Even though you may "feel good" about such models for whatever reason, you are about to make a major business decision!

What is the track record of such models? What are their inherent levels of uncertainty?

(B) *Estimation performance of the white-box models derived from each sample*
When you have access to data to assess the performance of vendors' estimation tools, you also have the data to build yourself productivity models in a white-box manner, and therefore the ability to compare a vendor's product against the models you yourself built directly from the data. This is illustrated as follows:

The performances of all the models built in a white-box manner from the same samples are presented in columns (2) and (4) of Table 6.1. In summary:

- These white-box productivity models had significantly lower estimation errors in terms of RRMS than the corresponding black-box models (column 2): from 15% for the Access 200 to 800 FP interval, to 120% for the Oracle 100–2000 FP interval.

  - Therefore, the number of white-box models with estimation errors is much lower than the corresponding number of errors of the vendor's estimation tool.

- For each sample, between 21% for the Oracle 100–2000 FP interval (column 4) and 91% of the project estimates for the Access 200–800 FP interval were within the targeted error range of PRED(0.25).

  - This means that the white-box productivity models perform much better than the vendor's estimation tool.

In summary, for all the programming language samples studied and for projects within the size interval of each corresponding sample:

- Practitioners can have greater confidence in the estimation results provided by the white-box productivity models they have built than those provided by the commercially available estimation tools studied in Kemerer [1987] and Abran et al. [2007].
- They should be aware, however, that the performance predictability of the white-box productivity models has not been tested on datasets other than the one that contributed to their own design (although they can use one of the testing strategies described at the end of Section 6.2.1).

6.6   LESSONS LEARNED: DISTINCT MODELS BY SIZE RANGE

While the general practice in software engineering is to build a single model without taking into account the size range of the independent variable, this is not supported by good practices in statistical analysis, which require that the assumptions of a model be verified and the results interpreted within the range for which there are enough data points.

For a dataset of projects *with a normal distribution*, represented approximately in Figure 6.2:

- A stated confidence interval is typically almost constant for the interval, which includes most of the data points on the independent variable – between the light-colored arrows.
- But the ranges of variation, i.e. the darker arrows in Figure 6.2, are much larger outside the range of the majority of data points, in particular with outliers.

Unfortunately, the usual approach in software engineering is still to look for a single model, overlooking the distribution of the data points and without considering the density of the data points across size intervals:

- Users of productivity models should be aware that levels of confidence cannot be assumed to be equal across most of the ranges, and outside them, in all models.

A much more cautious approach to building models is to segregate the available dataset into density ranges of projects. The following dataset is used for illustrative purposes – see Table 6.2 and Figure 6.3.

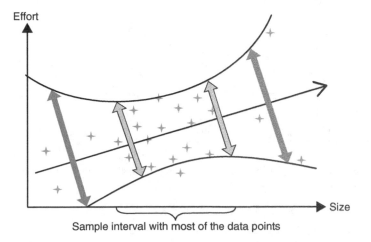

Sample interval with most of the data points

Figure 6.2   Confidence Intervals and Sample Intervals

Table 6.2   Illustrative Dataset with $N = 34$ Projects

ID number	Size (CFP)	Effort in Hours
1	15	15
2	18	13
3	22	35
4	25	30
5	25	38
6	33	43
7	37	35
8	39	32
9	40	55
10	50	55
11	55	35
12	63	90
13	66	65
14	70	44
15	80	79
16	83	88
17	85	95
18	85	110
19	93	120
20	97	100
21	140	130
22	135	145
23	200	240
24	234	300
25	300	245
26	390	350
27	450	375
28	500	390
29	510	320
30	540	320
31	580	400
32	1200	900
33	1300	950
34	1000	930

For example, in Table 6.2 and Figure 6.3, on the x-axis of the independent variable, functional size, there are:

- 22 projects within the 15–140 CFP size interval,
- 9 projects within the 200–580 CFP size interval, and
- 3 projects within the 1000–1300 CFP size interval.

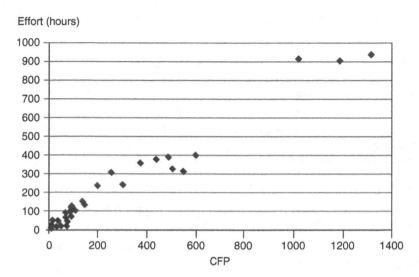

Figure 6.3   Two-Dimensional Representation of the 34 Projects in Table 6.1

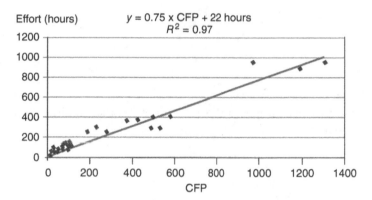

Figure 6.4   Single Linear Regression Model from Table 6.2 ($N = 34$)

Of course, a single productivity model can be built with this full dataset – see Figure 6.4.

For the full set of projects, the equation is

$$\text{Effort} = 0.75 * \text{FP} + 22 \quad \text{with an } R^2 \text{ of } 0.97$$

This model appears to have an excellent R^2 of 0.97.

- However, it is influenced too much by the three largest projects, and so it is not representative of the majority of the projects, which are much smaller.
- Also, for the full dataset, the normality distribution of the data is not met, and so its regression is correspondingly less statistically meaningful.

▶ By contrast, within the two smaller size intervals identified, each would be closer to a normal distribution – within their ranges, of course.

Considering the ranges of variations in functional size, the preferred approach is to build multiple regression models representative of the density of the data points, which can be represented graphically.

For practical purposes, a much more cautious approach to building productivity models for this example is to segregate the available dataset into the three density ranges of projects.

For this specific dataset, it would be much better

- to build two productivity models:
    ▶ one for the very small projects – equation A – Figure 6.5 and
    ▶ one for the mid-range projects – equation B – Figure 6.6
- to consider the three largest projects as an analogical base without statistical strengths – see Figure 6.3.

For the set of small projects (from 15 to 150 CFP), the equation model is – see Figure 6.5

$$\text{Effort} = 1.01 * \text{CFP} + 3$$

where

- $R^2 = 0.87$
- The fixed cost is low (i.e., $= 3$ hours)
- The slope close to 1, which means that this subset does not exhibit either economies or diseconomies of scale within this range.

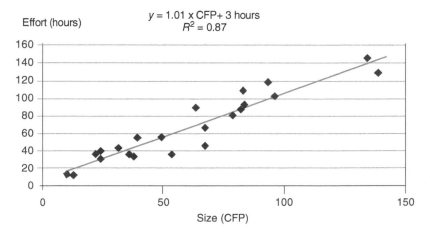

Figure 6.5   Regression Model for the 15–150 FP Interval ($N = 22$)

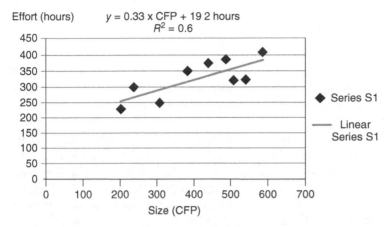

Figure 6.6   Regression Model for the 200–600 FP Interval ($N = 9$)

For the mid-size projects (within this dataset, of course), the equation is – see Figure 6.6

$$\text{Effort} = 0.33 \ \text{hours/FP} * \text{FP} + 192 \ \text{hours}$$

where

- $R^2 = 0.6$
- The fixed cost is much higher, at 192 hours
- The slope is lower, at 0.33 (which would be representative of economies of scale within this range of 200–600 CFP), instead of the steeper variable cost of 1.01 for the small projects.

Note that this model is built with only nine data points for the 200–600 FP size range, which is not sufficient, from a statistical viewpoint, to generalize its performance to another context. However, for projects within the same context, this information is still meaningful for estimation purposes within that size range.

Here are some examples:

(A) For the estimation of a small project of 50 CFP, equation A is preferable to the general equation.
- Equation A is built only for small projects, and is therefore much more appropriate for the project being estimated.
  - ▶ This equation is not influenced at all by the much larger projects.

(B) For the estimation of a mid-range project, for example one of 500 CFP, equation B is preferable to the general equation.
- Equation B is built for mid-range projects only, and is therefore much more appropriate for the project being estimated.
  - ▶ This equation is not influenced by either very small projects or much larger projects.

▶ Caution must still be exercised because of the limited number of projects available within that range when building the productivity model for this range.

(C) For the estimation of a very large project of 1000 FP, there is no statistical generalization significance to this equation. These three data points can still be used for purposes of analogy to estimate a project in the 1000–1400 FP size range.

(D) For the estimation of a project in the interval with missing data, i.e. the 600–1000 FP size range, the dataset in Table 6.2 and Figure 6.4 does not provide clues on whether projects within this interval have a size–effort relationship closer to the lower interval or to the higher interval. This level of uncertainty is not evident when we only look at the single model, but much more evident when the sample is subdivided into density intervals.
Effort $= 0.748 * $ FP $+ 22$ with an R^2 of 0.97

6.6.1   In Practice, Which is the Better Model?

• The one with a very high R^2 of 0.97 or
• The two submodels based on size range with an R^2 of 0.6 and 0.87, respectively?

The single model appears to have a very high R^2 of 0.97.

• However, it is influenced too much by the three largest projects, and is not representative of the majority of the projects, which are much smaller;
  ▶ So, if the magnitude of the relative error (MRE) were to be calculated, it would be larger for the model of the full dataset, and smaller for the model of a subset of projects in the size ranges identified.
• Moreover, the normality distribution of the data has not been met, which means that its regression results will be correspondingly less statistically meaningful.

In contrast, within each of the two size ranges identified, the distribution of the independent size variable is closer to a normal distribution, within their ranges of course.

6.7   SUMMARY

With the datasets illustrated, the model with the highest R^2 (0.97) is not the best model to use: it is poorly built, and uninformed users would be overconfident in its performance.

EXERCISES

1. List five criteria for verifying the performance of a model.
2. What does an R^2 of 1.0 mean?
3. What does an MMRE represent?
4. What does PRED (10) = 70% mean?
5. What are the three conditions that must be met to ensure the proper use of the statistical regression technique?
6. What is the recommended size of a dataset sample for a simple regression technique?
7. Does this mean that building a productivity model with your own productivity data for a small sample size is useless? Discuss.
8. Take the average productivity ratio of the software projects in your organization's repository of projects. What is the error range on this average productivity ratio? What criteria should you be using?
9. Look at whether or not authors and vendors have documented the quality of the productivity model they are proposing to practitioners. Comment on your findings. What are the short-term consequences for your organization? What are the long-term consequences for your profession?
10. What is a replication study? How do you carry out a replication study?
11. Table 6.1 presents a comparison of the results of two estimations models. For a project using Visual Basic, which model would you trust more? Up to what point?
12. If you are using (or plan to use) a statistically based productivity model, what should you be verifying?
13. If the data points for one of the cost factors in your model have a non-normal distribution, how do you take that into account in analyzing the quality of the productivity model built with such data?
14. Describe to your project management personnel, in layman's terms, the practical meaning of a coefficient of regression – R^2 – and its relevance to them when selecting a specific budget for a project on the basis of the productivity model (built from your organizational dataset or from an outside repository).
15. Take the data from Table 6.2 and Figure 6.3. Explain to your manager why it is preferable for him to have two or three productivity models rather than a single one.

TERM ASSIGNMENTS

1. Take project 10 in Table 6.2 and multiply the effort by 3. What impact does this have on the regression model? Take project 31 and multiply the effort by 3. What impact does that have on the regression model? Explain the impact of both on the quality of the regression model.
2. Select one of the estimation models available free of charge on the Web, and test it using any available dataset (from your own organization, from the literature, or from the ISBSG repository). Document its quality using the criteria listed in Section 4.1.

3. Typically, you need 20–30 data points for each variable in a statistical study. Look at a study on software productivity or productivity models and discuss the significance of the statistical findings based on the number of data points available and the number of cost factors taken into account in these models.

Chapter 7

Verification of the Adjustment Phase

OBJECTIVES

This chapter covers

- The contribution of adjustments to the decision-making process in estimation
- Some current practices in bundling the adjustments into the productivity models themselves
- The cost drivers structured as estimation submodels with a step function without known error ranges
- The impact of the propagation of errors in models

7.1 INTRODUCTION

When estimating, software managers want to take as many adjustments (often referred to as effort and cost drivers) as possible into account, expecting that each cost driver will contribute to improving the quantitative relationship with effort and cost. Such adjustment factors could be

- ▶ staff experience in software development,
- ▶ staff experience with the specific programming language,
- ▶ the database environment,
- ▶ the use of support tools for design and testing,
- ▶ and so on.

This leads to a number of challenges as follows:

- How do you quantify these cost drivers?
- What is the impact of each of these cost drivers?

Software Project Estimation: The Fundamentals for Providing High Quality Information to Decision Makers,
First Edition. Alain Abran.
© 2015 the IEEE Computer Society. Published 2015 by John Wiley & Sons, Inc.

- Which ones are the most important in a specific context?
- What is their real contribution in estimation models?
- Does taking them into account using current practices really decrease estimation risks and increase estimation accuracy?

There are very few studies on the impact of any of these cost drivers in software engineering, and the ones that have been carried out are usually based on such small samples that they are not statistically significant. Consequently, the basis for reusing these results in other contexts with confidence is weak (i.e. poor generalization power of limited experiments performed in less than optimal experimental conditions).

This chapter is organized as follows:

- Section 7.2 presents the contributions of the Adjustment Phase to the decision-making step in the overall estimation process.
- Section 7.3 looks at the current generic practice of bundling the adjustments into the estimation model itself, through categorization of the cost drivers and the predetermined impact factors for each.
- Section 7.4 discusses how some of these cost drivers are structured as estimation submodels without known uncertainty and error ranges.
- Section 7.5 illustrates how uncertainties and errors propagate in models.

The Advanced Reading section presents some examples of the propagation of uncertainties and errors in models.

7.2   ADJUSTMENT PHASE IN THE ESTIMATION PROCESS

7.2.1   Adjusting the Estimation Ranges

As indicated in Chapter 4, Section 4.4, the purpose of the adjustment phase (Figure 4.5, reproduced here as Figure 7.1) is to take into account the following additional considerations in the estimation process:

- Effort and cost drivers not explicitly included as independent variables in the statistical models based on historical data
- Uncertainties in the information on the inputs to the estimation process
- Project assumptions
- Project risks
- And so on.

The desired impact of this step is to obtain more accurate estimates. However, as we have seen in Chapter 5 on the quality of models, an expectation of accuracy is

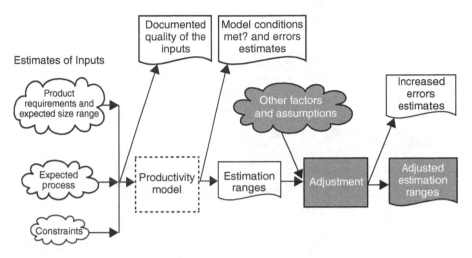

Figure 7.1 The Estimation Adjustment Phase

not appropriate in a software estimation context where the estimation process itself consists of identifying candidate plausible ranges of estimates, while it is the responsibility of managers, as we saw in Chapter 3, to select a specific project budget and a corresponding contingency, since the probability of being right on budget selection is statistically very small in most instances.

In the adjustment process, it cannot be taken for granted that an adjustment will automatically deliver smaller ranges of estimates, i.e. the smaller MMRE *hoped for* (as illustrated in Figure 7.2 by the gap between the *dashed lines*), in comparison with the larger initial MMRE of the productivity model (i.e. the gap by the *longer arrows* across the outside lines).

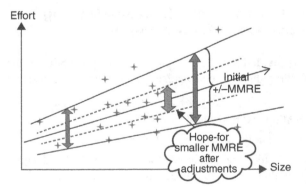

Figure 7.2 Desired Impact of Adjustments to Estimates

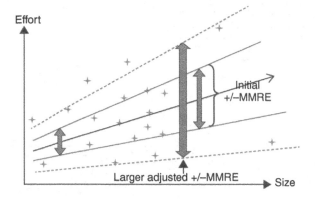

Figure 7.3 Plausible Greater Impact of Adjustments to Estimates

However, this is not the only possible outcome of an adjustment phase. When the adjustment process identifies a number of additional uncertainties and risk factors with a high negative impact, for example, the outcome may well be a larger MMRE – see Figure 7.3: the larger MMRE (longer arrow) in comparison with the initial MMRE from the model (shorter arrows).

Considering that:

(A) the initial MMRE of a productivity model is calculated based on completed projects without any uncertainty and

(B) at estimation time, there are typically both incomplete information and a number of uncertainties and risks,

it is more realistic to come up with a larger range of estimates, as in Figure 7.3, rather than the *desired* (but unrealistic) smaller range in Figure 7.2. This is discussed in greater detail later in this chapter.

7.2.2 The Adjustment Phase in the Decision-Making Process: Identifying Scenarios for Managers

On the basis of the information provided by the estimator, it is the responsibility of the management to make the following three specific decisions, considering all possible outcomes:

1. A specific budget to be allocated to the project manager.
2. A specific contingency fund at the project portfolio level.
3. The expected upper limit (which should include the project budget and a contingency reserve, along with a probability distribution).

This is illustrated in Figure 7.4 for an optimistic scenario, typically with a large contingency fund, and in Figure 7.5 for a pessimistic scenario, with a smaller contingency fund, which is common.

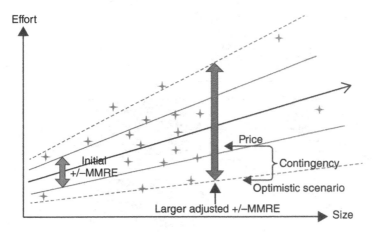

Figure 7.4   Project Budget + Contingency = Price in the *Optimistic* Scenario

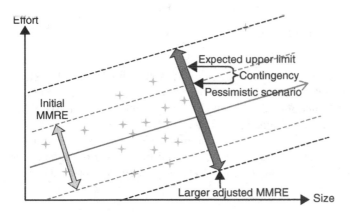

Figure 7.5   Project Budget + Contingency = Price in the *Pessimistic* Scenario

7.3   THE BUNDLED APPROACH IN CURRENT PRACTICES

7.3.1   Overall Approach

It has been observed for decades that a large number of factors impact project effort, and that size is not the only one. At the same time, there are a number of classical techniques available for building productivity models, which can handle multiple independent variables, as well as nonquantitative variables, concurrently. Some of these techniques are presented in Chapter 10.

However, many of these statistical techniques have been replaced in software estimation by practices bundling all the factors involved together. In this section, we present a number of these "craft" practices, which are frequently observed.

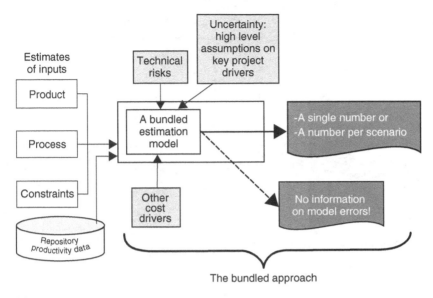

Figure 7.6 Estimation – the Bundled Approach

The big picture, presented in Figure 7.6, is this. What should be achieved in multiple distinct steps, with a quality analysis performed at each step, is bundled together into a single step and model, without a report presenting an analysis of the estimate errors. Typically, the outcome of a bundled model is either a single estimate or a few scenarios (optimistic or, most likely, pessimistic), each with a single estimate.

Note that the bundled estimation model represented in Figure 7.6 can be either a black-box or white-box mathematical model or, very often, an approach based entirely on expert judgment, referred to as the expert opinion-based estimation process.

7.3.2 Detailed Approach for Combining the Impact of Multiple Cost Drivers in Current Models

How is the impact of all of these cost drivers taken into account concurrently in many estimation models?

- By adding the impacts of each cost driver in a particular cost estimation model:

$$\text{Impact of all cost drivers} = \sum_{i}^{n} \text{PF}_i$$

Finally, the impact of the full set of cost drivers is obtained by multiplying them by the base equation of the size–effort relationship of the production (estimation) model selected.

$$\text{Effort} = a \times \text{Size} \times \left(\sum_{i}^{n} \text{PF}_i \right) + b$$

7.3.3   Selecting and Categorizing Each Adjustment: The Transformation of Nominal Scale Cost Drivers into Numbers

The traditional way to bypass these constraints in software engineering has been to use "judgment" categories for the cost drivers determined, either locally or collectively.

The approach often seen in many current estimation models is as follows:

1. The cost drivers are first characterized and described: for example, reuse and performance. At this stage, these cost drivers can only be "named," which means that they are arranged on a *nominal* scale.

2. These nominal variables are then organized into a number of *ordinal* categories: for example, from very low to ultra high – see Table 7.1:

   - These categories are based on descriptions of what could fit into (successively larger) ordered intervals.
   - The intervals will typically vary from the absence of this cost driver (i.e. the *very low* category label) to the other extreme, the *ultra high* category label, where it would be ubiquitous.
   - At the midpoint in such a classification, there would be a *nominal* category, which is considered as *neutral* in its impact on productivity.
   - The ranges in these ordered categories are not necessarily equal for a single cost driver (that is, their intervals may not be uniform).
   - These ordered categories do not necessarily have the same interval sizes as those in the same ordinal category of other cost drivers.

Table 7.1   Examples of the Categorization of Cost Drivers

Cost driver	Very low	Low	Nominal	High	Very high	Ultra high
Project management experience	None	1–4 years	5–10 years	11–15 years	16–25 years	25+ years
Reuse	None	0–19%	20–30%	31–50%	50–80%	Over 80%

These cost driver categories (for instance, from very low to ultra high, as in Table 7.1) are ordered categories (i.e. ranked): each category is ranked higher than the previous one, but they cannot be added or multiplied.

- Organizations will typically propose various criteria for each category, to reduce subjectivity when classifying a cost driver in one of these categories (e.g., the number of years considered for project management experience).
- These irregular intervals would not be similar across categories.

3. Next, each ordered category of cost drivers is assigned an impact factor:

- The impact factor is typically a percentage of the effort from the null impact of the nominal position (with increased effort to the left of the nominal position and decreased effort to the right of the nominal position – see Table 7.2). For example:
  ▶ For a project manager in the low category of project management experience (the factor F_1 here), expert opinion has determined a 5% loss of productivity (i.e. an increase of 5% in project work effort).
  ▶ For a project manager in the ultra high category (over 25 years of experience), a 20% gain in productivity would be assigned.

This process of assigning a number to a factor does not quantify the factor itself, but rather its impact in terms of effort, and these numbers do, in fact, correspond to (productivity) ratios.

7.4 COST DRIVERS AS ESTIMATION SUBMODELS!

7.4.1 Cost Drivers as Step Functions

Do these ratios come from well-documented and well-controlled experimental studies, as in sciences and engineering?

We should note that the cost drivers (such as F_1 and F_2 in Table 7.2) are now no longer direct inputs to an estimation model:

- Each corresponds to a stepwise production function – see the project management experience of cost driver F_1 in Figure 7.7).

Figure 7.7 depicts a step function estimation model *with regular intervals* PF_i, where the 5-interval classification is on the horizontal axis and the percentage impact on productivity is on the vertical axis.

However, *in practice, most of these intervals are irregular*, as illustrated in Figure 7.8.

Table 7.2 Opinion-Based Impact of Effort Drivers

Effort driver	Very low	Low	Nominal (neutral)	High	Very high	Ultra high
F_1: **Project management** experience	+15%	+5%	1	−5%	−10%	−20%
F_2: **Reuse**	+20%	+5%	1	−10%	−20%	−40%

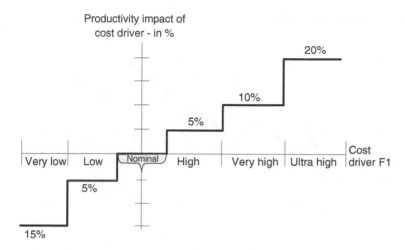

Figure 7.7   A Step Function Estimation Model – with *Regular* Intervals

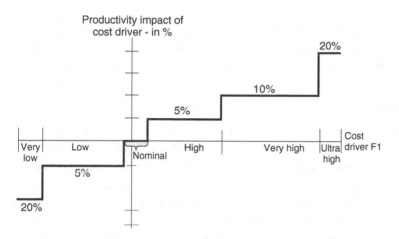

Figure 7.8   A Step Function Estimation Model – with *Irregular* Intervals

7.4.2   Step Function Estimation Submodels with Unknown Error Ranges

The stepwise production models in Figures 7.7 and 7.8 include 6 "crisp" values: from −5% to +20%.

However, in a particular estimation context, a stepwise estimation model has two major sources of inaccuracy, as illustrated by the arrows in Figure 7.9, which cut across adjoining impact ratios across an interval:

1. A specific instance of a cost driver could be anywhere within the interval of the category.

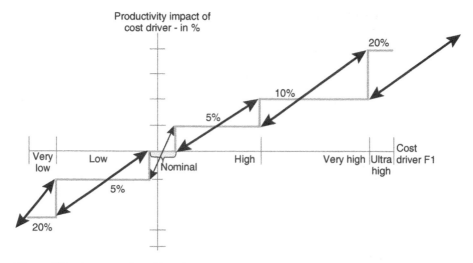

Figure 7.9   Approximation of Step Function Estimation Models with *Irregular* Intervals

2. It is unreasonable to expect that the crisp value of the effort impact would be the same across an interval, as a step function is a very crude approximation of the productivity across that interval, and across all the other intervals as well – see Figure 7.9.

In summary:

- Figure 7.8 shows one way of representing a step function estimation model for a single cost driver with a 5-category ranking with irregular intervals.
- Figure 7.9 shows the approximations embedded within these stepwise models.
- When an estimation model includes 20 cost drivers built with this approach, this model implicitly has 20 other subestimation models, even though each of these is inadequately labeled as a cost driver.
- Since these stepwise productivity estimation submodels are fixed by the designer of the models, they are embedded not as independent variables in statistical techniques, but as adjustments to the estimation model.
- For the purposes of this book, we will refer to these adjustments as *derived inputs* (because they are derived by the designer of the estimation model) as opposed to the direct inputs provided by estimation model users every time they undertake an estimation.

What Does This Mean?

It means that the categories selected for each of the cost drivers for the projects to be estimated are not direct inputs to the estimation model:

- They are estimation submodels, that is:
  - They are indirect or derived inputs from a category on an ordered scale based on a somewhat imprecise categorization process.
    - That is, from very low to extremely high.
  - The output of this transformation process is a constant.
    - That is, a single value is provided.
  - The basis for this transformation is not supported by documented empirical evidence.
    - But only by the subjective judgment of a single author or group of participants.
  - The error range of such an impact value is not known, nor is it taken into account in the analysis of the errors of the total estimation model.

Derived Inputs to Estimation Models: "Feel Good" Models

Most of the inputs to estimation models built using this technique are undocumented. As a result, the models themselves, which are not analyzed and so little is known about them to begin with, are not supported by documented empirical data.

In other words,

- The quality of the estimation models is unknown and
- They provide a weak basis for the estimation model itself, which takes these submodels as inputs.

Therefore, many cost drivers make the users of such estimation models overly confident that the models take into account many factors, which does not make sense!

The real issue should be: Are these cost drivers adequately taken into consideration?

The end result might well be that more uncertainty is being introduced into the estimates, rather than less.

7.5   UNCERTAINTY AND ERROR PROPAGATION[1]

7.5.1   Error Propagation in Mathematical Formulas

In science, the terms *uncertainty* and *error* do not formally refer to mistakes, but rather to the uncertainties inherent in all measurements and models, and which can never be completely eliminated.

---

[1] See also Santillo (2006) Error Propagation in Software Measurement and Estimation, International Workshop on Software Measurement – IWSM-Metrikom 2006, Postdam, Shaker Verlag, Germany.

Part of the effort of a measurer and estimator should be devoted to understanding these uncertainties (error analysis), so that appropriate conclusions can be drawn from n observations of the variables:

- Measurements can be quite meaningless without any knowledge of their associated errors.

In the sciences and in engineering, numbers without accompanying error estimates are not only suspect, but possibly useless.

- This also holds true in software engineering – for every measurement and model, the uncertainty inherent in the measured quantity should be analyzed, recorded, and taken into account.

In this section, we discuss some of the consequences of using measures with *unavoidable* errors in the application of some formula (algorithm) to derive further quantities, including productivity models. In science, this analysis is usually referred to as error propagation (or the propagation of uncertainty).

Here, we illustrate how the generic uncertainties in two or more quantities from which another is derived using a mathematical formula always add up to a larger uncertainty on the derived quantity.

When the quantity to be determined is derived from several measured quantities, and when the measured quantities are *independent* of each other (that is, their contributions are *not correlated*), the uncertainty, δ of each contribution can be considered separately.

For example, suppose that time, $t \pm \delta t$ and height, $h \pm \delta h$ have been measured for a falling mass (the δs refer to the relatively small uncertainties in t and h) and the measurement results are obtained as follows:

$$h = 5.32 \pm 0.02 \ \text{cm}$$

$$t = 0.103 \pm 0.001 \ \text{s}$$

From physics, we know that the acceleration due to gravity is

$$g = g(h, t) = 2h/t^2$$

Substituting the measurement results of h and t in this equation yields $g = 10.029 \ldots$ m/s^2.

From physics, the value for acceleration due to gravity is

$$g = 9.80665 \ldots \ \text{m/s}^2$$

To find the uncertainty in the derived value of g caused by the uncertainties in h and t, the uncertainty in h and the contribution due to the uncertainty in t are considered separately and combined in the following way:

$$\delta_g = \sqrt{\delta_{g_t}^2 + \delta_{g_h}^2}$$

where the contribution due to the uncertainty in t is denoted by the symbol δ_{g_t} (read as "delta-g-t" or "uncertainty in g due to t").

- The addition of the square of δ_{g_i} is based on the assumption that the measured quantities have a normal, or Gaussian, distribution about their mean values.

In summary, while the formula for gravity g gives a single crisp value, in practice it has a measurement uncertainty that is greater than the uncertainty of the individual measurement of its base quantities of time, t and height, h.

Table 7.3 shows the uncertainty of simple mathematical functions, resulting from independent variables A, B, and C, with uncertainties ΔA, ΔB, and ΔC, respectively, and a precisely known constant, c.

7.5.2   The Relevance of Error Propagation in Models

In practical situations, the scope of a software project is often not fully defined in the early phases:

- The main cost driver, the size of the project, cannot be known accurately at the beginning of a project, when software estimates are the most useful.
- Of course, different values estimated for size provide different estimates for effort, but this alone does not provide any indication of the precision of a single estimate.

No model can be seriously used without considering possible deviations between estimates (expected values) and true values.

Also, when deriving numbers from factors measured directly, we must consider the impact that a (small) error in a direct measure might have on the derived numbers, which would depend on the algorithm or formula used to derive them.

Consideration of error propagation provides an important perspective on the evaluation and selection of a software estimation approach:

Table 7.3   Uncertainty Functions for Some Simple Mathematical Formulas

Mathematical Formula	Uncertainty Function
$X = A \pm B$	$(\Delta X)^2 = (\Delta A)^2 + (\Delta B)^2$
$X = cA$	$\Delta X = c\,\Delta A$
$X = c(A \times B)$ or $X = c(A/B)$	$(\Delta X/X)^2 = (\Delta A/A)^2 + (\Delta B/B)^2$
$X = cA^n$	$\Delta X/X = |n|\,(\Delta A/A)$
$X = \ln(cA)$	$\Delta X = \Delta A/A$
$X = \exp(A)$	$\Delta X/X = \Delta A$

- The qualities and advantages claimed by any model can be improved or diminished when an objective analysis of the method or model is performed, in terms of error propagation and the overall accuracy that it can offer.
- Error propagation provides some useful insights into the model selection process, from both a theoretical (the form of the method/model) and a practical point of view (application in real cases).

The Further Reading section presents two examples of error propagation:

Example 1: Error propagation in the exponential form of a model.

Example 2: Error propagation in cost drivers bundled into an adjustment factor.

Therefore, model builders should find the right balance between all-inclusive cost driver formulas, which they might wish to use, and reasonable percentage errors in the practical application of those formulas.

For instance, in some cases, a decision must be made between:

- accepting the measured value of each cost driver in the model,
- improving its measurement accuracy (if possible, reducing its error), and
- avoiding some factors in the overall model completely, because of any unacceptable impact they may have on the overall uncertainty of the estimate.

FURTHER READING[2]

EXAMPLE 7.1

The exponential form of a model and its errors. To derive the development effort for a software project using a model, the exponent form is

$$y = A \cdot x^B$$

where

- y represents the expected work effort expressed in person-hours,
- x is the size of the software to be developed, and
- factors A and B are determined by statistical regression on a historical sample.

Note that having fixed statistical values for some parameters in the model does not necessarily mean that these values are accurate:

▶ Their associated errors can be derived from the standard deviation of the statistical sample from the fitting function y.

To evaluate the error on y, some partial derivatives have to be calculated, given the errors on the parameters A and B and on the independent variable x:

$$\frac{\partial}{\partial x}(A \cdot x^B) = A \cdot B \cdot x^{B-1}, \quad \frac{\partial}{\partial A}(A \cdot x^B) = x^B, \quad \frac{\partial}{\partial B}(A \cdot x^B) = A \cdot x^B \cdot \ln x$$

[2] Adapted from Santillo (2006) Error Propagation in Software Measurement and Estimation, International Workshop on Software Measurement – IWSM-Metrikom 2006, Postdam, Shaker Verlag, Germany.

EXAMPLE 7.2

- Consider a project with an approximate size of 1000 ± 200 FP, or a percentage uncertainty of 20%.
- Assume that the error ranges of the parameters A and B of the equation are equal to 10 ± 1 and 1.10 ± 0.01, respectively in the appropriate measurement units.

Collecting all the data and applying the error propagation for Δy, we obtain

$$y = A \cdot x^B = 10 \cdot 1,000^{1.10} = 19,952.6 \ (\text{person} - \text{hours})$$

$$\delta y = \sqrt{[(A \cdot B \cdot x^{B-1})\delta x]^2 + [(x^B)\delta A]^2 + [(A \cdot x^B \cdot \ln x)\delta B]^2}$$

$$= \sqrt{[21.948 \times 200]^2 + [1,995.262 \times 1]^2 + [137,827.838 \times 0.01]^2}$$

$$= 5,015.9 (\text{person} - \text{hours})$$

Taking only the first significant digit of the error, we obtain the following for y:
- an estimated range of $20,000 \pm 5000$ or
  - a percentage uncertainty of 25%.

Note that the percentage error on y is not simply the sum of the percentage errors on A, B, and x, because the function in this example is not linear.

EXAMPLE 7.3

Example 2: Adjustment factors bundled together in multiplicative form. Estimation models in software engineering are often adjusted by a series of (independent) cost drivers, c_i, bundled together in multiplicative form.

Even though, for simplicity, the cost drivers assume discrete values in practical applications, they can also be treated as continuous variables.

The derivation of the uncertainty for the adjusted effort estimate of this form of model is

$$y_{adj} = y_{nom} \cdot \prod_i c_i$$

$$\frac{\partial}{\partial y_{nom}}\left(y_{nom} \cdot \prod_i c_i\right) = \prod_i c_i, \qquad \frac{\partial}{\partial c_j}\left(y_{nom} \cdot \prod_i c_i\right) = y_{nom} \cdot \frac{\prod_i c_i}{c_j}$$

For instance, considering $y_{nom} = 20,000 \pm 5000$ hours (i.e. +/− 25%) and a set of only seven factors, c_i, for each of which (for the sake of simplicity) the same value $c = 0.95 \pm 0.05$ is assumed, then the following is obtained for y_{adj}:

$$y_{adj} = y_{nom} \cdot \prod_i c_i = 20,000 \cdot \prod_1^7 0.95 = 20,000 \cdot 0.95^7 = 13,966.7$$

$$\delta y_{adj} = \sqrt{\left[\left(\prod_i c_i\right)\delta y_{nom}\right]^2 + \left[\left(y_{nom} \cdot \frac{\prod_i c_i}{c_1}\right)\delta c_1\right]^2 + \ldots + \left[\left(y_{nom} \cdot \frac{\prod_i c_i}{c_7}\right)\delta c_7\right]^2}$$

$$= \left(\prod_i c_i \right) \sqrt{ (\Delta y_{nom})^2 + (y_{nom})^2 \left(\frac{\Delta c_1}{c_1} + \dots + \frac{\Delta c_7}{c_7} \right)^2 }$$

$$= 0.95^7 \cdot \sqrt{ (5,000)^2 + (20,000)^2 \left(\frac{0.05}{0.95} + \dots + \frac{0.05}{0.95} \right)^2 } = 5,146.8 \simeq 5000$$

So, *each additional factor* in the model and estimation process:

- *may appear* to make the estimation *more accurate*.
  - ▶ In the example given, y_{adj} is reduced with respect to its nominal value because all the factors are smaller than 1.
- but its percentage error has *increased*:
  - ▶ It is now about 36%, versus 25% in the nominal estimate.

Key Learning

The more cost drivers are introduced into a model in this bundled approach, the more uncertainty sources are added to the estimation process!

EXERCISES

1. *In your software organization*, what is expected when additional cost drivers, uncertainties, and risks are added to models?

2. *In engineering*, what is expected when additional cost drivers, uncertainties, and risks are added to models?

3. What is the contribution of the Adjustment Phase to decision-making in an estimation process?

4. Illustrate how an adjustment phase can help identify an optimistic scenario for decision-making.

5. Many models have the following form: $y = A \cdot x^B \times (\sum_n^i PF_i)$, where PF_i represents the values assigned to the impact of each cost driver. Does the combined impact of these cost drivers help improve the estimate ranges?

6. Cost drivers in many models are often structured as step functions with crisp values for each interval in a cost factor. How is uncertainty taken into account in this structure and use of these cost drivers?

7. When you have uncertainty and errors in the variables in input to a model of the linear form, how do you calculate the resulting uncertainty in a model of the form: Effort $= a \times$ Size $+ b$?

8. When you have uncertainty and errors in the variables in input to a model of an exponential form, how do you calculate the resulting uncertainty in a model of the form: $y = A \cdot x^B$?

9. When you have uncertainty and errors in the variables input to a model, how do you calculate the resulting uncertainty in a model of the form: $y = A \cdot x^B \times (\sum_n^i PF_i)$?

10. Take the mathematical formula for gravity. In your own words, describe how much time and experimentation was required to quantitatively figure out the relationship among the elements in this formula. Describe how much care is taken by industry to measure the various elements to determine gravity in a specific context (e.g., in rocket launches). Next, take the software estimation model used in your organization, and do the same as you did before for the mathematical formula for gravity.

TERM ASSIGNMENTS

1. Select one or more of the cost drivers in a model in exponential form in which multiple cost drivers are combined (i.e. bundled models), which are themselves estimation submodels, and document candidate ranges of variation on the one(s) you selected. Then, analyze the impact of these candidate variations on the outcome of the full model.

2. Select two software estimation models (from books or from the Web). Explain how the cost factors included in these models were "quantified." Comment on this quantification process.

3. What is the typical approach currently taken to build cost factors into the software estimation models proposed to practitioners: craft or engineering? Compare this approach to similar estimation practices in the construction industry, in business, or in medicine. Comment on the software engineering approach.

4. Identify the candidate error range of each cost factor in your organizational estimation model. What would be the rate of error propagation when they are combined in your estimation model?

5. Select one of the software estimation models available free of charge on the Web and determine its rate of error propagation.

6. Take one estimation model based on Use Case Points and determine its rate of error propagation.

7. Take one estimation model based on anecdotal user evidence and determine its rate of error propagation.

8. Access three software estimation models available on the Web. Document the basis for experimentation provided by the designers of each of these publicly available estimation models. To what point can you trust them? Explain your point of view to your management and customers. Look back at the reasons supporting that point of view and classify them as engineering-based or opinion-based.

9. Look back at the last three projects you estimated. What assumptions did you document? From what you know now about these completed projects, what assumptions should you have documented?

Part III

Building Estimation Models: Data Collection and Analysis

In this book, we take an engineering approach to the design of productivity and estimation models by first suggesting tackling a very limited number of cost factors, based on sound data collection practices and relatively simple statistical techniques, with the aim of building models realistically, one step at a time. Although they are simple, these models can provide significant and very useful insights into the perils of estimation.

This approach teaches how to build simple models to fit a specific environment – provided, of course, that the data are collected within that environment.

To help with this task, we introduce now what is currently world's best alternative to owning a historical dataset of completed projects, that is, the repository of projects collected and managed by the International Software Benchmarking Standards Data Group – ISBSG. We also present how to build single and multivariable estimation models using such datasets.

Chapter 8 presents the structure of the ISBSG repository of software projects and discusses the need for data collection standards and the challenges that must be met to ensure the consistency of data definitions in a multi-organizational context.

Software Project Estimation: The Fundamentals for Providing High Quality Information to Decision Makers,
First Edition. Alain Abran.
© 2015 the IEEE Computer Society. Published 2015 by John Wiley & Sons, Inc.

Chapter 9 illustrates the use of the ISBSG repository for benchmarking and for building and evaluating productivity models.

Chapter 10 discusses building models with multiple independent variables, including non quantitative variables.

Chapter 11 discusses the identification and analysis of projects with very large economies or diseconomies of scale, and provides insights relevant for estimation purposes.

Chapter 12 introduces the analysis of datasets, which makes it possible to determine, using economics concepts, whether or not there is more than one productivity model present in a single dataset.

Chapter 13 presents an approach to re-estimating projects that have gone off course.

In most estimation contexts, estimators and managers are looking for quick and free access to cost drivers for various software application domains. However, within the current state of the art and state of practice (in the software estimation, software productivity data, and estimation model areas), "quick and free" often goes hand in hand with both very low quality, or undocumented, published data and a misunderstanding of basic economics and statistical concepts.

Productivity values will, of course, be domain specific, but the appropriate use of statistical techniques to interpret them is critically important in any application domain.

The intention in this book is not to present specific values (of poor quality) for cost drivers by application domain or to highlight poor, and often used, estimation practices, but rather to present the best engineering practices for handling data collection and data analysis, no matter what the software application domain).

In this third part of this book (Chapters 8–12), examples and references are provided on how to use software industry data, including material collected by the ISBSG, the largest provider of such data.

The proper use of ISBSG and other data calls for knowledge of the basic statistics required for handling software engineering data and the proper interpretation of those data from an economics perspective, as taught in business schools, and of engineering economics for productivity analysis and subsequent estimation. It is guidance on how to proceed that is provided in this book – not specific values.

The ISBSG publications available on their website do provide some specific values for a large number of different contexts, but how they are applied in a particular organization's software productivity process is left to the users of such data.

Chapter 8

Data Collection and Industry Standards: The ISBSG Repository

OBJECTIVES

This chapter covers

- Data collection requirements for building benchmarking and productivity models
- The ISBSG organization and its data repository
- ISBSG data collection procedures
- How to prepare to use the ISBSG repository: data issues and data preparation in multi-organizational repositories

8.1 INTRODUCTION: DATA COLLECTION REQUIREMENTS

Productivity models are typically built using data from projects:

- which have been completed and
- for which there is enough documentation available:
  - ▶ to quantify the variables necessary for building quantitative models and
  - ▶ to qualitatively describe the characteristics of the project that might have impacted it either positively or negatively (e.g., leading to high or low productivity).

Software Project Estimation: The Fundamentals for Providing High Quality Information to Decision Makers, First Edition. Alain Abran.
© 2015 the IEEE Computer Society. Published 2015 by John Wiley & Sons, Inc.

When an organization has the ability to collect such information, as well as the ability to build its own models (either a single model or multiple models, depending on the project or product characteristics), it has the foundation:

- to quantitatively compare the performance of a project against its own portfolio of projects and
- to identify and analyze the factors that have led to its low or high productivity.

When performing comparisons of this kind, an organization is typically interested not only in estimation, but in benchmarking as well, that is, in

- identifying the best practices from previous projects with higher performance,
- reducing project risks by avoiding the factors that have reduced productivity in past projects,
- spreading the success factors that fostered high productivity to other projects, and
- designing process improvements to increase productivity in future projects.

A key requirement for data collection and meaningful data analysis, as well as for estimation purposes, is that the information gathered be described, and quantified whenever feasible, using the same definitions and standards of measurement, so that it will be available in a form that is useful in a comparison context.

This means that considerable work must be done upfront when collecting historical data to clearly identify, categorize, and measure using the same set of definitions, classification criteria, and rules for assigning quantitative values.

Without the establishment of a consensus on data collection standards for each data field collected, and clear documentation supporting it, the information gathered from different sources is highly susceptible to divergent (if not plainly erroneous) interpretations:

- All these definitions and standards must be agreed on, and committed to, before the data collection process.
- If not, the data collected will be meaningless for comparison purposes.

Building productivity models without good data collection standards does a disservice to both the organization itself and its peers, in a benchmarking exercise.

- If standards definitions and measures already exist, organizations participating in benchmarking exercises should adopt them – see Further Reading 1 on the various types of benchmarking.
- If not, the organizations should develop those standards jointly.

Detailed data collection procedures should always be prepared with great care, to ensure consistency in data collection, as well as completeness and nonambiguity of the information collected.

Organizational units in an organization tend to define their own data field definitions to ensure that those fields reflect their own project idiosyncrasies. This practice is understandable, however:

- it totally defeats the purpose of comparing performance across organizational units and with peers in industry and
- it prevents them from using industry performance data when they introduce a new technology for which they do not have any data of their own.

A strong recommendation to industry participants, as well as to researchers, is to reuse what already exists, in particular, when data collection procedures are recognized as *de facto* standards by industry, such as those supported by the International Software Benchmarking Standards Group – ISBSG (www.isbsg.org).

- Of course, organizations can always add to this foundation, but, without a basis on which to begin, benchmarking can become very expensive and time-consuming.

Furthermore, the ISBSG standards for data collection are available free of charge, and considered to be the best, by far, by national associations on software measurements.

In this chapter, we introduce the ISBSG repository and its use as a foundation of the estimation process. It is organized as follows:

- Section 8.2 presents the International Software Benchmarking Standards Group – ISBSG.
- Section 8.3 provides an overview of the ISBSG data collection procedures.
- Section 8.4 gives examples of individual ISBSG benchmarking reports of completed projects.
- Section 8.5 discusses how to prepare to use the ISBSG repository.

Further Reading 1 provides an overview of benchmarking types.
Further Reading 2 presents the detailed structure of the ISBSG Data Extract.

8.2 THE INTERNATIONAL SOFTWARE BENCHMARKING STANDARDS GROUP

8.2.1 The ISBSG Organization

In the 1990s, the International Software Benchmarking Standards Group (ISBSG) was set up to provide a worldwide repository of software projects.

- This repository provides data useful for multiple purposes, including project productivity comparison and estimation of the effort required to build productivity models.
- Productivity data and models can be used to improve the organization's overall capabilities, in terms of project planning and monitoring.

Typically, the ISBSG, as well as other project data repositories, contains descriptive variables and quantitative data from which a number of ratios can be derived for benchmarking purposes.

The ISBSG is a nonprofit organization created "to improve the management of IT resources by both business and government, through the provision and exploitation of public repositories of software engineering knowledge that are standardized, verified, recent, and representative of current technologies."[1]

- The ISBSG groups together national associations on software measurement, representing different countries, including Australia, India, Japan, the United Kingdom, and the United States, among others.

8.2.2   The ISBSG Repository

The ISBSG software project repository provides software development practitioners with industry-standardized data against which they may compare their aggregated or individual projects, and real international software development data that can be analyzed for benchmarking and estimation purposes [Hill and ISBSG 2010].

The ISBSG assembles the data collected into a repository and provides a sample of the data fields to practitioners and researchers in an Excel file, referred to from here on as the "MS-Excel data extract." Figure 8.1 presents the ISBSG process for collecting and storing data in its repository.

The full set of data fields in this ISBSG MS-Excel data extract is presented in the Further Reading 2 section of this chapter.

- The MS-Excel data extract is available at minimal cost to the industry, an amount that reflects what an organization would typically pay a consultant for one working day (this is significantly lower than the costs the organization would incur in collecting its own set of data).

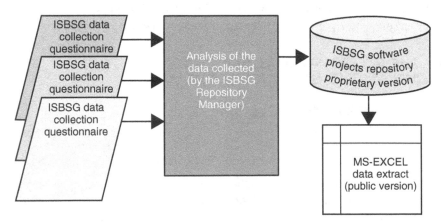

Figure 8.1   ISBSG Repository Process Organization [Cheikhi et al. 2006. Reprinted with permission from Novatica.]

[1]ISBSG mission at: http://www.isbsg.org/isbsgnew.nsf/webpages/~GBL~About%20Us accessed: Oct. 9, 2013

For example, Release 11 of the MS-Excel data extract (2009) includes 5052 projects from various industries and business areas, and from 29 countries around the world, such as Japan, the United States, Australia, the Netherlands, Canada, the United Kingdom, India, Brazil, and Denmark.

The R11-2009 extract contains different types of projects:

- Enhancement projects (59%)
- New development projects (39%)
- Redevelopment projects (2%).

According to the ISBSG, the software applications available in this MS-Excel data extract are grouped in the following categories [ISBSG 2009]:

- Telecommunications (25%)
- Banking (12%)
- Insurance (12%)
- Manufacturing (8%)
- Financial (excluding banking) (8%)
- Engineering (5%)
- Accounting (4%)
- Sales, Marketing (4%)
- Transport, Logistics (2%)
- Legal (2%)
- Government, Public Administration, Regulation (2%)
- Personnel (2%)
- Other (11%)

It is evident that some segments of the software industry have a culture of providing and sharing, anonymously, quantitative information with industry, such as telecommunications, banking, and insurance. These industry segments can then benefit from the data provided by their own data contributors.

Other industry segments have no tradition of investment in collecting and sharing information within these segments using industry standards: without such a tradition, it is unrealistic to expect them to benefit from a data repository for benchmarking and estimation purposes.

8.3   ISBSG DATA COLLECTION PROCEDURES

8.3.1   The Data Collection Questionnaire

The ISBSG makes available to the public a questionnaire designed to collect data about projects, including software functional size measured with any of the measurement standards recognized by the ISO.

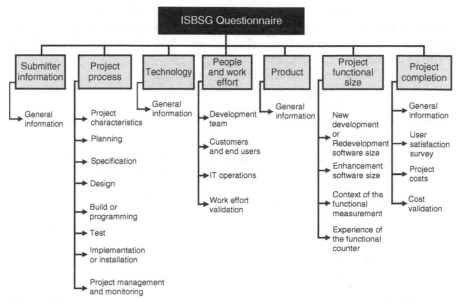

Figure 8.2 Structure of the ISBSG Data Collection Questionnaire [Cheikhi et al. 2006. Reprinted with permission from Novatica.]

The foundation of the ISBSG repository of projects is its internal view of the repository, as represented by the data collection questionnaire, with some additional fields added by the ISBSG repository manager. The ISBSG data collection questionnaire [ISBSG 2012] is available at www.isbsg.org.

Moreover, the ISBSG provides a glossary of terms and measures to assist in the collection of project data for the repository and to standardize the way the collected data are analyzed and reported.

The ISBSG data collection questionnaire consists of seven sections, divided into several subsections (see Figure 8.2).

- *Submitter information*: information about the organization and the individuals filling out the questionnaire.
  - ▷ This information is kept confidential by the ISBSG.
- *Project process*: information about the project process. The ISBSG provides well-defined terms in this section, offers a simple structure for gathering data, and allows precise comparisons to be made among projects.
  - ▷ The information collected here is structured in accordance with the various activities of a software life cycle, as specified in the ISBSG questionnaire: planning, specification, design, build or programming, test and implementation, and installation.
- *Technology*: information about the tools used for developing and carrying out the project.

- ▶ For each stage of the software life cycle, the ISBSG questionnaire proposes a list of tools.
- *People and work effort*: considering three groups of individuals – the development team, customers and end-users, and IT operations personnel.
  - ▶ The information collected here is about the people working on the project, their roles and expertise, and the effort expended for each phase of the software life cycle.
- *Product*: information about the software product itself.
  - ▶ For example, software application type and deployment platform, such as client/server.
- *Project functional size*: information about the functional size of the project and a few other variables related to the context of the measurement process.
  - ▶ This section is slightly different for each of the ISBSG-recognized measurement methods: COSMIC, IFPUG, NESMA, and Mark-II.
  - ▶ Some information is also collected about the expertise of the software functional size measurer.
- *Project completion*: provides an overall picture of the project, including project duration, defects, number of lines of code, user satisfaction, and project costs, including cost validation.

The number of data fields collected by the questionnaire is large. Only a few of these data fields are mandatory, most are optional.

8.3.2 ISBSG Data Definitions

The ISBSG has been particularly careful in defining the data fields. The scale type of the information collected by ISBSG is one of the following:

- Nominal (project management tool name, requirements tool name, etc.)
- Categorical (development platform: mainframe, mid-range, PC)
- Numerical (effort in hours, size in Function Points, etc.).

The organization has avoided, as much as possible, the inclusion of variables, the values of which are based on judgment, such as those on an ordering or interval scale (from very low to very high, e.g.) and for which is it next to impossible to achieve consistency and repeatability across organizations and countries.

Example: Avoiding a Overly Subjective Assignment of Values

Even though information about the expertise of the project staff would have been very interesting to collect, there is no industry consensus on how to order and categorize staff expertise.

The ISBSG is also using measurement standards, whenever available, adopted either by international bodies, such as the ISO, or by industry.

- For instance, effort is recorded in hours (in order to avoid variability in the length of the working day: in some countries it is 7 hours, while in others it might be 8.5 hours).
- All ISO standards on functional size measurement (FSM) methods are recognized by the ISBSG:
  - ISO 19761: COSMIC – Common Software Measurement International Consortium [ISO 2011]
  - ISO 20926: Function Point Analysis (e.g., IFPUG 4.2, Unadjusted Function Points only) [ISO 2009]
  - ISO 20968: Mark II Function Points – Mk II [ISO 2002]
  - ISO 24750: NESMA (A Dutch interpretation of FPA v. 4.1 which produces similar results) [ISO 2005]
  - ISO 29881: FISMA (Finnish Software Measurement Association).
- There exist guidelines on the use of some of these standards on functional size measurement (FSM) methods within an Agile context – see, for example, COSMIC [2011a].

Variations Across ISO Standards on Functional Size

Statistical studies should ideally be carried out using size data collected using exactly the same standards.

Those interested in building models using both IFPUG- and COSMIC-sized projects should be aware of the convertibility studies carried out on the two methods and take these studies into account if they are to include projects measured with either of these standards – see the convertibility section in the document, Advanced and Related Topics, published by the COSMIC Group on the Website www.cosmicon.com.

See also Chapter 13 'Convertibility across measurements methods' in (Abran 2010).

Of course, the number of hours collected will depend on the type of human resources for whom the hours are recorded for project monitoring purposes: in one organization, only directly assigned project staff-hours can be recorded in the organizational time reporting system, while another organization might require that all support staff working part-time on a project also charge their time to this project. To capture this diversity in recording project effort, the ISBSG has defined a "resource level" parameter, as presented in Table 8.1.

To provide insights into the reliability of the effort data collected, the ISBSG also asks for information about the time recording method used to collect the effort data – see Table 8.2.

Table 8.1   Resource Levels (ISBSG)

Resource level	Description

Level 1: Development Team	• Those responsible for the delivery of the application under development. The team or organization that specifies, designs, and/or builds the software also typically performs testing and implementation activities. This level comprises the following:
	
	    Project Team
	    Project Management
	    Project Administration
	    Any member of IT Operations specifically allocated to the project

Level 2: Development Team Support/IT Operations	• Those who operate the IT systems that support the end-users and are responsible for providing specialist services to the development team (but not allocated to the team). This level comprises the following:
	
	    Data Base Administration
	
	    Data Administration
	
	    Quality Assurance
	
	    Data Security
	
	    Standards Support
	
	    Audit and Control
	
	    Technical Support
	
	    Software Support
	
	    Hardware Support
	
	    Information Center Support

Level 3: Customers/ End-Users	• Those responsible for defining the requirements of the applications and sponsoring/championing the development of the application (including the software's end-users). The relationship between the project customer and the software's end-users can vary, as can their involvement in a software project. This level comprises the following:
	
	    Application Clients
	
	    Application Users
	
	    User Liaison
	
	    User Training

Table 8.2   Time Recording Methods (ISBSG)

Time recording method	Description
Method A: Staff-hours (recorded)	The daily recording of the entire *work effort* expended by each person on project-related tasks. For example, a person working on a specific project from 8 a.m. to 5 p.m. with a 1-hour lunch break will record 8 hours of *work effort*
Method B: Staff-hours (derived)	It is possible to derive the *work effort* when it has not been recorded on a daily basis as in Method A. It may only have been recorded in weeks, months, or even years
Method C: Productive time only (recorded)	The daily recording of only the productive effort (including overtime) expended by a person on project-related tasks. Using the same example as in Method A, when the nonproductive tasks have been removed, (coffee, liaising with other teams, administration, reading a magazine, etc.), only 5.5 hours can be recorded

8.4 COMPLETED ISBSG INDIVIDUAL PROJECT BENCHMARKING REPORTS: SOME EXAMPLES

For every project dataset sent to the ISBSG, the organization sends back an individual benchmarking report, which includes the following four sections:

1. Productivity benchmarking
2. Quality benchmarking
3. Assessment of the project data submitted
4. Normalization of the effort reported.

Section 1: Project delivery rate – PDR This ISBSG benchmarking report includes a comparison of the productivity of the project submitted with those in the repository.

   The ISBSG measures productivity using the PDR, that is, the number of hours to deliver a functional size unit (in FP for the IFPUG method; in CFP for the COSMIC Function Point method).

Project size	298 CFP
Project work effort	12670 hours
Project PDR	42.5 hours per CFP
Functional size method	COSMIC – ISO 19761
Development type	New

Table 8.3   Project Delivery Rate (PDR) by Range

Influencing factor	N	P10%	P25%	Med		P75%		P90%
Development platform: Multi, use all valid projects	25	1.5	4.9	10.2		40.7	*42.5	67.9
How methodology acquired: Developed in-house	10	1.8	5.0	7.7		23.6	*42.5	52.3
Language type: 3GL	19	1.5	5.2	28.3	*42.5	63.3		124.5

The report benchmarks the PDR for the following factors (provided the project submitted includes the required information on these data fields):

- Development platform
- Language type
- Maximum team size
- How the development methodology was acquired.

Table 8.3 also shows that, for this project, there was information available for three of the major factors (development platform, methodology, and language type), while no information had been provided for the fourth one (i.e., maximum team size).

EXAMPLE 8.1

Table 8.3 places the project's specific PDR relative to the PDR distribution of all the projects that involve the same development platform (line 1: the **PDR** of 42.5 hours per FP for the project being benchmarked is positioned in the 75% range (this means that the project PDR is higher than for 75% of the projects in the ISBSG repository for its specific platform category).

The ISBSG also reports, in the first column, N, the number of projects being compared to for each of the three variables for which this project has data.

EXAMPLE 8.2

Table 8.3 indicates that, with $N = 25$, the benchmarking on the development platform is performed with 25 projects, while the comparison by language type is performed with only 19 projects. The * in Table 8.3 represents the data value for the specific project being benchmarked.

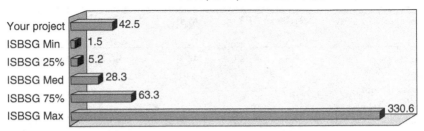

Figure 8.3 shows the PDR (Hr/FP) Benchmark chart.

PDR (Hr/FP) Benchmark chart

Your project	42.5
ISBSG Min	1.5
ISBSG 25%	5.2
ISBSG Med	28.3
ISBSG 75%	63.3
ISBSG Max	330.6

Figure 8.3   Project Delivery Rate (PDR) in Hours per FP

Table 8.4   Defect Density for the First Month of Operation

Defect type	Project	ISBSG		
		Min	Mean	Max
Total no. of defects	*0/1000 FP	*0	17	91

For the two factors with the most significant impact on productivity, Development Platform and Language Type, the related graph shows how the PDR of the project compares to projects with the same values *for both these factors*, that is, the same development platform and the same language type – see Figure 8.3.

Section 2: Project defect density If defect counts were provided in the project data submitted to the ISBSG, another table in the benchmarking reports – Table 8.4 – will show how the project's defect density (defects per 1000 Function Points) in the first month of operation compares to that of projects in the ISBSG repository.

Section 3: Assessment of the project data submitted The ISBSG data administrator assesses the quality of the data submitted by an organization and records the assessment in a Data Quality Rating (DQR) field for each project submitted.

- In the following box, a project has been given an overall rating of B, together with supporting comments explaining why this rating was assigned to this specific project.

Rating Assigned to the Project Being Benchmarked

B = Temporary rating until fully validated. Overall integrity appears all right. Complete dataset, no significant omissions.

Table 8.5 Assessment Code for the Quality of the Project Data

Rating code	Rating description
A	The data submitted were assessed as sound, with nothing identified that might affect their integrity.
B	The submission appears fundamentally sound, but there are some factors that could affect the integrity of the submitted data.
C	Owing to significant data not being provided, it was not possible to assess the integrity of the submitted data.
D	Owing to one factor or a combination of factors, little credibility should be given to the data submitted.

The set of DQR that can be assigned by the ISBSG data administrator is illustrated in Table 8.5.

Section 4: Normalization In order to make comparison meaningful, the ISBSG report indicates whether or not the project reported included the work effort for the whole development life cycle, or for only a portion of it:

- If the project reported effort for only a portion of the project life cycle, the ISBSG will calculate the normalized PDR – see also Section 8.5.3.

8.5 PREPARING TO USE THE ISBSG REPOSITORY

8.5.1 ISBSG Data Extract

Figure 8.4 presents the structure of the data fields made available to those purchasing the ISBSG data extract.

- It is, of course, highly recommended that anybody analyzing the data from the MS-Excel file become very familiar with the detailed definitions of all the fields included in this data extract.

8.5.2 Data Preparation: Quality of the Data Collected

Before analyzing data from any repository, including the ISBSG repository, it is important to understand how fields are defined, used, and recorded. In dataset preparation, two verification steps must be carried out:

- Data quality verification
- Data completeness verification.

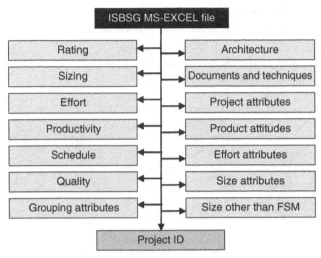

Figure 8.4 ISBSG Data Extract Structure [Cheikhi et al. 2006. Reprinted with permission from Novatica.]

Data Quality Verification

It is easy to verify the quality of effort data:

- The ISBSG data repository manager himself carries out the quality analysis – right at collection time – and he records his judgment, the DQR in that project field.
    ▶ This rating will vary from very good (A) to unreliable (D) – see Table 8.5.

It is thus advisable for analysis purposes to consider only those projects with a DQR of A or B (e.g., the data collected have a high degree of integrity).

- Correspondingly, to reduce the risk of poor quality data and to improve the validity of the analysis reported here, projects with a data quality rating of C or D should typically be removed before analysis.

Data Completeness Verification

Software engineers wishing to use the ISBSG repository should also look at other data fields that may provide important clues about the quality of the following two variables collected:

- Effort data
- Functional size.

To ensure the integrity, and credibility, of the information in these two key fields, the ISBSG collects additional information in three related fields to provide clues about the credibility of the information provided on effort and size:

- The time recording method – see Table 8.2

Significance of the Time Recording Method

A score of B in the time recording method field indicates that the effort data collected did not come from a daily data collection of work-hours, but rather were derived at a much higher level of frequency, such as weeks or months.

This typically means that the hours reported could have been guessed at (on a weekly or monthly basis, for instance), and this information has low credibility and should be handled with care in statistical analyses.

- The percentage of uncollected work effort:
  - ▶ This data field provides information on whether or not the work-hours reported have been under reported.
  - ▶ This data field provides clues about the potential percentage of underreported work-hours; of course, there is typically no time recording for this variable, and so this figure is usually an approximation.
  - ▶ The percentage provided should not be considered as accurate, but only an indication of the lack of accuracy of the work-effort hours recorded.
- The qualifications of the measurer who performed the software functional size measurement:
  - ▶ This data field provides a clue to determining the credibility of the functional size reported.
  - ▶ Of course, too little experience about functional size measurement might lead to much greater size measurement variations than those recorded by staff with over 5 years of experience in the application of a specific measurement method.

A source of variation in measuring functional size

An inexperienced or untrained functional size measurer might miss a significant portion of the functionality of the software being measured, particularly if the available project documentation is at a fairly high level of abstraction, rather than at the detailed level of approved specifications.

8.5.3   Missing Data: An Example with Effort Data

Another step is required to identify the level of missing data for fields of interest in data analyses [Déry and Abran 2005].

Effort data originate from an organization's time reporting system, which, in practice, can vary considerably from one organization to another:

- One time reporting system may include effort from initial planning to full deployment.

- Another time reporting system will only report effort for the programming and testing activities.

To capture information about disparities with respect to the total work effort across organizations reported in its repository, the ISBSG asks data collectors to map their own life cycle to a standardized ISBSG life cycle with six activities: Planning, Specification, Design, Build, Test, and Implement.

- Total project effort is a mandatory field in the ISBSG repository, but the detailed effort per project phase is an optional one, and is often missing.

This heterogeneity in the project activities included in the effort data collected means that the data in the total project effort[2] field have to be handled with great care, as the life cycle coverage is not identical across projects.

As a result, it is vital in data analysis using the ISBSG repository (as with many multi-organizational repositories where there is the possibility of variability in life cycle coverage for the effort data) to first assess the consistency of the data collected.

In the ISBSG repository, project effort may refer to any combination of the six activities defined by the ISBSG. The variability in the effort field is illustrated in Table 8.6 for the 2562 projects measured with the IFPUG method and for which data quality is considered to be high (in ISBSG Release 1999).

In this table, the columns indicate the project activities, while the rows indicate the combination of activities identified in the repository. We can see in Table 8.6 8 of the 31 different combinations of project activities in the repository.

For example:

- Rows 1 and 3 indicate the number of projects with a distinct single-phase effort
- Rows 2 and 4 indicate the number of projects with a distinct two-phase effort

Table 8.6   Projects and Their Activities in the ISBSG 1999 Release

Profile no.	No. of projects	Planning	Specification	Build	Test	Implement
1	11			√		
2	2			√		√
3	3					√
4	9	√	√			
5	405	√	√	√	√	
6	350	√	√	√	√	√
7	5	√	√		√	
8	1006					
Total	2562					

(Adapted from Déry and Abran 2005). Reprinted with permission from Shaker Verlag.

[2]The ISBSG refers to the total project work effort recorded as the "summary work effort."

- Row 6 indicates 350 projects with the full five-phase effort coverage
- Row 8 indicates 1006 projects with no information for the activities included.

With so much diversity in the actual content (and scope) of the field recording the effort collected, and, correspondingly, so many possible combinations of activities recorded, how can meaningful benchmarking comparisons be carried out and adequate models built?

- Of course, performing productivity benchmarking and building productivity models based on projects, where effort data do not share the same definition in terms of work activities, is challenging.
- Not taking such disparities into account would be hazardous. Indeed, average effort, for instance, can be calculated meaningfully only within a specific profile, and each profile should be dealt with separately,
  - ▶ unless, of course, some adequate statistical techniques are used to normalize such information.

To allow users of its repository to make meaningful PDR comparisons, the ISBSG provides an additional field, calculated data, which includes the derivation of normalized work-hours to represent projects as having been reported on a full life cycle.

Such a normalization process can be based, for instance, on the following:

- The average time spent per work phase (based on the subset of projects having reported detailed effort per work phase and including all activities).
- Looking at projects with no effort breakdown, but with information on the activities included, and then normalizing, for these projects, their effort based on the ratio of activities included versus the full life cycle.
  - ▶ If all the life cycle activities of a project have been reported, then no normalization is required and the Actual effort = Normalized effort.
  - ▶ If no phase breakdown has been reported for a project, then no normalization is possible.
  - ▶ If only one or two activities of a project are included in the effort reported, normalization can be performed, but its representativeness of the full life cycle is less reliable.

The use of values normalized in this way should be handled with care.

FURTHER READING 1: BENCHMARKING TYPES

Benchmarking for an organization involves

- comparing its performance against the performance of other organizations developing software,
- identifying the best practices that led to those higher levels of performance, and

- implementing, within their own organization, the best practices with objectively demonstrated higher performance levels.

Benchmarking is typically based on the following key concepts:

- Comparison of relevant characteristics of the products and services.
- Comparison of quantitative and documented evidence of the performance of the production process and/or service delivery.
- Identification of the best practices that have demonstrated a continuous ability to deliver superior products and services.

There are two major benchmarking categories: internal and external.

(A) *Internal benchmarking*
This type of benchmarking is typically performed within an organization.
- For instance, the productivity of a current project can be compared with the productivity of the projects completed by the same development organization in the previous year.
- Similarly, if an organization has multiple development groups, the comparison can be performed across the various groups within the organization.

(B) *External benchmarking*
This type of benchmarking is typically performed with other organizations, either within a geographical area in a specific market or without such constraints.

There can also be various subtypes of external benchmarking as follows:

- Competitive benchmarking
- Functional benchmarking

Competitive Benchmarking   This type of benchmarking is typically performed by collecting data about (and from) direct competitors, comparing direct quantitative performance, and then analyzing the causes of variations, which leads to the identification of best practices.

Of course, competitive benchmarking is difficult, since, on the one hand, competitors are very reluctant to provide such sensitive information, and, on the other, the organization is very sensitive to letting its competitors know how well the organization is performing and what its own recipes for higher performance are.

Benchmarking Outside Direct Competitive Markets   Benchmarking can be carried out with organizations delivering similar products and services, but outside the markets in which they directly compete.

- In such a context, organizations will be more amenable to exchanging information.

Functional Benchmarking   When direct competitive benchmarking is not an option (or even risky), functional benchmarking can be carried out with organizations delivering similar or related services in different markets.

Examples of Functional Benchmarking in Software

- A bank developing a payment system might find it useful to benchmark with insurance organizations or government agencies developing similar systems.
- An insurance organization developing an insurance system might find it useful to benchmark with governmental organizations providing insurance-type services at the national level.
- An organization developing an inventory system for the hotel industry might find it useful to benchmark with organizations providing reservation systems to the airline industry.

Benchmarking is a great deal more than data collection:

- Considerable data analysis capabilities are required
  - ▶ to carry out the benchmarking process and
  - ▶ to leverage benchmarking outcomes into successful and sustainable actions plans.

In the pursuit of an improved data analysis capability (for benchmarking and estimation purposes), repositories such as that of the International Software Benchmarking Standards Group – ISBSG – can help the software engineering community:

- better understand some of the cause-and-effect relationships across a number of variables available in the repository fields and
- figure out which relationships contribute most to the achievement of certain goals (increased productivity, shorter time-to-market, and so on).

FURTHER READING 2: DETAILED STRUCTURE OF THE ISBSG DATA EXTRACT

Category	Field
Project ID	Project ID
Rating (2)	• Data quality rating
	• Unadjusted function point rating
Sizing (4)	• Count approach
	• Functional size
	• Adjusted function points
	• Value adjustment factor
Effort (2)	• Summary work effort
	• Normalized work effort

Category	Field
Productivity (4)	<ul><li>Reported delivery rate (afp)</li><li>Project delivery rate (ufp)</li><li>Normalized productivity delivery rate afp: (adjusted function points)</li><li>Normalized productivity delivery rate ufp: (unadjusted function points)</li></ul>
Schedule (11)	<ul><li>Project elapsed time</li><li>Project inactive time</li><li>Implementation date</li><li>Project activity scope</li><li>Effort plan</li><li>Effort specify</li><li>Effort design</li><li>Effort build</li><li>Effort test</li><li>Effort implement</li><li>Effort unphased</li></ul>
Quality (4)	<ul><li>Minor defects – Defects reported in the first month of use of the software: the number of minor defects delivered.</li><li>Major defects – Defects reported in the first month of use of the software: the number of major defects delivered.</li><li>Extreme defects – Defects reported in the first month of use of the software: the number of extreme defects delivered.</li><li>Total defects delivered – Total defects reported in the first month of use of the software: the total number of defects (minor, major, and extreme), or, where no breakdown is available, the single value is shown here.</li></ul>
Grouping attributes (6)	<ul><li>Development type</li><li>Organization type</li><li>Business area type</li><li>Application type</li><li>Package customization</li><li>Degree of customization</li></ul>
Architecture (7)	<ul><li>Architecture</li></ul>

Category	Field
	• Client server
	• Client roles
	• Server roles
	• Type of server
	• Client/server description
	• Web development
Documents and techniques (16)	• Planning documents
	• Specification documents
	• Specification techniques
	• Design documents
	• Design techniques
	• Build products
	• Build activity
	• Test documents
	• Test activity
	• Implementation documents
	• Implementation activity
	• Development techniques
	• Functional sizing technique
	• FP standard
	• FP standards all
	• Reference table approach
Project attributes (23)	• Development platform
	• Language type
	• Primary programming language
	• First hardware
	• Second hardware
	• First operating system
	• Second operating system
	• First language
	• Second language

Category	Field
	• First database system
	• Second database system
	• First component server
	• Second component server
	• First Web server
	• Second Web server
	• First message server
	• Second message server
	• First debugging tool
	• First other platform
	• Second other platform
	• CASE tool used
	• Methodology used
	• How the methodology was acquired
Product attributes (4)	• User base: business units
	• User base: locations
	• User base: concurrent users
	• Intended market
Effort attributes (6)	• Recording method
	• Resource level
	• Maximum team size
	• Average team size
	• Ratio of project work effort: nonproject effort
	• Percentage of uncollected work effort
Size Attributes (8)	• This section will vary, depending on the Functional Size standards selected (IFPUG, COSMIC, NESMA, etc.)
	• Added size
	• Changed size
	• Deleted size
Size other than FSM (2)	• Lines of code
	• LOC, not statements

EXERCISES

1. Why would an organization spend effort and money on a benchmarking exercise?
2. Why is it important to adopt standards in data collection?
3. At what organizational process maturity level(s) is benchmarking worthwhile? Would the benefits be the same at each level? Explain.
4. Identify key success factors in benchmarking.
5. Identify key failure factors in benchmarking.
6. How is the ISBSG organized?
7. How is ISBSG data collection organized?
8. What sections of the ISBSG data collection questionnaire are devoted to software projects?
9. Which ISO standards have been adopted by the ISBSG for the collection of the functional size of the software delivered by a project?
10. What are the key differences between the three levels of human resources?
11. In the ISBSG benchmarking report, what is the Project Delivery Rate – PDR?
12. In the ISBSG benchmarking report, how does the PDR of your project compare to that of other projects in the ISBSG repository?
13. In Section 4 of the ISBSG benchmarking report, what is involved in effort normalization?
14. How does the ISBSG assess the quality of the data submitted to its data administrator?
15. Why is the normalization of effort data necessary for benchmarking purposes and for building productivity models?

TERM ASSIGNMENTS

1. Look at your time reporting system and map it to the ISBSG definitions for the time recording methods and work effort breakdown in Tables 8.2 and 8.6.
2. Of the data fields in the ISBSG questionnaire, what is the ratio of quantitative data to nominal data?
3. When you have to carry out a data analysis on the ISBSG dataset (or any other dataset), what preparation steps are important?
4. What is the significance (and impact) of bundling projects sized with different functional size measurement methods?
5. What is the significance (and impact) of bundling projects for which effort was collected with different time recording definitions?
6. If your organization does not have a repository of completed projects, how can you test the relevance for your organization of using an external dataset (such as the ISBSG, or any other similar repository) in your organization? What would you recommend to an organization in such a context?
7. Collect the data from a team project carried out in another software engineering course, and compare its performance with that of similar projects in the ISBSG repository. Discuss and comment on the interpretation context.

8. Take the documentation for a completed project, including the total effort that was needed to complete the project. Access the project estimation information based on which the project budget was initially allocated. Compare the figures, comment on them, and prepare recommendations for your management.

9. Identify five organizations you would like to propose to your CIO for a benchmarking exercise. Provide a detailed rationale for your recommendation. What do you know specifically about the software organizations you recommended to your CIO? Why would these five organizations be ready to share data with your organization?

10. The ISBSG publishes how many data are from which country on its Website. How many projects are from your country? Explain this number, relative to countries of similar size. Why would countries of similar size have more projects? What factors would lead to such a situation?

11. Download a Data Collection Questionnaire from the ISBSG Website. Use it to collect data from your project. For how many fields could you obtain data? What is the ratio of those fields to the total number of fields? Why were you not able to collect all the data in your organization? For the data you could not collect, were they meaningless for project monitoring and project management?

Chapter 9

Building and Evaluating Single Variable Models

OBJECTIVES

This chapter covers

- The engineering approach to building mathematical models
- Building models with the ISBSG repository
- Data preparation with the ISBSG
- Data analysis by sample

9.1 INTRODUCTION

The previous chapter illustrated the importance of standardized definitions for the inputs to software productivity models, and recommended the use of the data collection standards published by the ISBSG.

Of course, practitioners would like to take many other cost factors into account in their models, since it is expected that each cost factor will have an impact on the work–effort relationship. Rather than building models by taking into account as many cost factors as are deemed to be of interest, the engineering approach investigates the factors and studying them one at a time before combining them, to avoid potentially confusing their individual contributions to the work–effort relationship.

In this chapter, we show how models are built from an engineering perspective, that is, based on:

- Observation of past projects.

- Identification of the scale types of the variables, and taking them into account to ensure adequate use of those variables in productivity models.

- Analysis of the impact of each individual variable, one at a time.

Software Project Estimation: The Fundamentals for Providing High Quality Information to Decision Makers, First Edition. Alain Abran.
© 2015 the IEEE Computer Society. Published 2015 by John Wiley & Sons, Inc.

- Selection of relevant samples, and of samples of sufficient size, from a statistical viewpoint.
- Documentation and analysis of the demographics of the dataset used.
- No extrapolation to contexts other than those from which the data were collected.

The engineering approach does not take for granted that it is feasible to have a single model which can handle all sets of conditions:

- It searches instead for models that are reasonably good within a well-identified and understood set of constraints.

The approach taken in this chapter to provide the basis for building models is the following:

- Look at the work–effort relationship, one variable at a time, to gain insights for each variable, one variable at a time.

This also means initially obtaining a number of models for each variable, and acknowledging that

- no one model for a single variable will be perfect (because it will not take into account the other variables *directly*),
- but it will teach us something about the effect of that single variable on the dependent variable, that is, effort.

In this chapter, we show how to build models with examples of data from the ISBSG repository, taking into account some of the peculiarities of software engineering datasets. Building models with more than one variable is discussed in the next chapter – see Chapter 10.

The chapter is organized as follows:

- Section 9.2 describes the approach to building productivity models with software size as the key independent variable.
- Section 9.3 describes data preparation with the ISBSG repository.
- Section 9.4 illustrates the analysis of the quality and constraints of the models.
- Section 9.5 presents additional examples of models.
- Section 9.6 provides a summary of the chapter.

9.2 MODESTLY, ONE VARIABLE AT A TIME

9.2.1 The Key Independent Variable: Software Size

First, it is widely recognized that software size is a significant driver of project effort. A number of research reports based on statistical studies provide strong support for this. This is illustrated in Figure 9.1, where product size drives project effort.

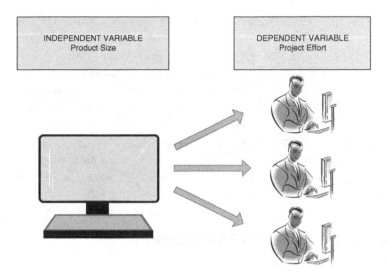

Figure 9.1   Product Size as the Key Driver of Project Effort

However, it is also recognized that size alone is far from a sufficient driver at all times, and that a number of other factors must be taken into account to improve the modeling of the relationship with effort.

In the ISBSG repository, there is a great diversity of projects

- from various countries and
- from various business application sectors, using
- different development and implementation platforms,
- various development approaches,
- various development tools, and so on.

All of these will have an impact on the work–effort relationship, as well as software size, of course.

The ISBSG dataset can therefore be considered a repository of heterogeneous projects:

- A model *built with the full ISBSG dataset* would not be expected to demonstrate a strong work–effort relationship with size as the single independent variable.

How can these factors be isolated, in order to study the size–effort relationship first?

- A typical strategy is to isolate samples in the full repository which are likely to behave in a similar (but not necessarily exactly the same) way given the same set of constraints.

- The criterion used for building each sample then becomes a constant within this sample, which no longer needs to be taken into account in the productivity model:
  - ▶ For each value of the criterion, a distinct productivity model can be built.
  - ▶ Once a model has been built for each value, the models can be compared to analyze the influence of the various values of the criterion used to build the samples.
    - ∘ For instance, if samples are built using programming languages, models can then be built for every group of projects with a similar programming language (and, within each sample, the programming language is a constant and no longer a variable).

9.2.2   Analysis of the Work–Effort Relationship in a Sample

The ISBSG repository is used as the empirical basis for the statistical analyses presented below.

- The variable "programming language" was selected as an example to illustrate how to build a productivity model.

Because programming language is a variable of the nominal type (e.g., C, C++, Access, COBOL, Assembler, and Visual Basic), its values cannot be directly treated as a single quantitative variable.

- In practice, every nominal programming language becomes a distinct variable for statistical analysis purposes.

In the ISBSG repository, there are projects developed with over 40 programming languages, some with a great deal of data and others with barely any.

Of course, the validity of a statistical technique depends on the number of data points used to build a model:

- Ideally, there should be 30 data points for every variable taken into account.
- In practice, 20 data points is still a statistically reasonable number.
- However, care must be exercised with a dataset of fewer than 20 points.

The approach selected in this chapter is to identify subsets within the ISBSG repository with enough projects for a statistical analysis according to their specific programming language.

The engineering approach requires that the parameters of the models be based not on judgment, but on data points from a sufficiently large sample to be statistically meaningful.

The following are some preparatory steps that are required when data are available:

- Data preparation
- Application of the statistical tools
- Data analysis.

This is illustrated next with the use of data from the ISBSG repository.[1]

9.3 DATA PREPARATION

9.3.1 Descriptive Analysis

The dataset used in this section is from the December 1999 Release (R9) of the ISBSG repository, which at that time included detailed information on 789 projects from 20 countries.

This version of the ISBSG repository was first analyzed to identify the projects that could qualify for this analysis.

The projects selected had to meet the following criteria:

- There is no doubt about the quality of the data points.
  - ▶ Each project has a quality tag assigned by the ISBSG registrar, based on whether or not the data fully meet ISBSG data collection quality requirements, that is, all the project data collected are considered fully credible by the ISBSG.
- The project effort (in person-hours) is available.
- The programming language is available.

In addition, for the purposes of this study, only projects with effort equal to or greater than 400 person-hours were selected, to eliminate the variations owing to very small projects most often executed by a single staff member, which introduces individual heterogeneity into the project performance.

The descriptive statistics of the 497 projects that met these criteria simultaneously are presented in Table 9.1. These projects took close to 7000 hours to complete on average, but with a large standard deviation of 13,000 hours, which explains a significantly different median at 2680 hours, with a minimum of 400 hours and a maximum of close to 140,000 hours.

The linear regression statistical technique was selected for building these productivity models, because it is better known by practitioners and simpler to understand and use.

9.3.2 Identifying Relevant Samples and Outliers

The qualified projects in ISBSG R9 were subdivided into samples by programming language, and analyses were carried out for each.

---

[1] See also Abran, A.; Ndiaye, I.; Bourque, P. (2007) "Evaluation of a Black-Box Estimation Tool: A Case Study", In Special Issue: "Advances in Measurements for Software Processes Assessment", Journal of Software Process Improvement and Practice, Vol. 12, no. 2, pp. 199–218.

Table 9.1   Descriptive Analysis of the ISBSG R9 Qualified Sample ($N = 497$)

Statistical function	Effort (person-hours)
Minimum	400
Maximum	138,883
Average	6949
Standard deviation	13,107
Median	2680

Abran et al. 2007. Reprinted with permission from John Wiley & Sons, Inc.

The independent variable available for the estimation was project size, that is, the input was measured in functional size units (e.g., Function Points – FP).

The constant for each sample was, of course, the programming language.

In addition to these criteria, two additional steps were taken as follows:

- A visual analysis of the datasets.
- An investigation of the obvious outliers (see Section 5.4) to interpret the results in the empirical context of size intervals (see Section 6.6).

Many software engineering datasets are heterogeneous, have wedge-shaped distributions [Abran and Robillard 1996; Kitchenham and Taylor 1984], and can, of course, have outliers that have an impact on the construction of the models and on their performance.

- Here, therefore, each sample was analyzed for the presence of outliers, as well as for visually recognizable patterns, which could provide an indication that a single simple linear representation would not constitute a good representation of the dataset.
    - ▶ For instance, a set of projects within one functional size interval might have one behavior with respect to effort, and another size interval could exhibit a different behavior.
    - ▶ If such recognizable patterns were identified, then the sample was subdivided into two smaller samples – if there were enough data points, of course. Both the samples with outliers and those without them were analyzed.

This approach was used on each sample identified by its programming language.

The next step in the construction of the samples consisted of subdividing the full set of 497 projects into samples by programming language.

- For reporting purposes, and because of the lack of statistical significance resulting from too small a sample size, programming languages with less than 20 projects were not retained for further analysis.

Table 9.2   Samples by Programming Language (with and Without Outliers) – ISBSG 1999 Release

Samples with all the data points and size intervals			Subsamples without outliers and with subsized intervals		
Programming language	N	Functional size interval	N	Functional size interval	No. of outliers excluded
Cobol II	21	80–2000	9	80–180	6
			6	181–500	
Natural	41	20–3500	30	20–620	2
			9	621–3500	
Oracle	26	100–4300	19	100–2000	7
PL/1	29	80–2600	19	80–450	5
			5	451–2550	
Telon	23	70–1100	18	70–650	5

Abran et al. 2007. Reprinted with permission from John Wiley & Sons, Inc.

A list of the five samples by programming language included in this analysis is presented in the left-hand side of Table 9.2, along with the number (N) of data points and the functional size intervals for each sample.

Each of the five samples by programming language is then represented graphically on two axes (functional size and effort) and analyzed.

- When the visual analysis indicated the potential for undue outlier impact in a sample, corresponding subsets without these outliers were created for further analysis (right-hand side of Table 9.2).

Visual Identification of Outliers

If a project in a sample has a significantly larger effort than other projects of similar size, this is an indication that, for this specific project, size has far less influence on effort when compared to the full sample of projects.

- In this case, we can hypothesize that there is at least one other variable that has a much greater influence on effort.

A project in the sample may have a much lower effort than other projects of similar size.

- It could also be considered as a productivity extreme – see Chapter 11.

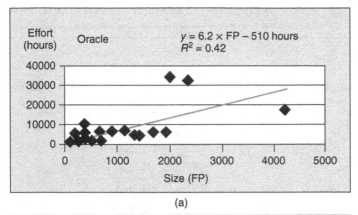

(a)

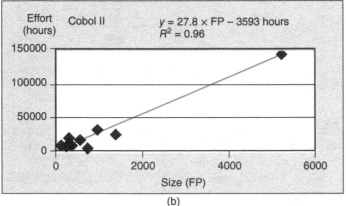

(b)

Figure 9.2   Full Dataset for (a) Oracle and (b) Cobol II, Including All Outliers [Abran et al. 2007. Reprinted with permission from John Wiley & Sons, Inc.]

Two cases are illustrated with the Oracle and Cobol II datasets (Figures 9.2a,b).

- Since we are interested mainly in analyzing the influence of size, the presence of such a clear indication, and major impact, of another influential variable provides sufficient reason to exclude it from the analysis.

Outlier Analogy

By analogy, this exclusion step corresponds to a study of the dynamics of a sample of people in good health, in which individuals not matching the study profile (who are terminally ill) are excluded from the study.

The numbers of outliers excluded for each programming language are listed in the right-hand-side column of Table 9.2.

- Outliers affecting the size–effort relationship are removed from a second set of samples, including considerably larger projects that had an undue influence on the regression models.
- Throughout this section, results are presented for both sets of samples (with and without outliers), to show the impact of leaving outliers out of the analysis.

In this section, outliers are identified using only graphical analysis. In Chapter 5, Section 5.4.2, more advanced techniques for identifying statistically significant outliers are provided (Figure 9.2).

Next, the distribution for each programming language is analyzed graphically, to identify potentially distinct patterns of size–effort relationships. Samples may be subdivided for one of the following two reasons:

- A potentially distinct linear relationship across size ranges.
- Different densities of data points across size intervals (with a distinct dispersion pattern across those intervals).

For the programming language samples in question, a single linear model would not have represented the samples best. Nonlinear models could have been explored, but the visual analysis indicated that, for both size intervals, a linear model for each interval could be representative of the subsets, and would be easier to understand. We can see in Figure 9.2 that, for these two programming languages

- the lower intervals have more data points and a smaller interval range and
- the second intervals contain fewer observations across a much larger size interval.

9.4 ANALYSIS OF THE QUALITY AND CONSTRAINTS OF MODELS

In this section, we present an analysis of a single sample, that is, the one for the programming language Natural with $N = 41$ projects.

- Natural, a programming language popular in the late 1990s, was specific to a particular database management system (DBMS).

This sample is illustrated in Figure 9.3, with the functional size in Function Points on the x-axis, and the actual effort on the y-axis.

A linear regression on this full data sample gives the following model:

$$Y = 10.05 \times FP - 649 \text{ hours,}$$

with a regression coefficient $R^2 = 0.86$.

However, the constant (649 hours) in the equation has a negative sign, which does not have a valid empirical interpretation:

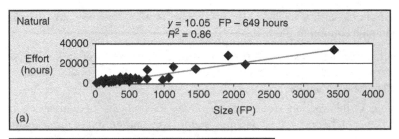

(a)

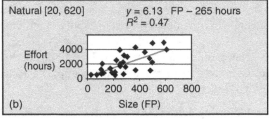

(b)

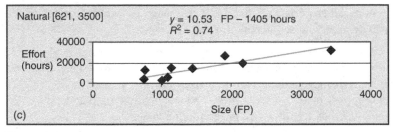

(c)

Figure 9.3 Regression Analyses for Projects in Natural Programming Language, (a) $N = 41$ (Includes Outliers); (b) Size < 620 FP ($N = 30$); (c) Size > 620 FP ($N = 9$) [Abran et al. 2007. Reprinted with permission from John Wiley & Sons, Inc.]

- In a project of size $= 0$, a minus sign should be interpreted as a negative effort, which, of course, is not possible.

Furthermore, a visual analysis of Figure 9.3a reveals that there are some candidate outliers that might have an undue impact on the regression model. For example:

- A project of around 3700 FP is almost three times as large as the majority of the projects. This means that this very large project might unduly influence the model. If this single project is taken out of the sample, the expressiveness of the model with respect to effort might be reduced significantly (i.e., its regression coefficient of R^2 might be lower than 0.86).

The visual analysis provides another clue. We can identify two different groups (subsets) of projects within this dataset as follows:

- One subset of projects between 20 and 620 FP, with a good sample size of 30 observations (Figure 9.3b).

- One with a more sparsely populated subset of nine projects between 621 and 3700 FP, which is a much larger size interval (Figure 9.3c).

9.4.1 Small Projects

We can now see that, in the sample of projects with a functional size between 20 and 620 FP, there is only a fair relationship between the independent and dependent variables: its productivity model (Figure 9.3b) is

$$Y = 6.13 \times FP + 265 \, \text{hours}, \text{with an } R^2 = 0.47.$$

This regression coefficient of 0.47 illustrates the dispersion of the data points, while still representing an increasing size–effort relationship.

In this model, the constant of 265 hours represents the portion of the effort that is not dependent on an increase in size, and hence the positive slope would correspond to the variable cost, which is dependent on the size of the projects.

9.4.2 Larger Projects

For projects larger than 620 FP (Figure 9.3c), the model is

$$Y = 10.53 \times FP - 1405, \text{ with } R^2 = 0.74,$$

but, with only nine data points, caution must be exercised in the interpretation of the data.

For this larger size interval, the constant of the equation is negative (−1405 hours), which is, of course, counterintuitive.

- This means, in particular, that the model should not be extrapolated outside the range of values from which it was derived, that is:
  - ▶ This regression model is not valid for projects smaller than 620 FP.

9.4.3 Implication for Practitioners

While the model for the full sample has the highest regression coefficient of $R^2 = 0.86$, *this is not the best model to use in practice.*

When a practitioner has to estimate a specific project, this project will have a predetermined size:

- If the project to be estimated has, say, a size of 500 FP, the practitioner should ultimately select the productivity model derived from the set of small projects:
  - ▶ The sample used to build it contained projects within the same range, with a large enough sample size, a regression coefficient of 0.47 (indicating, correctly for this range of size values, a much larger relative variation that was hidden in the full model for this size range), and a plausible fixed cost at the origin for a project within that size range.

- If the project to be estimated has, say, a size of 2500 FP, then the practitioner has the option of using the full model built for the full sample, or the model derived from the corresponding size range subset. The advantages and disadvantages of each are discussed below.

  ▶ The model for the full sample is built from a larger set of data points and has a higher regression coefficient ($R^2 = 0.86$.).
  ▶ The model for the subset of large projects has a smaller basis of nine projects and a smaller regression coefficient ($R^2 = 0.74$), and therefore a much smaller statistical representativeness, with only nine projects.

In spite of the above-mentioned criteria, the model derived from the subset of large projects should be the one to select for estimation purposes, since it is the one that provides the most relevant information to managers:

- The models built with these nine large projects correctly indicate that the sample is small and that care should be exercised in using it.

  ▶ The information needed by the manager is a number for an estimate. However, he also needs *information* about the quality of that number and the risks involved in using it. *This model provides the manager with the most relevant information.*

- The model built with the full set is less reliable in the range for which it is sparsely populated.

  ▶ If this fact is ignored, management gains a false sense of confidence when estimating large projects (2500 FP), even though the dataset does not allow for such a high level of confidence. This model *does not provide the manager with the most relevant information* available from that dataset.

9.5 OTHER MODELS BY PROGRAMMING LANGUAGE

In this section, we present the models derived for the five programming language categories with over 20 projects.

Table 9.3 presents the set of linear regression models derived directly from the ISBSG R9 repository:

- On the left-hand side are the five samples, including outliers and the size interval for which data were available.
- On the right-hand side is the group of samples, excluding outliers.

  ▶ Some samples were subdivided by size interval, where warranted by graphical analysis, using the same approach as described in the previous section.

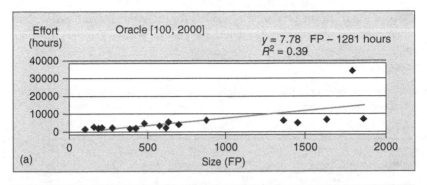

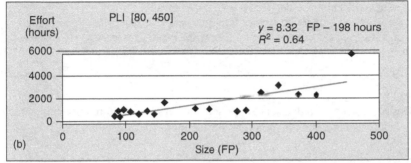

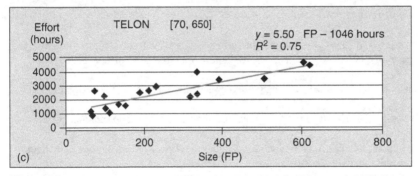

Figure 9.4   (a–c) Directly Derived ISBSG Productivity Models [Abran et al. 2007. Reprinted with permission from John Wiley & Sons, Inc.]

In Table 9.3, the coefficient of regression (R^2) is presented for each model. Three of the productivity models built directly from the ISBSG repository are presented in Figures 9.4a–c:

- Oracle (100, 2000)
- PL1 (80, 450)
- Telon (70–650).

Analysis of the R^2 of the productivity models for the samples (with and without outliers) illustrates how the outliers can distort the general behavior of the size–effort relationship.

For example:

(A) Outliers can hide a significantly higher size–effort relationship for the majority of the data points:

PL1 sample

The PL1 sample (including outliers) has a very low R^2 of 0.23.

However, when 5 outliers are excluded from the sample of 29 projects, the size–effort relationships has an R^2 of 0.64 and 0.86 for the two interval ranges identified in this sample, respectively.

(B) Outliers can cause a dataset to appear to have a size–effort relationship, which is much stronger than it should be for the majority of data points.

C++ Sample

The R^2 of 0.62 for the C++ sample (including outliers) with 21 projects (not shown in the previous tables) could lead us to believe that the size–effort relationship is strong.

However, four outliers have a major and undue influence on the regression model of the full sample.

Excluding them leads to models indicating almost no size–effort relationship (R^2 of less than 0.10).

(Of course, this conclusion is valid only for this sample in this dataset, and should not be generalized to all C++ datasets.)

The subdivision of samples (with and without outliers) yields different linear models, as well as different strengths in the size–effort relationship.

For the Cobol II sample:

- R^2 is 0.45 for the 80–180 FP size interval and
- R^2 is 0.61 for the 181–500 FP size interval.

This gives managers more fine-tuned and more representative models of the information contained in the datasets.

We can see that the models in each sample vary considerably in the slope of the line representing the relationship with effort. The slopes vary from

- a low of 5.5 hours per Function Point for Telon (size interval: 70–650 FP) to
- a high of 26.7 hours per Function Point for Cobol II (size interval: 181–500 FP).

This would indicate that the variable cost is five times higher with Cobol II than with *Telon* for projects within approximately the same small size intervals.

- However, it should be observed that there are only six Cobol II projects in the 181–500 size interval, and that the fixed cost is negative for the Cobol II sample. This limits the lessons learned from such a comparison.

From the right-hand side of Table 9.3 (productivity models, excluding outliers), the samples can be classified into two groups with respect to their size–effort relationship:

(A) languages with an $R^2 >$ 0.70, representing a strong relationship between functional size and effort:

- Natural, for the size interval of 631–3500 FP and
- Telon, for the size interval of 70–650 FP.

(B) languages with an R^2 <0.70, representing a much weaker relationship between functional size and effort for the other programming languages and size intervals:

- Note that for some subsamples, there are not enough data points in the samples ($N < 20$) or their range intervals are much too large for the number of data points.

PL1 Sample

For PL1 with five data points between 451 and 2550 FP, the slope is reasonable and the fixed cost is negative (but minimal), but the R^2 of 0.86 can only be indicative and tentative, since the sample range is much too sparsely populated.

The performance of each regression model is analyzed in Table 9.4, with both the following quality criteria explained in greater detail in Chapter 6, Section 6.2.3:

- Relative Root Mean Square (RRMS) error and
- Prediction level PRED (0.25).

The best three models with an RRMS error <30% and a PRED(25%) greater than 55% are as follows:

- Cobol II [80, 180]
- PL1 [451, 2550]
- Telon [70, 650]

Table 9.3 Direct ISBSG Regression Models (with and Without Outliers)

| | Samples (including outliers) | | | | Samples without outliers and within size intervals | | | |
Language	No. of projects	Size interval	Productivity model (linear regression equation)	R^2	No. of projects	Functional size Interval	Productivity model (linear regression equation)	R^2
Cobol II	21	80–2000	$Y = 28 \times FP - 3593$	0.96	9	80–180	$Y = 16.4 \times FP - 92$	0.45
					6	181–500	$Y = 26.7 \times FP - 3340$	0.61
Natural	41	20–3500	$Y = 10 \times FP - 649$	0.85	30	20–620	$Y = 6.1 \times FP + 265$	0.47
					9	621–3500	$Y = 10.5 \times FP - 1405$	0.74
Oracle	26	100–4300	$Y = 6.2 \times FP + 510$	0.42	19	100–2000	$Y = 7.8 \times FP - 1281$	0.39
PL/1	29	80–2600	$Y = 11.1 \times FP + 47$	0.23	19	80–450	$Y = 8.3 \times FP - 198$	0.64
					5	451–2550	$Y = 5.5 \times FP - 65$	0.86
Telon	23	70–1100	$Y = 7.4 \times FP + 651$	0.85	18	70–650	$Y = 5.5 \times FP + 1046$	0.75

Abran et al. 2007. Reprinted with permission from John Wiley & Sons, Inc.

Table 9.4   Performance of ISBSG Regression Models (on Samples Excluding Outliers)

Programming languages and size intervals	RRMS(%)	PRED(0.25)
Cobol II [80, 180]	29	78
Cobol II [181, 500]	46	33
Natural [20, 620]	50	27
Natural [621, 3500]	35	33
Oracle [100, 2000]	120	21
PL1 [80, 450]	45	42
PL1 [451, 2550]	21	60
Telon [70, 650]	22	56

Abran et al. 2007. Reprinted with permission from John Wiley & Sons, Inc.

Sample of Projects Written in Natural Language

For the sample with Natural as the programming language, the RRMS indicates the following:

An overestimation/underestimation of 50% for the subsample of 30 small projects within the [20, 620] range, and of 35% for the sample of 9 projects within the [621, 3500] range, with a PRED (0.25) of 27% and 33%, respectively.

These levels of performance of the models are obtained from multi-organizational datasets, on the basis of

- a single independent variable (functional size),
- one fixed constraint on the programming language, and excluding obvious outliers in the samples,
- subdivision of the samples into two size intervals where warranted by a visual analysis of the samples on the basis of the potential size–effort relationship, and
- enough data points to warrant a subdivision of the samples.

In Tables 9.2 and 9.3, a number of models have a negative constant. In the context of productivity models, this suggests that further analysis can be carried out to investigate their practical meaning and what to do about this. The practical suggestions presented in the box in Section 2.4.1 are reproduced below for those who would like to carry out further analysis.

Linear Regression Models with a Negative Constant

Practical suggestions:

(A) Identify on the horizontal axis the size at which the model crosses this axis.

(B) Split the dataset into two subsets:

B1: a data size between 0 and the size threshold at the crossing point on the *x*-axis
B2: a data size greater than the threshold.

(C) Build two models for each subset (B1: for a data size smaller than the threshold; B2: for a data size greater than the threshold).

(D) For estimation purposes, select the B1 or B2 model, depending on the size of the project to be estimated.

9.6 SUMMARY

In this chapter, we have illustrated an engineering approach to building single-variable models based on

- analysis of data from completed projects,
- analysis of the relationship to effort, one variable at a time,
- segmentation of a large dataset into meaningful samples relevant for estimation purposes, that is:
  - excluding significant outliers
  - creating subsets of data taking into account the number of data points within size intervals.

Note: the construction of multivariable productivity models is presented in Chapter 10.

In the engineering approach, the objective is not a single productivity model, but models that provide information and not merely meaningless numbers.

To build these models, we used the repository of the ISBSG, and subdivided it to create samples, by programming language, with enough data points for statistical analysis. For each sample, a different size–effort relationship was observed. We also saw that the strength of this relationship differed by

  ▶ programming language and
  ▶ size interval and range.

- The directly derived models performed as well as the models built by other researchers for smaller and older multi-organizational datasets [Albrecht 1983; Kemerer 1987], and did so in similar conditions and for more recent software applications.

- For some programming languages, the relationship of the models was within the range reported in the literature (i.e., an R^2 of around 0.40) for multi-organizational datasets combining projects independently of their programming language.

These results illustrate that

- size, as measured with a functional size measurement method, is a major independent variable explaining a significant portion of the effort variation in projects in the MIS domain, which have been developed with the same programming language.

EXERCISES

1. How would you build a model using an engineering approach?
2. Why is it important to look at the descriptive statistics of a dataset before building a model? Use Table 9.1 to explain why this is important.
3. The data points in Figure 9.2b for the programming language COBOL II leads to a model with a very high R^2 of 0.96. Explain why this R^2 for this dataset is misleading.
4. If you have a large dataset of completed projects (such as in the ISBSG repository), how would you go about determining the impact of a single cost factor? Provide an example with a specific cost factor.
5. How do you recognize a project outlier in a dataset of completed projects?
6. What is the impact of project outliers on the quality of your models? What is the impact on your next project estimate when outliers are embedded within the initial model?
7. Look at Figure 9.3 and compare the three models. Which model is the best for estimating a project with an expected size of 400 FP?
8. In Table 9.3, there are a number of estimation equations with negative constants. How do you interpret this negative constant? What precaution(s) do you need to take when using models with negative constants?
9. Of the various models in Table 9.3, which have the lowest fixed costs in terms of effort, and which have the lowest variable costs in terms of effort?
10. On the basis of Table 9.4, which is better for estimation purposes, a higher RRMS or a lower PRED(0.25)?

TERM ASSIGNMENTS

1. If your organization does not have a repository of completed projects, how can you test the relevance for your organization of using an external dataset (such as the ISBSG, or any other similar repository) in your organization? What would you recommend to an organization in such a context?
2. Think back over the past three projects you worked on. What are the 3–5 cost factors that had the most impact on the difference in productivity on those projects? List another 10 cost factors. What was the relative importance of the 5 most important cost factors in explaining project productivity (as compared to the other 10 you listed)?

3. Benchmark your organization's productivity model with a set of comparable projects from the ISBSG repository.

4. Select, using criteria of your choice, a subset of data from the ISBSG repository. What is the shape of the resulting graphical representation (with the Functional Size and Effort variables)? Explain.

5. Three major steps are recommended for building productivity models based on historical data: data preparation, application of statistical tools, and data analysis. Document how these steps have been applied within your own organization.

6. If your organization has not built a productivity model based on past projects, select a model proposed in the literature and carry out a similar analysis. Which step is particularly weak and which is particularly strong?

7. Select a model documented in the literature and built from a statistical analysis. How were outliers handled in the data preparation and in the statistical analyses?

Chapter 10

Building Models with Categorical Variables[1]

OBJECTIVES

This chapter covers

- How to build models using multiple variables
- How to define categorical variables in a simple way
- How data from an industrial case study are used to illustrate the contribution of an additional variable in deriving multiple models from a single dataset

10.1 INTRODUCTION

Productivity models are based on the generic concept of productivity defined as the ratio of the amount of outputs produced over the amount of units of inputs to produce them

Software size is recognized as a key factor in the construction of models estimating project effort. In addition, many other factors can influence project effort. For instance

- ▶ the need for a full system test,
- ▶ severe constraints on resource availability,
- ▶ functional complexity,
- ▶ technical complexity,
- ▶ a low or high level of reuse,
- ▶ and so on.

[1]See also Abran, A.; Silva, I.; Primera, L. (2002), *"Field Studies Using Functional Size Measurement in Building Estimation Models for Software Maintenance"*, Journal of Software Maintenance and Evolution: Research and Practice, Vol. 14, pp. 31–64.

Software Project Estimation: The Fundamentals for Providing High Quality Information to Decision Makers, First Edition. Alain Abran.
© 2015 the IEEE Computer Society. Published 2015 by John Wiley & Sons, Inc.

Typically, the datasets available to researchers and practitioners are too small for all these independent variables to be investigated simultaneously. Even the 2013 release of the ISBSG repository with over 6000 projects is much too small to analyze all of its over 100 variables at the same time.

▶ For example, for the nonmandatory fields in the ISBSG repository, there is typically a very large number of missing values, which leads to a fairly small number of data points with the information required for the statistical analysis.

Furthermore, many of the variables of interest in such repositories are not expressed in a quantitative manner, but rather by category:

▶ Development methodology

▶ Development platform

▶ Database management system

▶ Business area

▶ Application type

▶ And so on.

This chapter presents an approach to building multivariable models, including nonquantitative ones. The approach is presented through the analysis of a dataset documented in Abran et al. [2002].

This chapter is structured as follows:

• Section 10.2 presents the dataset available.

• Section 10.3 introduces the initial model with a single variable, size.

• Section 10.4 presents regression models with two independent variables.

10.2   THE AVAILABLE DATASET

The dataset used for building the productivity models presented in this chapter comes from a single organization which designs, develops, and implements systems for the defense industry.

• This organization is a subsidiary of an international organization, and the software unit of this organization develops and maintains real-time embedded software.

In this context, the projects measured and analyzed were carried out on the same software application, and consisted of adding and modifying the functionality of that application. This means, therefore, that a number of specific factors were held constant, some of which are as follows:

• Software application

• Software domain

• Development and exploitation environment (platform, DBMS, testing tools, etc.)

- Programming language
- Enhancement methodology
- And so on.

Therefore, compared to multi-organizational datasets such as the ISBSG repository, this dataset has considerably more homogeneity with respect to both the application domain and the technological environment.

- This means that, in this specific context and for our purposes here, these factors can be considered to be held constant and not influence the relationship to effort.

The size of the functionality (added or modified) of the projects was measured with the COSMIC functional size method.

- In the context of addition/modification to the functionality of existing software, the COSMIC functional size of a change to the Functional User Requirements within each piece of software is calculated by aggregating the sizes of the corresponding data movements impacted, according to the following formula:

$$\text{Size}_{\text{CFP}}(\text{Change}) = \sum \text{size}(\text{added data movement}_i)$$
$$+ \sum \text{size}(\text{changed data movement}_i)$$
$$+ \sum \text{size}(\text{deleted data movement}_i)$$

The work effort (in person-hours) was obtained from the organization's time reporting system, which made it possible to identify the effort expended on each specific functional enhancement project.

For some of the projects, the effort expended on the analysis phase of a project was not recorded. Therefore, only the effort expended, excluding analysis, on all the projects was taken into account to ensure consistency of the data recorded for this independent variable.

This industrial dataset included information on 21 enhancement projects implementing functional enhancements to the software components of the defense system. Two outliers were identified, and then removed, using both visual analysis and the statistical tests reported in Chapter 5, Section 5.4.2.

Visual analysis (Figure 10.1) of the remaining 19 projects without outliers in this dataset suggests that there is a positive correlation between an increase in functional size and the increase in effort, even though this correlation appears to be weak.

In addition, we can see that there is some degree of heteroskedasticity in this dataset (the data are wedge-shaped), which suggests that regression models with only a single variable would not necessarily be very good models.

- Such a distribution shape provides a clue that there is, for this organization, at least one other important variable which has significant impact on project effort.

Effort (hours)

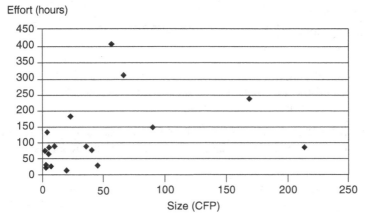

Figure 10.1 Data Graph – Excluding Two Outliers ($N = 19$) [Abran et al. 2002. Reprinted with permission from John Wiley & Sons, Inc.]

10.3 INITIAL MODEL WITH A SINGLE INDEPENDENT VARIABLE

10.3.1 Simple Linear Regression Model with Functional Size Only

The linear regression model with functional size as the independent variable gives the following linear equation for the sample of 19 observations (Figure 10.2):

$$\text{Effort} = 0.61 \times \text{CFP} + 91 \text{ hours } (R^2 = 0.12; n = 19)$$

This linear model is not strongly positive, with an R^2 of only 0.12, which means that

- only 12% of the total variability of the effort in the projects is explained by the variation in its functional size, as measured in CFP.

10.3.2 Nonlinear Regression Models with Functional Size

Other forms of regression model were investigated, and these results are presented in Table 10.1, where R is the coefficient of correlation between the actual values of Y and the values derived from the equation. The nonlinear models developed are

- power,
- exponential,

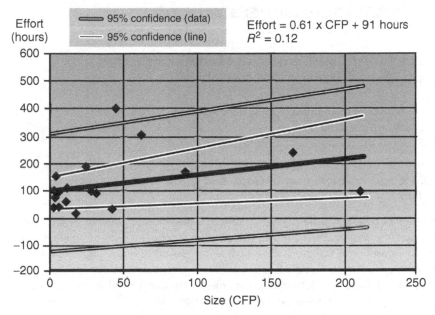

Figure 10.2   Linear Regression ($N = 19$) [Abran et al. 2002. Reprinted with permission from John Wiley & Sons, Inc.]

Table 10.1   Nonlinear Regression Models ($N = 19$)

		N	A	B	R	R^2
$Y = A \times X^B$	Power	19	43.808	0.245	0.50	0.245
$Y = A \times e^{(B \times X)}$	Exponential	19	63.067	0.006	0.39	0.15
$Y = A + B \times \ln(X)$	Logarithmic	19	44.121	29.29	0.51	0.26
$Y = A + B/X$	Hyperbolic 1	19	132.463	−48.330	0.32	0.10
$Y = 1/(A + (B \times X))$	Hyperbolic 2	19	0.022	−8.8E-05	0.31	0.09

Abran et al. 2002. Reprinted with permission from John Wiley & Sons, Inc.

- logarithmic, and
- two forms of hyperbolic model.

High values of R (maximum $= 1.0$) indicate a high correlation, and R^2 is the percentage of the variance of the dependent variable, which can be explained by the given equation.

From Table 10.1, we can see that none of the nonlinear regression models represents a significant improvement over the linear model.

10.4 REGRESSION MODELS WITH TWO INDEPENDENT VARIABLES

10.4.1 Multiple Regression Models with Two Independent Quantitative Variables

Regression models with multiple independent variables (functional size and another variable) are investigated next to analyze how these additional variables contribute individually to the relationship between size and effort.

The Second Variable: Lines of Code and Number of Programs Modified

A second independent quantitative variable, such as the total number of CFP for an application, the total number of lines of code, the number of lines of code modified, or the total number of programs modified, is introduced in linear regression models of the form $y = ax + bz + c$.

For this dataset, the introduction of these quantitative independent variables does not bring about significant improvement in the explanatory power of regression models.

For example, the model with two independent variables (functional size and number of programs modified) is

$$Y = a \times \text{CFP} + b \times (\text{no. of programs modified}) + c$$

$$Y = 0.78 \times \text{CFP} - 3.62 \times (\text{no. of programs modified}) + 98$$

- This multiple regression model with the number of programs modified has the same R^2 value, 0.12, which is not an improvement over the simple linear regression model.

10.4.2 Multiple Regression Models with a Categorical Variable: Project Difficulty

A Categorical Variable as the Second Project Variable

The second independent variable selected to attempt to improve the models is project *difficulty*.

Since there is no accepted definition of project difficulty, nor is there a recognized way to measure this variable quantitatively, four levels of project difficulty have been defined:

- Not difficult
- Difficult
- Very difficult
- Extremely difficult.

This variable is therefore defined as a categorical value with an ordinal scale (from not difficult to extremely difficult).

The level of project difficulty for each of the enhancement projects was assigned by the staff who had carried out those projects.

- The staff performed this assignment on the basis of project documentation and their own experience.

  ▶ In industry, this is referred to as assignment of values by *subject matter experts*.

The use of these four initial difficulty levels in a sample of this size (19 observations) is problematic from a statistical viewpoint, as there are insufficient data observations for certain difficulty values (only one or two observations), which means that some difficulty categories will not be representative enough for building productivity models.

A simpler classification of a categorical variable would be desirable.

- To achieve this, the difficulty variable with four levels was reclassified into a two-level classification: low difficulty and high difficulty.

Additive Form for the Second Variable   Even though categorical variables are not quantitative variables, they can still be taken into account in regression models through the addition of dummy variables (one for each of the groups of categorical variables). This is illustrated below.

The next regression model constructed takes into account the low to high level of the difficulty of the categorical factor in the following way:

$$\text{Difficulty} = 1, \text{ for a high level}$$

$$\text{Difficulty} = 0, \text{ for a low level}$$

An additive model with the low to high difficulty factor gives each level the same importance in the relationship between size and work effort, and takes the following form:

$$y = ax + bz + c$$

where

$$\text{if } z = 0 \rightarrow y = ax + c, \text{ or,}$$

$$\text{if } z = 1 \rightarrow y = ax + (b + c)$$

For this sample of 19 projects, the general form of the model is

$$\text{Effort} = 0.92 \times \text{CFP} + 126 \times \text{difficulty} + 26$$

with an R^2 of 0.46

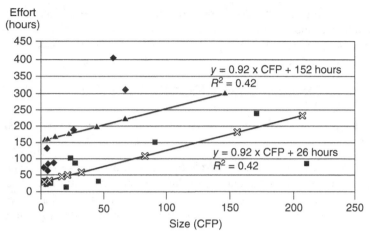

Figure 10.3   Additive Model ($N = 19$) [Abran et al. 2002. Reprinted with permission from John Wiley & Sons, Inc.]

When taking the low to high difficulty level into account, the following two models, as illustrated in Figure 10.3, are obtained:

If Difficulty $= 0 \rightarrow$ Effort $= 0.92\,\text{CFP} + 26$ hours.

If Difficulty $= 1 \rightarrow$ Effort $= 0.92\,\text{CFP} + 126 + 26 = 0.92\,\text{CFP} + 152$.

This model, with the difficulty level variable, has a coefficient of determination $R^2 = 0.46$, which is better than that of the simple linear regression model, but still not good enough.

As we can see in Figure 10.3, the two regression lines have

- the same slope (0.92).

They are represented by parallel lines and have

- different points at the origin when CFP $= 0$ (i.e., 26 hours when the level of project difficulty is low, and 152 hours when the level of project difficulty is high).

This is typical of additive models.

In Figure 10.3, the square points represent the projects categorized as low-difficulty projects, and the losange points, those categorized as high-difficulty projects.

Multiple Regression Model: Multiplicative Form   With the additive model, the size effect is considered independently of the low to high difficulty variable. To take this size effect into account, a new variable is added, that is

- the interaction of difficulty and size, as represented by the multiplication of the two variables as follows:
  ▶ (Difficulty × CFP)

  Including the variable in the model makes it possible to recognize the multiplicative impact of these two variables on the positive relation between size and effort.
- Of course, it will eliminate the parallelism of the two lines in the additive model.

The general form of the multiplicative model becomes

$Y = \alpha X + \beta Z + \gamma(X \times Z) + \mu$, that is,

Effort $= \alpha\, \text{CFP} + \beta\, \text{Difficulty} + \gamma(\text{CFP} \times \text{Difficulty}) + \mu$

If difficulty $= 0 \rightarrow$ Effort $= \alpha\text{CFP} + \mu$.

If difficulty $= 1 \rightarrow$ Effort $= (\alpha + \gamma)\text{CFP} + (\mu + \beta)$.

The difficulty variable, represented by γ, has an influence on the behavior of the size variable CFP, modifying the slope and the constant of the regression line during the analysis of its values of 0 and 1.

The general multiple linear regression equation obtained is

Effort $= 0.64\, \text{CFP} + 41.94\, \text{Difficulty} + 3.85(\text{Difficulty} \times \text{CFP}) + 41$

with $R^2 = 0.75$

- This multiplicative model has a coefficient of determination $R^2 = 0.75$, which is a significant improvement over both the model with one variable and the additive model with two independent variables.
- Furthermore, the coefficient of the categorical variable linked to both difficulty and size is statistically significant, that is, it has a p value < 0.05.

The specific equations for each difficulty level are as follows:

If difficulty $= 0 \rightarrow$ Effort $= 0.64 \times \text{CFP} + 42$ with $R^2 = 0.47$ and $n = 8$.

If difficulty $= 1 \rightarrow$ Effort $= 4.49 \times \text{CFP} + 83$ with $R^2 = 0.78$ and $n = 11$.

These equations, which are presented in Figure 10.4, clearly illustrate that the effort level of projects depends on both their functional size and their level of difficulty as significant variables to be taken into account during estimation.

In addition, the graphical analysis in Figures 10.3 and 10.4 shows that the largest project in terms of size (216 CFP for project no. 1) is classified in the low-difficulty category, and has a much lower level of effort than smaller projects, which is not consistent with the balance of the dataset.

- The behavior of project no. 1 could be considered to be significantly different from the others in terms of some unspecified factor.

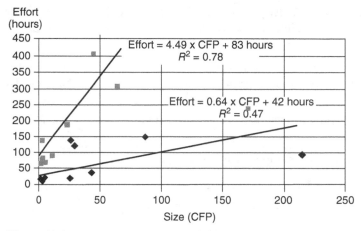

Figure 10.4   Multiplicative Model ($N = 19$) [Abran et al. 2002. Reprinted with permission from John Wiley & Sons, Inc.]

▶ It could, therefore, be excluded from the sample and reserved for further analysis to verify its impact on the multiplicative model.

On this reduced sample of 18 projects, we apply the general multiplicative model given by $(Y = \alpha\,X + \beta\,Z + \gamma\,(X \times Z) + \mu)$, which gives

$$\text{Effort} = 1.25 \times \text{CFP} + 56 \times \text{Difficulty} + 3.24 \times (\text{Difficulty} \times \text{CFP}) + 27$$

with $R^2 = 0.84$ and $n = 18$

The specific models for each difficulty class are then as follows:

If difficulty $= 0 \rightarrow$ Effort $= 1.25$ CFP $+ 27$ with $R^2 = 0.87$ and $n = 8$.

If difficulty $= 1 \rightarrow$ Effort $= 4.49$ CFP $+ 83$ with $R^2 = 0.78$ and $n = 10$.

With a regression coefficient $R^2 = 0.84$, this model is better than the previous one, and the CFP variable is statistically significant with a p value <0.05, as is the multiplicative term of both variables (Figure 10.5).

Table 10.2 presents a comparison of the results of the multiplicative models for sample $N = 19$ and sample $N = 18$.

In addition to the improvement in the regression coefficient (R^2) from 0.75 to 0.84, the MMRE has dropped from 0.51 to 0.40 (i.e., the lower the MMRE, the better)

- PRED(25%) is still higher than the 25% recommended by Conte [1986] with a PRED(25%) of 56% for 10 projects.
- This is a significant improvement, with some other projects fairly close to this level.
  ▶ With PRED(35%), 77% of the projects are inside this interval, which is quite good in the context of software enhancements, where there could be

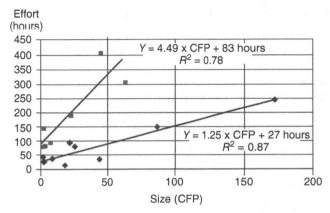

Figure 10.5   Multiplicative Model ($N = 18$) [Abran et al. 2002. Reprinted with permission from John Wiley & Sons, Inc.]

Table 10.2   Comparison of Model Quality Criteria

Model (sample size)	R^2	MMRE (%)	PRED(±25%)		PRED(±30%)		PRED(±35%)	
			No. of projects	%	No. of projects	%	No. of projects	%
Multiplicative ($N = 19$)	0.75	0.51	10	52.6	12	63.2	14	73.7
Multiplicative ($N = 18$)	0.84	0.40	10	55.5	12	66.7	14	77.8

Abran et al. 2002. Reprinted with permission from John Wiley & Sons, Inc.

considerable variation because of the involvement of individuals that is not mitigated by a team balanced by management in the case of larger development projects.

10.4.3   The Interaction of Independent Variables

It should be observed that this way of adding each individual impact of the set of cost drivers as independent variables is based on the assumption that these cost drivers are independent of one another and that there are no relationships across factors.

- In practice, most of these factors may have a cross impact on effort, which should be taken into account in building models.

There are statistical techniques to isolate and quantify the cross impact of multiple variables.

For instance, models with two factors would be of the form

$$\text{Effort} = a \times (\text{Size} \times \text{F1}) + b \times (\text{Size} \times \text{F2}) + c \times (\text{Size} \times \text{F}_1\text{F}_2) + d$$

where c represents the impact of the combined interaction of F1 and F_2, and, when there is no interaction between F1 and F2

$$\text{Effort} = a \times (\text{Size} \times \text{F1}) + b \times (\text{Size} \times \text{F2}) + d$$

EXERCISES

ID number	Effort (hours)	Total functional size of the program (CFP)	Functional size of the modification (CFP$_{modified}$)	Difficulty rating (2-level: Low, High)
1	88	360	216	L
2	956	984	618	L
3	148	123	89	L
4	66	40	3	H
5	83	16	3	H
6	34	18	7	L
7	96	120	21	L
8	84	88	25	L
9	31	151	42	L
10	409	75	46	H
11	30	36	2	L
12	140	7	2	H
13	308	125	67	H
14	244	232	173	L
15	188	53	25	H
16	34	44	1	L
17	73	22	1	H
18	27	6	1	L
19	91	53	8	H
20	13	37	19	L
21	724	248	157	–

1. Discuss the difference between a quantitative variable, a categorical variable, and a nominative variable. Discuss how you can correctly handle each of these types of variable in a regression model.

2. The table presented above represents the full dataset of the case study presented in this chapter. Identify the projects considered as outliers, using both graphical analysis and statistical tests.

3. Delete the five largest projects. What is the impact of this on the linear regression model? Delete the five smallest projects. What is the impact of this on the linear regression model? Comment on the difference between these various regression models. On the basis of what you observed, what would you recommend to your management; that is, what productivity model should be used, and under what conditions?

4. Repeat Exercise 3, this time using an exponential regression technique.

5. Change the project difficulty category of project 10 (from high to low), and rerun the additive and multiplicative regression models.

6. Build a multiplicative regression model taking into account both the quantitative variables: the total size of programs (column 3) and the size of the modified functionality (column 4).

TERM ASSIGNMENTS

1. Using project data collected in your organization, identify categorical variables and build both additive and multiplicative regression models.

2. Using project data from the ISBSG, identify categorical variables and build both additive and multiplicative regression models.

Chapter 11

Contribution of Productivity Extremes in Estimation

OBJECTIVES

This chapter covers

- Identification of large productivity ranges in datasets
- Investigation of projects with very low unit effort
- Investigation of projects with very large unit effort
- How to use such information for estimation purposes

11.1 INTRODUCTION[1]

At times, software project productivity can vary considerably: one project may require much more effort than another of comparable functional size. Such projects do exist, and the next one may be just around the corner.

Can they be identified early on, so that the necessary budgeting precautions can be taken at estimation time?

For estimation purposes, it is of the utmost importance to identify large productivity variations in software project repositories and to analyze the causes of such significant variations in order to be able to explain why the productivity of these projects is much higher or much lower.

- If these causes (i.e., the cost drivers as independent variables) can be identified early on in the project life cycle, they can be introduced into the estimation

---

[1]For more information, see: Paré, D., Abran, A., "Obvious Outliers in the ISBSG Repository of Software Projects: Exploratory Research," Metrics News, Otto Von Gueriske Universitat, Magdeburg (Germany), vol. 10, no. 1, August 2005, pp. 28–36 [Paré 2005].

---

process either as additional independent variables or as adjustments with significant effort impact.

To discuss this issue, this chapter uses the ISBSG repository for the following tasks:

- Identification of projects which have significantly different productivity behaviors from those of most other projects.

- Discovery of factors that have such a strong influence (positive or negative) on the productivity of these projects.

The criterion for identifying such projects is whether productivity is considerably lower or higher, that is, with very low or high unit effort.

Once these projects can be identified, other project variables can be investigated by heuristics to identify candidate explanatory variables that might explain the behaviors of those projects at the extremes of the productivity ranges within similar size intervals.

This chapter is structured as follows:

- Section 11.2 shows how to identify productivity extremes.

- Section 11.3 provides the findings of an analysis of productivity extremes.

- Section 11.4 presents some lessons learned that can be used in the adjustment phase to support decision-making.

11.2 IDENTIFICATION OF PRODUCTIVITY EXTREMES

Figure 11.1 presents 118 projects programmed in C, from ISBSG R9: the functional size in function points (FP) is on the x-axis and the effort in hours is on the y-axis.

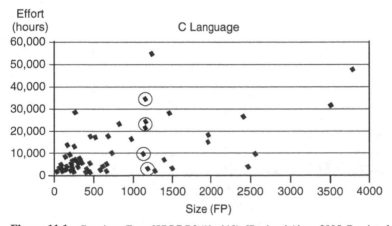

Figure 11.1   C projects From ISBSG R9 ($N = 118$) [Paré and Abran 2005. Reprinted with permission from Otto von Gueriske Universitat, Magdeburg, Germany]

In this figure, we can see that, for a similar functional size of approximately 1300 FP, some projects (identified with red circles) may have a very low effort (a few hundreds of hours) while others have orders of magnitude more effort required (from 20,000 to 30,000 hours); that is, a number of projects have either a very high productivity or very low productivity for an equivalent size.

Figure 11.2 shows some Cobol 2 projects from ISBSG R9. For illustrative purposes, 15 projects have been circled, because they have very low effort for their size (within a functional size range of 500–2500 FP), and they did not cost more than many projects 10–20 times smaller:

- This means that these projects benefited from very high unit effort (by a factor in the 10–20 range).

It is obvious that a number of other cost drivers (independent variables) could explain the minimal effort expended on these projects.

11.3 INVESTIGATION OF PRODUCTIVITY EXTREMES

Once the projects at the extremes of the productivity ranges have been identified, they can be compared to other projects of similar size or effort, to explore whether or not there are other variables recorded that might explain the size–effort relationship of such projects.

For the analysis of the ISBSG repository, various tests selected by heuristics were carried out on some of the variables available in the ISBSG repository.

- Only eight variables yielded results that enabled a practical interpretation leading to the formulation of candidate explanatory variables for the productivity extremes. These are discussed next by looking first at projects with very low unit effort, and second, at projects with very high unit effort.

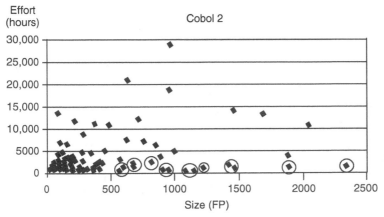

Figure 11.2   Projects with Very Low Unit Effort – (ISBSG R9, Cobol 2) $N = 115$ [Paré and Abran 2005. Reprinted with permission from Otto von Gueriske Universitat, Magdeburg, Germany]

Table 11.1 Explanatory Variables for Very Low Unit Effort for C Projects (ISBSG R9, $N = 118$)

Variable analyzed	Value observed in the variable analyzed	Extreme projects with the value observed (ratio and %)	Non-extreme projects with the value observed (ratio and %)
O/S	AIX	**3/7** (43)	**4/89** (4)
Primary DBMS	Sysbase	**4/7** (57)	**4/111** (4)

Paré and Abran 2005. Reprinted with permission from Otto von Gueriske Universitat, Magdeburg, Germany.

Table 11.2 Explanatory Variable for Very Low Unit Effort for Cobol 2 Projects (R9, $N = 115$)

Variable analyzed	Value observed	Extreme projects with the value observed (ratio and %)	Non-extreme projects with the value observed (ratio and %)
DQR	D	**13/14** (93)	**8/101** (8)
RL	2	**14/14** (100)	**36/101** (36)
Organization type	Insurance	**14/14** (100)	**21/101** (21)
Reference table approach	Counted as inputs	**14/14** (100)	**21/101** (21)

Paré and Abran 2005. Reprinted with permission from Otto von Gueriske Universitat, Magdeburg, Germany.

11.3.1 Projects with Very Low Unit Effort

Tables 11.1 and 11.2 present several variables that have been identified by heuristics as partially responsible for the behavior of these projects in terms of productivity extremes. These variables are as follows:

1. The operating system (O/S) on which the software measured runs.
2. The primary database management system (DBMS) for the software measured.
3. The Data Quality Rating (DQR), as evaluated by the ISBSG repository manager – see Chapter 8, Table 8.5 for definitions.
4. The resource level (RL): the personnel recording the effort – see Chapter 8, Table 8.1 for definitions.
5. The type of organization that sent the data.
6. The reference table approach: the IFPUG Function Points version used to count the tables of codes in the software.[2]

---

[2]This is a peculiarity of the IFPUG method: Depending on which IFPUG version is selected for the measurement of tables of code, there can be large differences in the numbers of Function Points.

In these tables

- the variables tested by heuristics are in the left-hand side column,
- the value most often observed in these projects for the variable tested are in the next column,
- the other two columns on the right-hand side present the number of observations of the observed value over the full sample[3]:
  - ▶ the middle column: within the subset of extreme projects and
  - ▶ the right-most column: within the sample, but excluding the extreme projects.

C Projects with Very Low Unit Effort

For the sample with the projects in C, there are two candidate explanatory variables for the very low unit effort (Table 11.1) as follows:

- The AIX Operating System, which appears in 47% of the extreme projects and in only 4% of the non-extreme projects.
- Sysbase as the primary DBMS, which appears in 57% of the extreme projects and in only 4% of the non-extreme projects.

COBOL 2 Projects with Very Low Unit Effort

For the sample of projects in Cobol 2, there are four candidate explanatory variables for the very low unit effort projects (Table 11.2). For instance, almost all the projects with the very low unit effort share the same values for the four variables identified (middle column of Table 11.2):

- Thirteen out of fourteen (i.e., 93%) have a poor DQR (i.e., DQR = D).
- Effort RL = 2 (i.e., it includes hours for both direct development staff and support staff).
- Organization type = Insurance.
- The IFPUG version used for size measurement takes into account each code table as an External Input.

In contrast, for the 101 projects considered to be non-extreme (Table 11.2, right-most column), these characteristics are much less common: from 8% to 36% of the projects.

11.3.2   Projects with Very High Unit Effort

In this section, we look at projects with very high unit effort in Java, Cobol, C, and SQL.

---

[3]Out of the 118 C projects, only 7 + 89 = 96 had information in the O/S field.

In Tables 11.3–11.6, four variables have been identified by heuristics as partially responsible for the behavior of these projects in terms of project productivity ratios. The ISBSG definitions of these variables are as follows:

- Standard FP: IFPUG standard used to count Function Points.
- Max Team Size: Maximum number of people who worked on the project at the same time (peak time).
- Resource Level (RL) – see Chapter 8, Table 8.5 for definitions.
- Project Elapsed Time (PET): Duration, in months, to complete the development of the project.

For the Java, Cobol, and C samples, a single discriminative variable has been identified by heuristics for very high unit effort, that is

- the IFPUG version 4 variable for the Java projects (Table 11.3) and
- a Max Team Size of more than 10 people for the Cobol and C projects (Tables 11.4 and 11.5).

Finally, in Table 11.6 for the SQL sample, the two most discriminative variables for very high unit effort are

Table 11.3 Very High Unit Effort for Java, R9 projects ($N = 24$)

Variable tested	Value observed	Ratio of extreme projects	Ratio of non-extreme projects
FP Standard	IFPUG version 4	**4/4** (100%)	**2/20** (10%)

Paré and Abran 2005. Reprinted with permission from Otto von Gueriske Universitat, Magdeburg, Germany.

Table 11.4 Very High Unit Effort for Cobol, R8 Projects ($N = 412$)

Variable tested	Value observed	Ratio of extreme projects	Ratio of non-extreme projects
Max Team Size	>10	**5/7** (71%)	**27/405** (7%)

Paré and Abran 2005. Reprinted with permission from Otto von Gueriske Universitat, Magdeburg, Germany.

Table 11.5 Very High Unit Effort for C, R9 Projects ($N = 16$)

Variable tested	Value observed	Ratio of extreme projects	Ratio of non-extreme projects
Max Team Size	>10	3/4 (75%)	3/12 (25%)

Paré and Abran 2005. Reprinted with permission from Otto von Gueriske Universitat, Magdeburg, Germany.

Table 11.6   High Unit Effort of Scale for SQL, R9 projects ($N = 26$)

Variable tested	Value observed	Ratio of extreme projects	Ratio of non-extreme projects
RL	>2	3/4 (75%)	1/22 (4%)
PET	>15 months	3/4 (75%)	2/22 (9%)

Paré and Abran 2005. Reprinted with permission from Otto von Gueriske Universitat, Magdeburg, Germany.

- a Resource Level greater than 2, that is, with a resource level that includes customers and users, and
- a Project Elapsed Time of over 15 months.

11.4 LESSONS LEARNED FOR ESTIMATION PURPOSES

In many software engineering datasets, there are some projects that have had either very low unit effort or very high unit effort: it is obvious that there are some cost drivers (i.e., independent variables) at work that lead to such large productivity variations. Some very important lessons for estimation purposes can be learned if the causes of these variations can be identified. For instance, in the previous analyses of R9 of the ISBSG repository, the criteria used for the identification of extreme projects were whether productivity is significantly lower (high unit effort) or higher (low unit effort) in relatively homogeneous samples.

Once the extreme projects had been identified, other project variables were investigated by heuristics to identify candidate explanatory variables that might explain the behaviors of these projects.

Candidate variables identified as potentially related to *low unit effort* in the ISBSG repository for some programming languages were identified as follows:

- Resource Level 2 (i.e., including only development and support staff).
- Insurance as the organization type.
- The peculiarity of the reference table approach in the IFPUG Function Points sizing method (which "inflates" size, artificially improving the productivity ratio).
- The D rating for data quality.

Candidate variables identified as potentially related to *high unit effort* in the ISBSG repository for some programming languages were identified as follows:

- A Maximum Team Size of more than 10 people.
- A Project Elapsed Time greater than 15 months.
- Effort data which include not only development and support staff, but also operators' and customers' project-related effort (i.e., effort level >2).

The specific version of the IFPUG Function Points method is also a variable identified as a candidate explanatory variable.

Of course, this list of candidate explanatory variables is far from exhaustive. Further analyses are required:

- on the one hand, using more robust methods for identifying these extreme projects in a systematic manner and
- on the other hand, for investigating the causes of the behaviors of these extreme projects.

These analyses will be challenging and time-consuming.

Practitioners can, however, derive immediate benefits from this information in the following way:

- Monitoring the candidate explanatory variables can provide valuable clues for early detection of potentially extreme projects for which the most probable estimates should be selected:
  - ▶ not within a close range of values predicted by a productivity model,
  - ▶ *but rather at their upper or lower limits.*

By this we mean that *either the most optimistic or the most pessimistic value* that can be predicted by the productivity model used *should be selected.* Such projects do exist, and there may be one right around the corner in any organization. It is clearly important not to be caught with an estimate that would need to be tripled or quadrupled later on!

EXERCISES

1. In Figure 11.1, what is the range of variation of productivity for projects of a similar size of around 700 FP?
2. In Figure 11.2, what is the range of variation of productivity for projects of a similar size, around 1000 FP?
3. Do the projects circled in red in Figure 11.2 exhibit low or high unit effort?
4. In Figure 11.1, which candidate variables are identified as candidate factors of very low or very high unit effort for the projects in C?
5. In Table 11.6, which candidate variables are identified as candidate factors for high unit effort for the SQL projects?
6. Are the variables identified as candidate factors in Question 5 known only at the end of the project? Or, by contrast, are they known up front? If the latter, how can you integrate these factors into your risk analysis and estimation process?

TERM ASSIGNMENTS

1. Select a dataset documented in the literature (or from the ISBSG repository). Represent it graphically and identify the ranges of productivity.

2. Study the dataset from your organization. Select the most productive project and the least productive one. What is the difference in productivity? What are the most obvious factors influencing the most productive one and the least productive one?

3. You have identified a few key factors in your responses to Exercise 4 that have a major impact on productivity (for either very high or very low productivity). Are these factors known only at the end of the project, or are they known up front? If the latter, how can you integrate these factors into your risk analysis and estimation process? On the basis of your findings, propose an enhancement to your organization's estimation process.

4. Select samples from the ISBSG repository. Compare them in terms of their extremes in unit effort.

5. Using the samples from the previous exercise, compare the factors of the extreme projects and identify factors common to projects with very low or very high unit effort.

Chapter 12

Multiple Models from a Single Dataset

OBJECTIVES

This chapter presents an example with real data to illustrate

- The analysis of data based on economics concepts, with fixed effort and with variable effort
- The identification of the productivity capability of an organization
- The impact of major risk factors on productivity for an organization
- Comparison of the projects of this single organization with comparable projects from the ISBSG repository

12.1 INTRODUCTION[1]

The classical approach to developing productivity models in software engineering is to build a single productivity model and include as many cost factors (i.e., independent variables) in it as possible. An alternative to this search for a single productivity model that would be ideal in all circumstances is to look for a number of simpler models which would better reflect the major variations in an organization's performance in terms of fixed and variable costs.

In Chapter 2, we looked at some concepts from the field of economics (such as fixed/variable costs and economies/diseconomies of scale) to identify a new approach to software benchmarking and estimation. This chapter 12 reports on an empirical study that explored the contribution of these economics concepts in developing

---

[1]For more information, see Abran, Desharnais, Zarour, Demirors, "Productivity Based Software Estimation Model: An Economics Perspective and an Empirical Study, 9th International Conference on Software Engineering Advances – ICSEA 2014, Publisher IARA, Oct. 12–16, 2014, Nice (France), pp. 291–201.

---

tailor-made productivity models representing the performance of the major processes within the organization studied.

This chapter is organized as follows:

- Section 12.2 provides a summary of concepts of production models, including fixed and variable costs, as well as economies and diseconomies of scale.

- Section 12.3 describes an example of an empirical study conducted using many of the data collection procedures recommended in Part 2 of this book.

- Section 12.4 provides a descriptive analysis of the data collected in this dataset.

- Section 12.5 presents the multiple productivity models identified from this single dataset.

- Section 12.6 provides an external benchmarking analysis using comparable data from the ISBSG repository.

- Section 12.7 identifies adjustment factors that have a positive or negative impact on productivity.

12.2 LOW AND HIGH SENSITIVITY TO FUNCTIONAL SIZE INCREASES: MULTIPLE MODELS

When the increase in output units requires a correspondingly smaller increase in the number of input units, the production process is said to benefit from economies of scale: the larger the number of units produced, the more productive the production process becomes.

By contrast, when an increase in output units requires a larger increase in the number of units for each additional output, then the production process is said to exhibit diseconomies of scale. Each additional unit produced reduces the productivity.

Here, we revisit a pattern of software projects in the form of a wedge-shaped dataset which is often encountered, and assume that the dataset is free from statistical outliers – see Figure 12.1. When looked at with the analytical grid of the concepts of low and high sensitivity to size, this single wedge-shaped dataset can be decomposed into three subsets as follows – see Figure 12.2 (same as Figure 2.19):

- Zone 1: The lower part of the dataset, which is populated with a subset of projects demonstrating little sensitivity to increases in size. In fact, for this subset, even large increases in size do not lead to corresponding increases in effort that are noticeably large. In practice, it is as if, in this subset, the effort required is almost insensitive to an increase in the number of functions in the software being developed.

- Zone 3: The upper part of the dataset, which is populated with a subset of projects demonstrating high sensitivity with respect to functional size as the independent variable (that is, a small increase in size requires a much larger increase in effort – in either fixed or variable costs, or both).

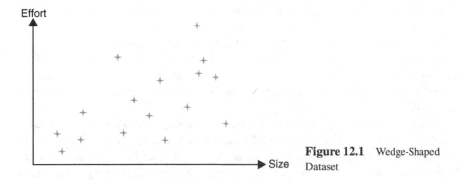

Figure 12.1   Wedge-Shaped Dataset

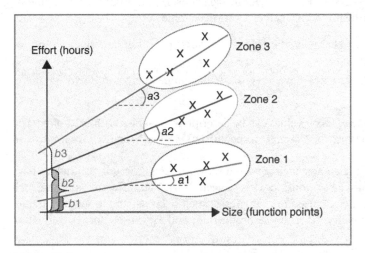

Figure 12.2   Data Subsets with Distinct Sensitivities to Increases in Functional Size
[Abran and Cuadrado 2009. Reprinted with permission from Knowledge Systems Institute Graduate School]

- Zone 2: Finally, there is sometimes a third subset, which lies somewhere in the middle range of the dataset.

These data points may then be representative of three distinct production processes – and their corresponding distinct models (often referred to as "productivity models" in the software engineering literature):

- $f_1(x) = a_1 * x + b_1$, which corresponds to a data sample in Zone 1.
- $f_2(x) = a_2 * x + b_2$, which corresponds to a data sample in Zone 2.
- $f_3(x) = a_3 * x + b_3$, which corresponds to a data sample in Zone 3.

Each of these three models has its own slope (a_i), as well as its own fixed costs (b_i). The next question is, what causes these different behaviors?

Of course, the answer cannot be found by graphical analysis alone, as there is only a single independent quantitative variable in a two-dimensional graph. This single variable does not provide, by itself, any information about the other variables, or about similar or distinct characteristics of the completed projects for which data are available.

When a dataset is large enough (that is, 20–30 data points for each independent variable), the impact of the other variables can be analyzed by statistical analysis. In practice, most software organizations do not have a dataset large enough for valid multivariable analysis. However, within a single organization, the projects included in a dataset can be identified nominally by the organizations that collected the data [Abran and Gallego 2009]. Each project in each subset, as in Figure 12.2, should be analyzed next, as illustrated in Chapter 11, to determine

- which of their characteristics (or cost drivers) have similar values within the same subset and
- which characteristics have very dissimilar values across the two (or three) subsets.

Of course, some of these values can be descriptive variables with categories (i.e., on a nominal scale type; for example, a specific DBMS has been used for a subset of projects).

At this point, it becomes necessary to discover which descriptive variables have the most impact on the relationship with project effort. The different values of such characteristics can then be used to characterize such datasets, and to set the parameters for selecting which of these three production models to use later for estimation purposes.

12.3   THE EMPIRICAL STUDY

12.3.1   Context

The data presented in this chapter come from a governmental agency providing specialized financial services to the public, and its software applications are similar to those of banking and insurance providers. This organization was interested in:

1. measuring the productivity of its individual projects,
2. identifying the productivity model(s) that would represent the performance capability of this organization in terms of fixed and variable costs, using mostly a single quantitative independent variable (functional size) and a limited number of descriptive variables,
3. identifying and explaining any significant deviation from their process capability, and

4. comparing and positioning the productivity of the organization's work processes with one or a group of meaningful external datasets, that is, external benchmarking.

12.3.2   Data Collection Procedures

The projects selected

- had been developed in the previous 2 years and
- had project documentation and related data available to be measured in terms of function point size, effort, and duration.

All the data for the projects selected for this study were recorded using ISBSG definitions and data questionnaire [ISBSG 2009].

12.3.3   Data Quality Controls

As indicated in Chapter 5 on the verification of the inputs to productivity models, the quality control of the data collection process is important for any productivity study and for productivity models. Here, two quantitative variables were critical: the effort reported for each project and the functional size of each project:

(A) Effort data: in this organization, the time reporting system was considered highly reliable and used for decision-making, including payment of invoices when external resources were hired to complement project staffing.

(B) Measurement of functional size: the quality of the measurement results depends on the expertise of the measurers and on the quality of the documentation available for the measurement process. For this study:

- All functional size measurements were carried out by the same measurer with years of expertise in functional size measurement.
- The quality of the documentation used for measuring functional size was observed while the functional size of each project was being measured, and it was assessed using the criteria listed in Table 12.1 [COSMIC 2011b].

12.4   DESCRIPTIVE ANALYSIS

12.4.1   Project Characteristics

Table 12.2 presents the 16 projects measured in terms of their functional size, effort in hours, project duration in months, quality of their project documentation, and their maximum team size:

- Project sizes vary from a minimum of 111 FP (project 7) to a maximum of 646 FP (project 2).

Table 12.1   Criteria for Assessing Documentation Quality [COSMIC 2011b]

Rank	Criteria
A	Every function is completely documented
B	Functions are documented, but without a precise data model
C	Functions are identified at a high level, but without any detail
D	An approximation of the number of functions is available, but with the individual functions not listed
E	Some functions are not explicitly described in the documentation, but information is added by an expert measurer based on his expertise, e.g., missing validation functions

Table 12.2   Descriptive Information ($N = 16$)

No	Function points	Effort (hours)	Duration (months)	Documentation quality (%)	Unit effort (hours per FP)
1	383	20,664	33.6	A: 11 B: 85 C: 4	53.2
2	646	16,268	18	B: 100	25.2
3	400	19,306	18	A: 54 B: 42 C: 2 D: 2	48.3
4	205	8442	16.8	B: 68 C: 38	41.2
5	372	9163	9.6	B:100	24.6
6	126	12,341	16.8	B:100	97.9
7	111	4907	9.6	B:100	44.2
8	287	10,157	27.6	B: 31 C: 69	35.4
9	344	5621	12	E:100	16.3
10	500	21,700	24	B:100	43.4
11	163	5985	10	C: 74 E: 26	36.7
12	344	4879	19.2	A: 17 B: 83	14.2
13	317	11,165	24	B: 71 C: 29	35.2
14	258	5971	12	A:76 B: 24	23.1
15	113	6710	12	B:100	59.4
16	447	29,246	35	B:100	65.4
Average	313	12,033	18.3	–	45.5

- Effort varies from 4879 to 29,246 hours.
- Duration varies from 9.6 to 33.6 months.
- Maximum development team sizes for 12 of the 16 projects were available, and ranged from 6 to 35 employees.

The staff who developed these projects included both internal and external developers, distributed equally overall.

The descriptive statistics of this dataset are as follows:

- Average effort = 12,033 hours (1718 person-days or 82 person-months).
- Average duration = 18.3 calendar months.
- One-third of the projects are newly developed software.
- Two-thirds of the projects are functional enhancements to existing software.

12.4.2 Documentation Quality and Its Impact on Functional Size Quality

The fifth column of Table 12.2 reports on the documentation quality of each project and specifies what proportion of the project documentation met the various criteria listed in Table 12.1. Note that this is not a global assessment of the documentation, but an assessment of the documentation of each of the functional processes based on an assessment of the documentation elements available for measurement. This was done considering each functional process measured by the measurer. Using these criteria, the documentation is considered to be of good quality when it is ranked A or B in Table 12.1.

From Table 12.2, column 5, we can observe the following:

- For 11 projects, the documentation of more than 95% of the functional processes measured was rated as being of good quality (= A or B).
- For projects 4 and 13, the documentation quality was rated as being of good quality (criterion B) for 68% and 71% of the functional processes, respectively.
- The documentation of project 8 was rated as being of good quality for only 31% of the functional processes.
- The documentation of project number 11 was rated as being of average quality (criterion C). This could also impact the quality of the size measured, because it used less-detailed documentation.
- For project 9 (criterion E = 100%), most of the functions measured had to be derived from documentation at a very high level.

That is, 85% of all the processes measured for the 16 projects had a good level of documentation. In summary, 13 projects were rated as well documented (ranking A and B), while only 3 projects were rated as poorly documented.

12.4.3   Unit Effort (in Hours)

Unit effort is measured in hours per functional size unit, that is, hours/FP. Figure 12.3 presents the projects in ascending order of unit effort: the horizontal axis represents the project number and the vertical axis the unit effort in person-hours per function point for each project individually.

For the 16 projects, the average unit effort by project is 45.5 hours/FP (FPA). There is a large gap in the unit effort of the projects in this organization; for instance, from the smallest unit effort of 14.2 hours/FP for project 12, to the highest unit effort of up to 97.9 hours/FP for project 6: this is almost one order of magnitude within the same organization, that is, a factor of 9 between the least productive and the most productive in terms of unit effort.

12.5   PRODUCTIVITY ANALYSIS

12.5.1   Single Model with the Full Dataset

The dispersion of points is illustrated in Figure 12.4 for all 16 projects, along with the regression model:

$$\text{Effort} = 30.7\,\text{hours/FP} \times \text{project size} + 2411 \;\; \text{hours.}$$

The coefficient of determination (R^2) of this model is relatively low, at 0.39.

The practical interpretation of the equation given above for this organization is as follows:

- (Fixed) effort not sensitive to software size = 2411 hours
- (Variable) effort sensitive to an increase in software size = 30.7 hours/FP

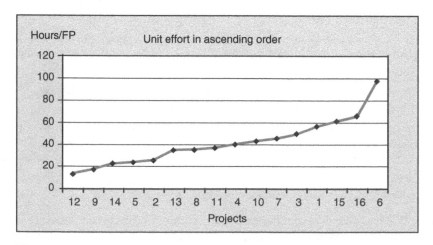

Figure 12.3   Projects in Ascending Order of Unit Effort (Hours/FP)

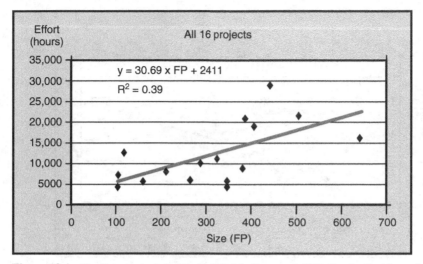

Figure 12.4   The Organization's Production Model. Abran et al. 2014. Reprinted with permission from IARA publication.

The possible reasons for the rather high fixed unit effort values have been discussed with the managers, and the following points raised:

- The acquisition process is highly procedural and time-consuming.
- The projects have tight constraints and procedural documentation.
- The projects require lengthy consensus building procedures.
- The projects require a relatively high number of inspections.

12.5.2   Model of the Least Productive Projects

From Table 12.2 and Figures 12.3 and 12.4, we can see that, for this organization, five projects have an effort 100% higher than do projects of comparable functional size:

- Project 6 with 126 FP required twice as much effort as projects of similar size (projects 7 and 15).
- Four large projects (between 400 and 500 FP) required two or three times as much effort as similarly sized projects. The effect of these projects is to pull up the linear model (and the corresponding slope) and to influence both the fixed and variable portion of the effort considerably.

This data sample was therefore split into two groups for further analysis as follows:

- **(A)** A group of five projects that are above the regression line in Figure 12.5 and have a very high unit effort.

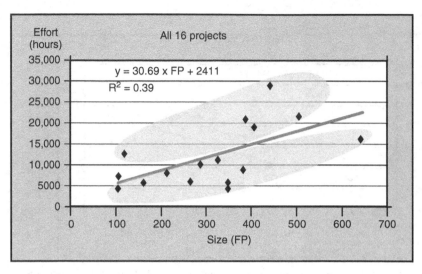

Figure 12.5   Two Subsets of Projects Within the Single Dataset

(B) A group of 11 other projects which are under the regression line and have lower unit effort.

For the five projects in group A, the effort relationship model in Figure 12.6 is as follows:

$$\text{Effort} = 33.4 \ \text{hours/FP} \times \text{project size} + 8257 \ \text{hours} \ (\text{Figure 12.4})$$

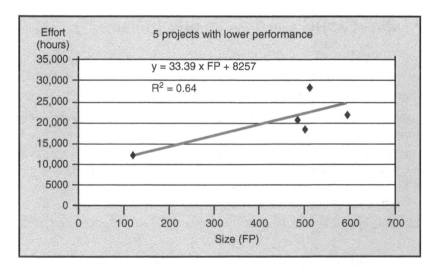

Figure 12.6   Least Productive Projects

The coefficient of determination (R^2) of this model is significantly better, at 0.637. Of course, with a sample of only five projects, this number is not statistically significant, but still of interest to this organization.

The practical interpretation of the equation given above is as follows:

- Fixed effort = 8.257 hours
- Variable effort = 33.4 hours/FP

This group of the five least productive projects is characterized by a fixed cost, which is almost four times higher than that of the full set of projects (8257 hours vs 2411 hours), and a relatively similar variable effort unit (33.4 hours/FP vs 30.7 hours/PF).

12.5.3   Model of the Most Productive Projects

Figure 12.7 presents the 11 projects with a much lower unit effort per project, that is, the most productive ones. For these projects, the linear regression model is

Effort = 17.1 hours/FP × size of the project + 3208 hours (Figure 12.5)

The coefficient of determination (R^2) of this model is 0.589, higher, relatively, than that for the overall model.

The practical interpretation of this equation is the following:

- Fixed effort not sensitive to the size of the software = 3208 hours
- Variable effort sensitive to the increase in functional size = 17.1 hours/FP

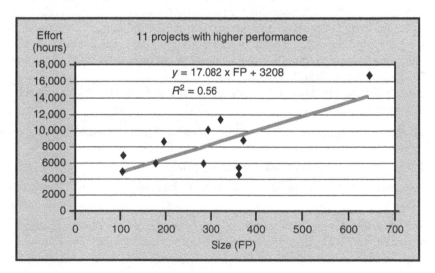

Figure 12.7   Most Productive Projects

Table 12.3   Fixed and Variable Efforts – Internal. Abran et al. 2014. Reprinted with permission from IARA publication.

Samples/regression coefficients	All 16 projects	Least productive: 5 projects	Most productive: 11 projects
Fixed effort (hours)	2411	8257	3208
Variable effort (hours/FP)	30.7	34.4	17.1

This group of 11 most productive projects is characterized by a fixed cost, which is approximately 40% lower than that of the least productive projects (3208 hours vs 8257 hours), and a variable unit effort, which is almost 50% lower (17.1 hours/FP vs 32.4 hours/FP); that is, with greater economies of scale and an R^2 of 0.55.

A summary of each group is presented in Table 12.3. While 5 projects are considered the least productive, the other 11 represent the "capability" of the organization to deliver under normal conditions.

12.6   EXTERNAL BENCHMARKING WITH THE ISBSG REPOSITORY

12.6.1   Project Selection Criteria and Samples

Benchmarking is the process by which measurement results of a specific entity are compared with those of similar entities – see also Chapter 8, Further Reading 1. Traditional benchmarking models in software engineering are typically based first on the concept of productivity, defined as a single ratio of output to input (or its corollary, unit effort as the ratio of input to output), then on using the more generic concept of performance, and, finally, on combining the productivity ratio with various additional factors [Cheikhi *et al.* 2006]. Benchmarking can be performed either internally with data collected within the organization, or externally with data collected outside the organization or available from multi-organizational datasets [ISBSG 2009; Chiez and Wang 2002; Lokan *et al.* 2001].

For external benchmarking, the following criteria were used to select a benchmarking repository:

1. A repository of projects, from both the private and public sectors, representative of software applications providing financial services.

2. A repository of projects from various countries.

3. A repository with information available at the data field level (not at the aggregate level).

The ISBSG, introduced in Chapter 8, meets all these criteria. For this benchmarking exercise, the ISBSG 2006 release with 3854 projects was used. The following criteria were used to select projects for benchmarking purposes for this organization:

1. Projects with a similar size range (0–700 FP).

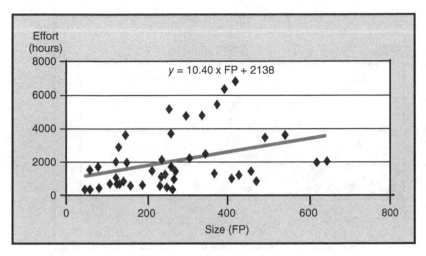

Figure 12.8 3GL ISBSG Governmental Projects

2. Projects developed in a development environment using third-generation programming languages (3GL).

Projects that met these criteria were further classified into two groups:

(A) *Projects from governmental organizations*
This data selection step identified 48 projects developed in a 3GL environment
in a governmental organization and within a size range of 0–700 FP. These
ISBSG data points are presented graphically in Figure 12.8, along with the
corresponding model that best represents this dataset using a linear regression
model:

$$\text{Effort} = 10.4 \ \text{hours/FP} \times \text{project size} + 2{,}138 \ \text{hours}$$

(B) *Financial institutions (insurance and banking)*
This data selection step identified 119 ISBSG projects developed in a 3GL
environment in the private sector of financial institutions and within the 0–700
FP size range – see Figure 12.9. The corresponding regression model is

$$\text{Effort} = 16.4 \ \text{hours/FP} \times \text{project size} + 360 \ \text{hours}$$

12.6.2   External Benchmarking Analysis

Table 12.4 presents a summary of the fixed and variable costs of the models for both
the organization (column 2) and the two reference groups from the ISBSG repository
(columns 3 and 4):

- The organization's fixed effort of 2411 hours is

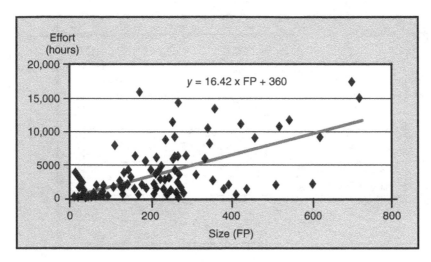

Figure 12.9   3GL ISBSG Financial Projects

Table 12.4   Summary of Fixed and Variable Effort

	Organization (1)	ISBSG: Government (2)	ISBSG: Financial (3)
Number of projects	16	48	119
Fixed effort (hours)	2411	2138	360
Variable effort (hours/FP)	30.7	10.4	16.4

- comparable to the fixed effort of governmental institutions (2138 hours) and
- seven times higher than that of private financial sector organizations, at 360 hours.
- Moreover, the variable effort of 30.7 hours/FP is
  - almost triple that of the reference group of ISBSG governmental institutions, at 10.4 hours/FP and
  - almost double that of ISBSG private sector financial institutions, at 16.4 hours/FP.

12.6.3   Further Considerations

The ISBSG considers that the data in its repository represent organizations that are among the top 25% in the industry in terms of efficiency. Benchmarking with the ISBSG repository is, therefore, a comparison with some of the best in the industry, excluding less-efficient organizations that are unable to collect such data (often characterized by unstable or undocumented processes, high-risk projects, or projects abandoned along the way).

It should also be noted that the organizations that provide data to the ISBSG repository are able to measure their own performance and are willing to share such data with industry at large.

12.7   IDENTIFICATION OF THE ADJUSTMENT FACTORS FOR MODEL SELECTION

12.7.1   Projects with the Highest Productivity (i.e., the Lowest Unit Effort)

Projects above the regression line in Figure 12.5 have the highest unit effort, while those below the line have the lowest unit effort.

The question is, what are the factors that lead to such an increase or decrease in unit effort? What are the cause–effect relationships?

To identify and investigate these relationships, available project managers were interviewed to obtain their feedback on what they believed had contributed to either an increase or a decrease in the productivity of their respective projects. The project managers interviewed had managed 7 of the 16 projects:

(A) Three projects with the lowest productivity (i.e., the highest unit effort)

(B) Two projects with average productivity

(C) Two projects with the highest productivity (i.e., the lowest unit effort).

The aim of the interviews was to obtain qualitative information from the project managers on the factors they believed had contributed, or not, to the increase in project effort compared to that of other projects of similar size developed in the organization's environment or elsewhere during their project management practice. The feedback obtained is summarized in the following factors:

(A) Customer requirements that were poorly expressed, or a customer representative who did not know his environment (business area), leading to frequent change requests during a project life cycle.

(B) Customers not familiar with the software development process in the organization.

(C) High turnover of users involved in the projects, leading to instability in the requirements and delays in decision–making.

(D) New technologies unknown to the developers.

(E) Multiple links with the organization's other software applications.

(F) A severely compressed schedule as the project top priority, with resources having been thrown at the problem to make it disappear from the public view as quickly as possible.

An example of factor E in this organization is project 6, with the highest unit effort (98 hours/FP): this project had a small functional size, but required twice as much effort as a project of similar size, and it involved almost all the software applications of the organization and was dependent on other organizational units.

By contrast, the most productive projects had the following characteristics:

1. Users familiar with both the business and software development processes.
2. Users involved throughout the project.
3. Software developers working on the projects who were experienced in the use of the development environment.

Even though it was possible to identify these major positive and negative factors, the impact of each factor could not be quantified.

12.7.2 Lessons Learned

Over the past 40 years of research on software project estimation, expert practitioners and researchers have come up with various models with different mixes of cost drivers, but with little in common, and to date most of these models have not been generalized to contexts other than the one on which they were based.

This analysis did not postulate the existence of a single productivity model that can be considered ideal in all circumstances, even within a single organization. Rather, it looked for concepts which could contribute to the identification of distinct models corresponding to distinct production processes. This chapter has reported on an empirical study which took into account relevant concepts from the economics field.

In Section 12.2, for instance, a few economics concepts were presented that have been used to model a production process, as well as corresponding characteristics that may be relevant to software, such as fixed and variable costs, and production processes with either low or high effort sensitivity to functional size.

For this organization, two productivity models were identified:

- A model representing the capability to deliver a software project within a fixed/variable effort structure.
- A second model representing a twofold increase in effort when one or a number of major disruptive factors materialize during the project life cycle.

Of course, the limited number of projects available in the empirical study does not permit generalization to other contexts.

This notwithstanding, these models are representative of the organization studied, especially since, in this organization, the software development processes are widely implemented and represent not varying individual practices, but rather well-used corporate ones.

At estimation time for new projects, the organization's process capability model should be used, provided that a concurrent risk analysis has not detected the presence of any of the historical factors that typically increase effort twofold in this organization. Whenever such negative factors are identified with a high probability of occurrence, the organization should always select its second productivity model.

EXERCISES

1. Wedge-shaped datasets often occur in software engineering. Is it always necessary to look for a single productivity model? If not, which economics concepts can help in data analysis and identify models?

2. Identify some criteria to analyze the quality of the documentation available for the measurement of the functional size of the software to be developed.

3. In Table 12.2, are there statistical outliers on the independent variable, functional size?

4. In Table 12.2, are there statistical outliers on the dependent variable, effort?

5. For the dataset in Chapter 12, what are the ratios of fixed and variable effort between the two productivity models developed?

6. Compare the performance of the ISBSG projects developed by government organizations and those developed by financial institutions?

7. Compare the performance of the data reported in this chapter with that of the data from ISBSG governmental organizations.

TERM ASSIGNMENTS

1. Collect software project data from your organization, and provide a descriptive analysis of them.

2. Carry out a graphical analysis on size and effort data, and determine whether or not you are looking at candidate multiple models.

3. If you have candidate multiple models, interview the project managers to identify positive and negative productivity factors.

4. Compare your organization's performance with that of similar organizations in the ISBSG repository.

Chapter 13

Re-Estimation: A Recovery Effort Model

OBJECTIVES

This chapter covers

- Issues leading to the need for re-estimation
- The impact of delays in acknowledging an underestimation situation
- A proposed recovery effort model and calculation of additional staff resources

13.1 INTRODUCTION[1]

When a project in progress has been seriously underestimated, it is essential to figure out a strategy to complete the project:

- When increasing the budget and postponing the delivery date is not an option, cutting features in order to deliver within the same budget and the same deadline is one possible strategy.

- However, if, for whatever reason (regulatory, business constraints, etc.) all the expected features still have to be delivered, the project budget must be revised. This of course requires re-estimation.

How much additional effort is required to complete the project with its original scope and delivery date? How do you estimate this effort?

Is going back to the initial set of estimates sufficient? Is using the contingency identified at the outset of the project still relevant and prudent (i.e., is the amount

---

[1] See also Miranda, E., Abran, A., "Protecting Software Development Projects Against Underestimation," Project Management Journal, Project Management Institute, September 2008, pp. 75–85.

Software Project Estimation: The Fundamentals for Providing High Quality Information to Decision Makers, First Edition. Alain Abran.
© 2015 the IEEE Computer Society. Published 2015 by John Wiley & Sons, Inc.

what would have been required had the project been adequately planned right from the start?) – see Chapter 3 for a discussion on the management of contingencies at the portfolio level.

In this chapter, we identify a number of additional issues that must be addressed when a project has gone off-track (budget-wise) and must be re-estimated. In particular, we present, an approach to identifying the additional project budget required to recover from the underestimation.

This chapter is organized as follows:

- Section 13.2 provides examples of issues leading to the need for re-estimation.
- Section 13.3 presents key concepts for a recovery effort model.
- Section 13.4 presents a recovery model when a re-estimation need is recognized at time $T > 0$.

13.2   THE NEED FOR RE-ESTIMATION AND RELATED ISSUES

When a software project goes significantly off-track and is greatly overshooting its budget, and it is becoming clear that the project deadline will be missed, the project must obviously be re-estimated and a number of constraints must be handled and decisions taken as follows:

- Increasing the budget (e.g., re-estimating), while keeping the same deadline and the same set of functions.
- Increasing the budget (e.g., re-estimating) to deliver the same number of functions, but postponing the deadline.
- Staying within the budget, but postponing a number of functions to a later project phase.
- Staying within the budget and deadline, but stopping testing early (i.e., skipping a number of quality controls).
- And so on.

When the need for re-estimation arises, the human and organizational considerations that dictate decision-making in real-world projects cannot be ignored, such as

- management's preference for schedule over cost,
- Management's tendency toward inaction, and
- the "money allocated is money spent" (MAIMS) behavior [Kujawski et al. 2004].

A good example of the preference for schedule over cost is given by Grey [1995]:

"While most people will be willing to accept that cost could exceed expectations, and might even take a perverse delight in recounting past

examples, the same is not true for deadlines. This is probably due to the fact that cost overruns are resolved in-house, while schedule issues are open and visible to the customer" (p. 108).

In other words, project delays and scope cuts are not great career builders:

- When faced with a schedule overrun, management's preferred course of action is not to revisit the plan to achieve the best economic outcome, but to attempt to keep to the schedule by adding staff, despite the fact that adding resources midway through a project will result in one or more of the following [Sim and Holt 1998]:

  - The need to break down the work into additional segments, so that they can be allocated to newcomers to the project.
  - The need to coach the new staff.
  - Additional integration work.
  - Additional coordination effort.

This means that it is recognized that additional funds are often used first and foremost to maintain a schedule, and not just to pay for underestimated work. A re-estimation process should acknowledge the extra cost incurred by the above-mentioned activities.

13.3 THE RECOVERY EFFORT MODEL

13.3.1 Key Concepts

Figure 13.1 illustrates the effort makeup of a project in recovery, assuming that the objective is to preserve the original scope and respect the delivery date to which a commitment has been made.

In Figure 13.1, the top part represents the addition of person-months, which may include:

- Recognition by management, at time t, of an underestimation, and the approval of overtime for the current staff.

- Recognition by management, at time T_a, that additional overtime by current staff will not be enough and that an increase in staff is needed, on top of overtime. Since not all the additional staff can be hired at once (e.g., a step function), the progressive addition of new staff is represented, for simplicity's sake, as a linear increasing function, starting at T_a and for duration T_j. The overtime of current staff is represented by E_{ob}.

- Then, at some time, overtime is also requested from the additional staff – after period T_j. The overtime contributed by the additional staff is represented by E_{oa}.

- Finally, a decreasing function (darker black in the figure) is represented in the overtime by both current and additional staff.

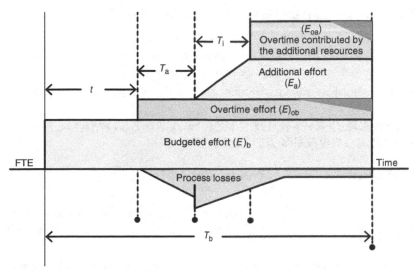

Figure 13.1   Recovery Cost of An Underestimated Project [Miranda and Abran 2008. Reprinted with permission from John Wiley & Sons, Inc.]

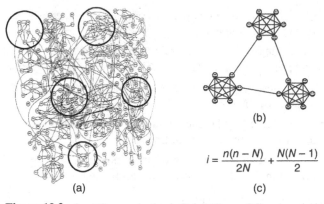

$$i = \frac{n(n - N)}{2N} + \frac{N(N - 1)}{2}$$

Figure 13.2   (a–c) Communication in R & D Teams [Miranda and Abran 2008. Reprinted with permission from John Wiley & Sons, Inc.]

13.3.2   Ramp-Up Process Losses

Adding staff midway through a project creates additional work (process losses) that would not have existed otherwise. These losses correspond to the ramp-up process leading to the incorporation of the newcomers and the effort expended by the original staff coaching them respectively. Both efforts are modeled in Figure 13.1 as triangular areas.

In addition, another variable is necessary to capture the extra effort expended coordinating the activities of the extended team – see Figure 13.2 – and on previous work by Miranda [2001]:

(a) Patterns of communication in R & D teams [Allen 1984];

(b) Stylized graph mimicking Allen's observations:

  ▷ Everyone talks to everyone else in a subsystem team, while communications across subsystems are carried out by a few individuals;

(c) A mathematical equation to calculate the number of communication paths.

13.4   A RECOVERY MODEL WHEN A RE-ESTIMATION NEED IS RECOGNIZED AT TIME $T > 0$

13.4.1   Summary of Recovery Variables

- The budgeted effort (E_b) is the amount of effort originally allocated to the project, and is the product of the time budgeted (T_b) and the original staff (FTE_b).

- t is the time at which the underestimation is acknowledged, and a decision to do something about it is finally made.

- T_a is the mean time between the time the decision to bring in new staff was made and the time when the new staff arrive.

- The additional effort (E_a) is the effort that will be contributed by the resources brought in to help recover from the delay.

  ▷ The sloped left-hand side of the quadrilateral models the fact that there will be a certain time interval (T_1) before the new staff become fully productive.

- The overtime efforts (E_{ob} and E_{oa}) are the efforts contributed through overtime by both the original and additional resources.

  ▷ Overtime efforts are affected by fatigue, as modeled by the dark triangles in the upper-right corners of the corresponding rectangles.

- The process losses (P_1) include all the extra effort: ramp-up, coaching, and communication overhead imposed on the original staff by newcomers.

The simplicity of this makeup is deliberate:

- While other effort breakdowns are certainly possible, these would come at the expense of more complicated mathematical expressions, perhaps based on hypothesized parameters, which would make the model harder to explain.

In the next sections, we present the mathematical models to address the above-mentioned re-estimation problem taking these variables into account.

13.4.2   A Mathematical Model of a Recovery Course in Re-Estimation

Wishful thinking and inertia are examples of inaction that result in postponing the acknowledgement of a delay until the last possible moment.

Todd Little [2006] commented on the unwillingness to acknowledge project delays:

> "This is the result of the project manager holding onto a deadline in hopes that a miracle will occur and the software will release. Finally, the day of reckoning occurs, with no miracle in sight. At this point, the project estimate is usually reset. In many cases, this cycle repeats until the software releases" [Little 2006, p. 52].

The tendency to procrastinate should also be factored into the calculation of contingency funds, because, other things being equal, the later the underestimation is acknowledged, the larger the number of extra staff required, and, consequently, the higher the cost.

These two premises lead to the postulation that

$$\text{Contingency funds} = \iint \text{Recovery cost}(u, t)p(t)p(u)dtdu \qquad (13.1)$$

Equation (13.1) asserts that contingency funds must equal the expected recovery cost of a project, that is, the effort necessary to recover from an underestimation of magnitude u on which we act at time t by the probability of u and the probability of t.

Having considered management's predilection for schedule over budget and their tendency toward inaction, we now look at the third behavior that affects the use of contingency funds:

- The MAIMS behavior [Gordon 1997; Kujawski et al. 2004].

With this behavior, once a budget has been allocated, it will, for a variety of reasons, tend to be spent in its entirety, which means that funds not spent as a result of cost underruns are seldom available to offset overruns.

- This negates the basic premise that contingency usage is probabilistic, and hence managing the funds over and above the project level becomes the obvious and mathematically valid solution for its effective and efficient administration.

13.4.3 Probability of Underestimation – $p(u)$

The probability distribution of the underestimation, u is identical to the effort distribution in Figure 13.1 shifted by the project budget (see also Figure 3.5, in Section 3.3 of Chapter 3).

The selection of a right skewed triangular distribution is justified for the following three reasons:

1. While the number of things that can go right in a project is limited, and in most cases have already been factored into the estimate, the number of things that can go wrong is virtually unlimited.

2. It is simple.

3. Since the actual distribution is not known, it is as sensible as any other.

Equation (13.2) gives $F(u)$, the cumulative probabilities for $p(u)$.

$$F(u) = \begin{cases} \text{if } u \leq u_{min} \text{ then} \\ 0 \\ \text{else if } u_{min} < u \leq u_{ml} \text{ then} \\ \dfrac{(u-u_{min})^2}{(u_{max}-u_{min})(u_{ml}-u_{min})} \\ \text{else if } u_{ml} < u < u_{max} \text{ then} \\ 1 - \dfrac{(u_{max}-u)^2}{(u_{max}-u_{min})(u_{max}-u_{ml})} \\ \text{else if } u \geq u_{max} \text{ then} \\ 1 \\ \text{end if} \end{cases}$$

u_{min} = Best-case estimate − Project budget

u_{ml} = Most likely estimate − Project budget

u_{max} = Worst-case estimate − Project budget (13.2)

13.4.4 Probability of Acknowledging the Underestimation on a Given Month − $p(t)$

Figure 13.3 shows the ratio of the actual remaining duration to the current estimated remaining duration plotted as a function of relative time (the ratio of elapsed time to total actual time) for each project at each week.

- In the case of a schedule overrun, the estimated remaining duration will be shorter than the actual duration, and, as time passes, the estimated remaining duration will grow toward zero and the ratio will grow toward infinity.
- One such function is Eq. (13.2) − see Figure 13.3.

This, of course, is not the only possibility, but it resembles the patterns in Figure 13.3 and it is simple.

- Other possibilities for the probability function would include the use of Bayesian probabilities to model the effect of the underestimation; for example, larger underestimations will be easier to notice than smaller ones, but this treatment is beyond the scope of this book.

$$p(t) = \frac{t}{\sum\limits_{i=1}^{T_b-T_a-T_1-1} i} \qquad (13.3)$$

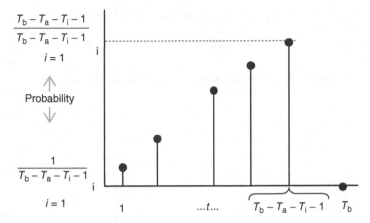

Figure 13.3   Probability Distribution for *t* [Miranda and Abran 2008. Reprinted with permission from John Wiley & Sons, Inc.]

In Figure 13.3, the probability function does not extend to T_b, since the time required for recruiting, the time required for training, and at least 1 month to do some work must be taken into account. Mathematical examples are presented in Miranda and Abran [2008].

EXERCISES

1. List four strategies which can be looked at when a project schedule and budget is seriously off-track.
2. When additional staff are added to a project, what are the positive and negative productivity impacts that you must take into account for re-estimation purposes?
3. Is there a penalty to having to re-estimate a project at some point? Is the impact on total effort the same across the whole life cycle?
4. What is the impact on delaying re-estimation when the schedule must stay fixed?
5. When re-estimating, where should the additional funding be coming from?

TERM ASSIGNMENTS

1. Some say that adding new staff to a late project makes it even later! Comment and discuss when this assertion is valid and when it is not.
2. Look back at your last five projects. Which ones had to be re-estimated? When in the life cycle were re-estimates performed? What were the consequences of re-estimation on the budget and schedule?
3. What was the basis for re-estimation? Does your organization have a specific recovery model?

4. Your project is significantly late, and, to finish on schedule, you will need to hire five new staff. How would you calculate the process loss resulting from hiring these individuals and getting them up to speed? Does your organization take such a loss into account when re-estimating projects?

5. How can you take schedule penalty costs into account when re-estimating a project?

References

Abran A, Desharnais JM, Zarour M, Demirors O. (2014) Productivity based software estimation model: an economics perspective and an empirical study, 9th International Conference on Software Engineering Advances – ICSEA 2014, Publisher IARA, Oct. 12–16, 2014, Nice (France), pp. 291–201.

Abran A. (2010) *Software Metrics and Software Metrology*. Hoboken, New Jersey: IEEE-CS Press & John Wiley & Sons; 2010. p 328.

Abran A, Cuadrado JJ. (2009) Software estimation models & economies of scale, 21st International Conference on Software Engineering and Knowledge Engineering – SEKE'2009, Boston (USA), July 1–3, pp. 625–630.

Abran A, Ndiaye I, Bourque P. (2007) Evaluation of a black-box estimation tool: a case studyin special issue: "advances in measurements for software processes assessment". J Softw Proc Improv Prac 2007;12(2):199–218.

Abran A, Silva I, Primera L. (2002) Field studies using functional size measurement in building estimation models for software maintenance. J Softw Maint Evol: R 2002;14:31–64.

Abran A, Robillard PN. (1996) Function points analysis: an empirical study of its measurement processes. IEEE Trans Softw Eng 1996;22:895–909.

Albrecht AJ. (1983) Software function, source lines of code and development effort prediction: a software science validation. IEEE Trans Softw Eng 1983;9(6):639–649.

Allen T. (1984) Managing the Flow of Technology, MIT Press, January 1984.

Austin R. (2001) *The Effects of Time Pressure on Quality in Software Development: An Agency Model*. Boston: Harvard Business School; 2001.

Boehm BW, Abts C, *et al.* (2000) *Software Cost Estimation with COCOMO II*. Vol. 502. Prentice Hall; 2000.

Bourque P, Oligny S, Abran A, Fournier B. (2007) "Developing project duration models", software engineering. J Comp Sci Tech 2007;22(3):348–357.

Cheikhi L, Abran A, Buglione L. (2006) ISBSG software project repository & ISO 9126: an opportunity for quality benchmarking UPGRADE. 2006;7(1):46–52.

Chiez V, Wang Y. (2002) Software engineering process benchmarking, Product Focused Software Process Improvement Conference - PROFES'02, Rovaniemi, Finland, pp. 519–531, LNCS, v. 2559.

Conte SD, Dunsmore DE, Shen VY. (1986) *Software Engineering Metrics and Models*. Menlo Park: The Benjamin/Cummings Publishing Company, Inc.; 1986.

Software Project Estimation: The Fundamentals for Providing High Quality Information to Decision Makers, First Edition. Alain Abran.
© 2015 the IEEE Computer Society. Published 2015 by John Wiley & Sons, Inc.

COSMIC (2014a) Guideline for approximate COSMIC functional sizing, Common Software Measurement International Consortium – COSMIC Group, Draft version http://www.cosmicon.com/dl_manager3.asp?cat_id=18&cat=05+%2D+Guidelines, accessed February 8, 2015.

COSMIC (2014b) The COSMIC functional size measurement method – Version 4.0 - measurement manual, Common Software Measurement International Consortium – COSMIC Group, http://www.cosmicon.com/dl_manager3.asp?cat_id=11&cat=01+%2D+COSMIC+method+standards, accessed May 16, 2014.

COSMIC (2011a) Guideline for COSMIC FSM to manage Agile projects, Common Software Measurement International Consortium – COSMIC Group, http://www.cosmicon.com/dl_manager3.asp?cat_id=18&cat=05+%2D+Guidelines, accessed: May 16, 2014.

COSMIC (2011b) Guideline for assuring the accuracy of measurement, Common Software Measurement International Consortium – COSMIC Group, http://www.cosmicon.com/portal/public/COSMIC_Assuring_accuracy_measurements_Guideline_v10.pdf, accessed: July 25, 2014.

Déry D, Abran A. (2005) Investigation of the effort data consistency in the ISBSG Repository, 15th International Workshop on Software Measurement – IWSM 2005, Montréal (Canada), Sept. 12–14, 2005, Shaker Verlag, pp. 123–136.

Desharnais, JM (1988), "Analyse statistiques de la productivité des projets de développement en informatique à partir de la technique des points de fonction," Master Degree thesis, Dept Computer Sciences, Université du Québec à Montrëal – UQAM (Canada), 1988.

Ebert C, Dumke R, Bundschuh M, Schmietendorf A. (2005) *Best Practices in Software Measurement*. Berlin Heidelberg (Germany): Springer-Verlag; 2005. p 295.

El Eman K, Koru AG. A replicated survey of IT software project failures. IEEE Softw 2008;25(5):84–90.

Eveleens J, Verhoef C. (2010) The rise and fall of the Chaos report figures. IEEE Softw 2010;27(1):30–36.

Fairley RD. (2009) *Managing and Leading Software Projects*. John Wiley & IEEE Computer Society; 2009. p 492.

Flyvbjerg B. (2005) Design by deception: The politics of megaprojects approval. Harvard Design Magazine 2005;22(2005):50–59.

Gordon, C. (1997) Risk Analysis and Cost and Cost Management (RACM): A Cost/Schedule Management Approach using Statistical, 1997

Grey S. (1995) *Practical Risk Assessment for Project Management*. New York: John Wiley & Sons; 1995.

Hill P, ISBSG. (2010) *Practical Software Project Estimation: A Toolkit for Estimating Software Development Effort and Duration*. McGraw-Hill; 2010.

IEEE (1998) *IEEE Std 830–1998 - IEEE Recommended Practice for Software Requirements Specifications*, IEEE Computer Society, Ed. IEEE New York, NY, pp. 32.

ISBSG (2012), Data collection questionnaire new development, redevelopment or enhancement sized using COSMIC function points, version 5.16, International Software Benchmarking Standards Group, http://www.isbsg.org/ISBSGnew.nsf/WebPages/286528C58F55415BCA257474001C7B48?open, accessed: May 16, 2014

ISBSG (2009), Guidelines for use of the ISBSG data, International Software Benchmarking Standards Group – ISBSG, Release 11, Australia, 2009.

ISO (2011). *ISO/IEC 19761: software engineering – COSMIC - a functional size measurement method*. Geneva: International Organization for Standardization - ISO; 2011.

ISO (2009). *ISO/IEC 20926: Software Engineering - IFPUG 4.1 Unadjusted Functional Size Measurement Method - Counting Practices Manual*. Geneva: International Organization for Standardization - ISO; 2009.

ISO (2007a). *ISO/IEC 14143–1: Information Technology - Software Measurement - Functional Size Measurement - Part 1: Definition of Concepts*. Geneva: International Organization for Standardization - ISO; 2007a.

ISO (2007b). *VIM ISO/IEC Guide 99 International vocabulary of metrology - Basic and general concepts and associated terms (VIM)'*. Geneva: International Organization for Standardization - ISO; 2007b.

ISO (2005). *ISO/IEC 24750: Software Engineering - NESMA Functional Size Measurement Method Version 2.1 - Definitions and Counting Guidelines for the Application of Function Point Analysis*. Geneva: International Organization for Standardization - ISO; 2005.

ISO (2002). *ISO/IEC 20968: Software Engineering - Mk II Function Point Analysis - Counting Practices Manual*. Geneva: International Organization for Standardization - ISO; 2002.

Jorgensen M, Molokken K. (2006) How large are software cost overruns? A review of the 1994 CHAOS report. Infor Softw Tech 2006;48(4):297–301.

Jorgensen M, Shepperd M. (2007) A systematic review of software development cost estimation studies. IEEE Trans Softw Eng 2007;33(1):33–53.

Kemerer CF. (1987) An Empirical Validation of Software Cost Estimation Models. Comm ACM 1987;30(5):416–429.

Kitchenham BA, Taylor NR. (1984) Software cost models. ICL Tech J 1984;4(1):73–102.

Kujawski E, Alvaro M, Edwards W. (2004) Incorporating psychological influences in probabilistic cost analysis. Sys Eng 2004;3(7):195–216.

Lind K, Heldal R. (2008) Estimation of real-time software component size. Nordic J Comput (NJC) 2008;(14):282–300.

Lind K, Heldal R. (2010), Categorization of real-time software components for code size estimation, International Symposium on Empirical Software Engineering and Measurement - ESEM 2010.

Little T. (2006) Schedule estimation and uncertainty surrounding the cone of uncertainty. IEEE Softw 2006;23(3):48–54.

Lokan C, Wright T, Hill P, Stringer M. (2001) Organizational benchmarking using the ISBSG data repository. IEEE Softw 2001:26–32.

Miranda E. (2010), Improving the Estimation, Contingency Planning and Tracking of Agile Software Development Projects, PhD thesis, École de technologie supérieure – Université du Québec, Montréal, Canada.

Miranda E. (2003) *Running the Successful High-Tech Project Office*. Boston: Artech House; 2003.

Miranda E. (2001) Project Screening: How to Say "No" Without Hurting Your Career or Your Company, European Software Control and Measurement Conference, London, England.

Miranda E, Abran A. (2008) Protecting software development projects against under-estimation. Proj Manag J 2008;2008: 75–85.

Paré D, Abran A. (2005) Obvious outliers in the ISBSG repository of software projects: exploratory research, Metrics News, Otto Von Gueriske Universitat, Magdeburg (Germany), Vol. 10, No. 1, pp. 28–36.

Petersen K. (2011) Measuring and predicting software productivity: a systematic map and review. Infor Softw Technol 2011;53(4):317–343.

PMI. (2013) *A Guide to the Project Management Body of Knowledge (PMBOK® guide)*. 5th ed. Newtown Square, PA.: Project Management Institute (PMI); 2013.

Santillo L. (2006) Error propagation in software measurement and estimation, International Workshop on Software Measurement – IWSM-Metrikom 2006, Postdam, Nov. 2–3, Shaker Verlag, Germany.

Sim S, Holt R. (1998) The ramp-up problem in software projects: A case study of how software immigrants naturalize, 1998 International Conference on Software Engineering. Piscataway, NJ: IEEE, pp. 361–370.

Stern S. (2009) Practical experimentations with the COSMIC method in the automotive embedded software field, 19th International Workshop on Software Measurement - IWSM-MENSURA 2009, Amsterdam, Netherlands.

Victoria (2009). *SouthernSCOPE Avoiding Software Projects Blowouts*. Australia: State Government of Victoria; 2009.

Index

Note: Page numbers in *italics* refer to Figures; those in **bold** to Tables

Software Project Estimation: The Fundamentals for Providing High Quality Information to Decision Makers,
First Edition. Alain Abran.
© 2015 the IEEE Computer Society. Published 2015 by John Wiley & Sons, Inc.

Printed in the USA
J099399SCI033015   01S29053000000000273